BATTLE CHRONICLES
OF THE
CIVIL WAR
1865

JAMES M. McPHERSON, Editor
Princeton University

RICHARD GOTTLIEB, Managing Editor
Grey Castle Press

MACMILLAN PUBLISHING COMPANY
New York

COLLIER MACMILLAN PUBLISHERS
London

Text © 1989. *Civil War Times Illustrated*, a division of Cowles Magazines, Inc., Box 8200, Harrisburg, PA 17105.

Introduction, Transitions, Index and Format © 1989. Grey Castle Press, Inc., Lakeville, CT 06039.

Published by Macmillan Publishing Company
866 Third Avenue, New York, NY 10022

ILLUSTRATION CREDITS—Some sources are abbreviated as follows: CWTI Collection (*Civil War Times Illustrated* Collection), JC (Collection of Col. G.B. Jarrett), KA (Kean Archives), LC (Library of Congress), NA (National Archives), RC (Collection of Col. Julian E. Raymond), USAMHI (U.S. Army Military History Institute). Illustrations without credits are part of the *Civil War Times Illustrated* Collection.

Library of Congress Cataloging-in-Publication Data

Battle Chronicles of the Civil War.

    Includes bibliographies and indexes.
    Contents: 1. 1861—2.1862—3. 1863— [etc.]
    1. United States—History—Civil War, 1861–1865—
Campaigns.   I. McPherson, James M.
E470.B29   1989   973.7'3   89-8316
ISBN 0-02-920661-8 (set)

Printed in the USA

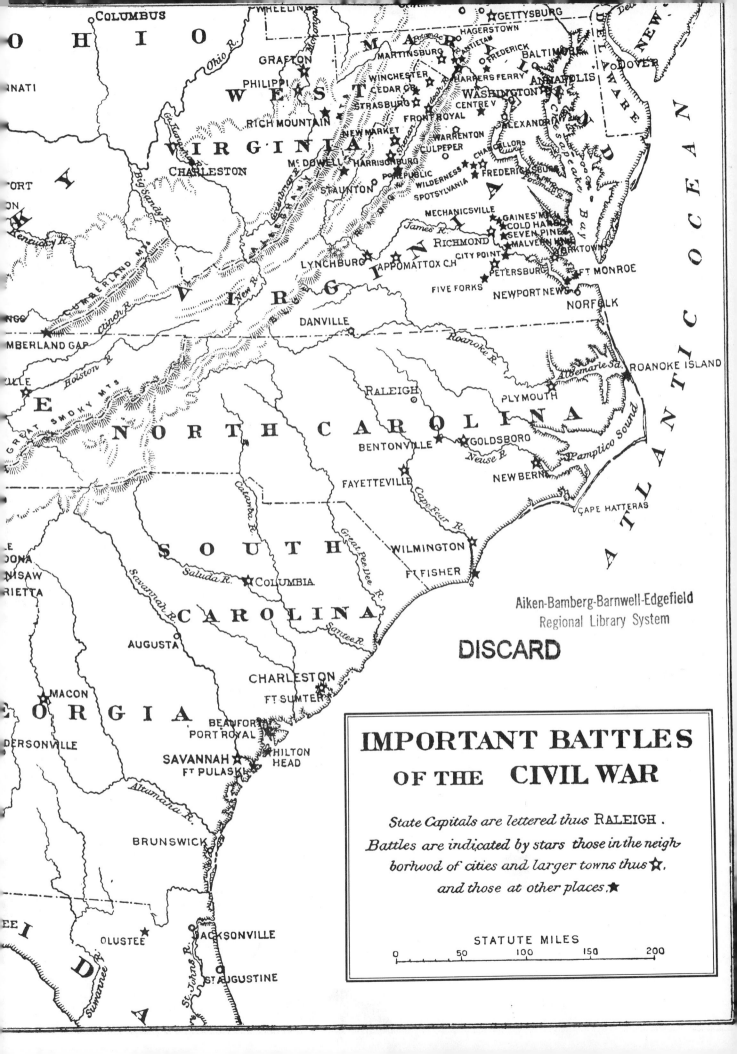

IMPORTANT BATTLES
OF THE CIVIL WAR

State Capitals are lettered thus RALEIGH.

Battles are indicated by stars those in the neigh-

borhood of cities and larger towns thus ☆.

and those at other places ★

STATUTE MILES

0   50   100   150   200

Contents

1865—AN OVERVIEW

In the East . . .

By spring of the war's fourth year, the Army of Northern Virginia was in critical condition. Federal thrusts at the weak Confederate lines during the nine-month siege had drained much from "Lee's Miserables." Sharp clashes, such as occurred at Reams's Station, Deep Bottom, Globe Tavern, Boydton Plank Road, Tom's Brook, Weldon Railroad, and Hatcher's Run, reduced Lee's ranks and tightened the Federal noose. Sickness, malnutrition, and lack of clothing accentuated the suffering. Desertion among Confederate units jumped dangerously. In February, morning reports for Lee's army "became a sickening and bewildering story of desertion"—as attested by a ten-day period in which 1,094 Southerners disappeared from the Petersburg trenches.

On March 2, Sheridan captured most of Early's Valley command at Waynesboro and then destroyed the Virginia Central Railroad as he rode eastward to join Grant. Lee realized that a climax was now approaching—just as Grant became fully determined not to allow Lee to escape from the Petersburg line. On March 25, Lee made a strong attack at Fort Stedman. The onslaught was intended either to break Grant's tight hold or to be at least a diversion while Lee readied the rest of his army for withdrawal. Federal troops repelled the assaults with losses to Lee of 4,500 men.

Grant now delivered the blow for which he had been preparing for months. On April 1, Federal infantry and cavalry crushed the Southern position at Five Forks, seventeen miles southwest of Petersburg; and the following day Grant's entire forty-mile front surged forward. The Confederate line bent in several places, then snapped into fragments. Lee abandoned Petersburg and Richmond (both of which were promptly occupied by elements of Grant's army) and retreated westward. The long siege had cost the Federals 42,000 casualties. However, Lee's 28,000 losses during those nine months had reduced the Confederate army to a skeleton no more than one fourth the size of Grant's forces.

Confederate strategy was to follow the route of the Richmond & Danville Railroad. Lee wished to use this one remaining line as a source for badly needed supplies. Then, if his army could reach Danville, it had a chance of uniting with the Army of Tennessee; together they might withstand Grant's punishing blows.

All of this proved to be a forlorn hope. When Lee's footsore, half-starved men reached the railroad at Amelia Court House, they found not boxcars loaded with food but empty tracks. A supply train from Danville had mysteriously continued on to Richmond—and been captured. Forage parties, hastily dispatched into the countryside by Lee, brought back only the news of a citizenry equally impoverished.

Now Lee could only trust that his smaller force might be able to outdistance the great hordes moving after him. But on April 5, Sheridan's cavalry swung into the Confederates' path and compelled Lee to veer northwestward toward Lynchburg. The next day almost a third of the Confederate army was trapped at Sayler's Creek. Lacking artillery and an escape route, 8,000 disheartened Rebels surrendered. The remainder of Lee's ragged army plodded wearily on, somehow managing to endure painful skirmishes at Farmville and High Bridge. On the night of April 8, artillery flashes and the glow of campfires revealed the worst to Lee: Grant's rapidly moving army had blocked all escape avenues.

Tired and thirsty, Confederate soldiers gather around a well near Farmville during their retreat from Petersburg. Drawing by W. L. Sheppard. (Battles and Leaders of the Civil War)

The Union army enters Richmond, the enemy capital, on April 3, 1865. They were soon followed by Abraham Lincoln, who had been at the fall of Petersburg. (Harper's Weekly, April 22, 1865)

Ragged yet proud: The surrender of the Army of Northern Virginia to the Army of the Potomac at Appomattox on April 12, 1865. Drawing by John R. Chapin. (Library of Congress)

Around 2 p.m. on Palm Sunday, April 9, Lee and Grant met in the front parlor of Wilmer McLean's Appomattox farmhouse. Grant proposed extremely generous terms that included allowing paroled Confederate soldiers to retain their mounts for the spring plowing they would shortly need to do. Lee accepted the terms with a mixture of gratitude and despair.

The actual surrender ceremony occurred on April 12, when 28,231 exhausted Confederates representing the Army of Northern Virginia relinquished their arms and battle flags. A Federal general, deeply moved by the scene, described it as "an awed stillness, and breath-holding, as if it were the passing of the dead."

In the West . . .

Sherman gave his men a month's rest at Savannah before resuming his surgery of the South. The resultant "March Through the Carolinas" was like a "devouring flame" to a Confederacy already near death.

On February 1, the 60,000 battle-hardened bluecoats again abandoned their supply lines and slashed into South Carolina. Sherman was content to leave the remaining Confederate coastal fortresses to Union naval and amphibious forces, which captured Fort Fisher on January 15 and thereby closed the last major Confederate access to the sea. Charleston likewise fell to the U.S. Navy on the day (February 17) after Sherman left Columbia, the capital of the Palmetto State, in flames.

Robert E. Lee, belatedly named General in Chief of Confederate military forces, reinstated Joseph E. Johnston as commander of the Army of Tennessee. Johnston moved into North Carolina from Mississippi to try to contain Sherman. His fragmen-

The Bennett House in Durham, North Carolina, where Joseph E. Johnston, head of the Army of Tennessee, surrendered to William T. Sherman on April 26. (North Carolina Museum of History)

tary regiments totaled about 20,000 men—a pitiful shadow of a once-proud army. Sherman's veterans occupied Fayetteville and its valuable arsenal on March 10, then turned eastward toward the important rail junction of Goldsboro.

Johnston now made a do-or-die gamble: He concentrated his meager forces at Bentonville and savagely attacked Sherman's left wing, hoping to force Sherman's withdrawal by defeating in turn the two Federal lines of advance. The battle of Bentonville raged for three days (March 19-21); on the third day, Sherman's two wings united and drove Johnston from the field. Sherman's occupation of Goldsboro shortly thereafter ended the great "march."

Lee's surrender at Appomattox two weeks later left Johnston's battered army completely alone. Yet a Sherman terrible in war proved to be a man compassionate in victory. His initial surrender terms to Johnston were so generous that Washington authorities rejected them and directed Sherman to re-negotiate. On April 26, at the Bennett house near Durham, Johnston signed the revised terms. His army had been reduced by deaths, wounds, and desertion in the final days to about 10,000 men.

Other Confederate armies throughout the South soon furled their banners. Early in April, three divisions of Federal cavalry under General James H. Wilson overwhelmed Bedford Forrest's troopers at Selma, Alabama. Wilson reported inflicting 1,200 Southern casualties and taking 6,820 prisoners. The few survivors of Forrest's command joined General Richard Taylor's army, which in turn surrendered May 4 at Citronelle, Alabama, to General Edward R. S. Canby's forces. The Confederacy's last significant army, under Kirby Smith, laid down its arms May 26 at New Orleans.

By then Lincoln was dead from an assassin's bullet, the Southern states were prostrate from four years of destruction, the cream of American manhood had been slain, a heritage of hate had been planted in many quarters, and the Union that men had sought to preserve had been irrevocably shattered and replaced by a new one.

—*James I. Robertson, Jr.*

"South Carolina Must be Destroyed"

By January 1865 it was clear to all but bitter-end southerners, who vowed to die in the last ditch, that the downfall of the Confederacy was near. In mid-January the largest fleet yet assembled in the war, fifty-eight Union ships carrying 627 guns, rendezvoused near Fort Fisher at the mouth of the Cape Fear River below Wilmington, North Carolina. This fort had protected the Confederate blockade-runners that had made Wilmington the Confederacy's major port and virtually its only lifeline to the outside world by the end of 1864. For two days the fleet pounded Fort Fisher with heavy shells, disabling most of its guns and softening it up for an assault by infantry and marines, who captured the fort on January 15. This important victory coiled the tentacles of the Union anaconda even more tightly around the South. Confederate Vice-President Alexander Stephens pronounced the fall of Fort Fisher "one of the greatest disasters which had befallen our Cause from the beginning of the war."

This was perhaps an exaggeration. But the loss of Fort Fisher did bring to a head a growing sentiment for peace. Stephens himself was a prominent advocate of peace negotiations. Jefferson Davis was a hard-liner who still hoped for Confederate victory.

Union troops captured Fort Fisher in January 1865. By then Lee's Army of Northern Virginia was the only substantial military force left in the Confederacy. (Library of Congress)

But in a gesture to the advocates of negotiations, he appointed Stephens and two other Confederate officials to meet Union representatives "with a view to secure peace to the two countries." Lincoln responded with an expression of willingness to receive commissioners "with the view of securing peace to the people of our one common country."

This crucial difference in wording should have alerted southerners to the futility of expecting peace on any terms short of unconditional surrender. For that, in effect, was what Lincoln insisted on when he and Secretary of State Seward met personally with the Confederate envoys February 3 on board a Union ship at Hampton Roads, Virginia. To every proposal for an armistice or preliminary terms, Lincoln replied that the Confederates must lay down their arms, give up slavery, and rejoin the Union. But this meant "unconditional submission," gasped the Confederate commissioners. Precisely, said Lincoln. The southerners returned empty-handed to Richmond, where they reported glumly to Jefferson Davis, who had expected exactly this outcome. He used Lincoln's demands for "humiliating surrender" to stir up flagging southern morale and rekindle war spirit. Lincoln and Seward would soon find that "they had been speaking to their masters," Davis told a cheering crowd in Richmond, for southern armies would yet "compel the Yankees, in less than twelve months, to petition us for peace on our own terms."

If he read these words, William Tecumseh Sherman must have uttered a sigh of exasperation. It was to break the back of this last-ditch resistance that he had embarked on the destructive march from Atlanta to the sea. And now his 60,000 soldiers were moving north from Savannah on a sequel to that march which would prove even more destructive. As Sherman's army had approached Savannah back in December 1864, Georgians asked them: "Why don't you go over to South Carolina and serve them this way? They started it." Sherman had meant to do so all along. On February 1 his army left Savannah, heading toward Virginia with the intention of coming up on Lee's rear and pitching in if the Army of the Potomac had not ended the war before they got there. As matters turned out, Sherman got as far as Raleigh, North Carolina, when word came of Lee's surrender. But the progression of Sherman's wrecking crew through the Carolinas in February and March had much to do with the final Confederate collapse.

South Carolina bore the brunt of Sherman's avengers. This was the state that had defied the national government in the nullification crisis of 1832. It had done so again at the time of the Compromise of 1850, when South Carolinians tried to persuade other slave states to secede. It was the first state to secede in 1860, and the state whose troops had started the war by firing on Fort Sumter. So when Sherman's soldiers crossed the Savannah River into South Carolina in February, they were not in a generous mood. "The truth is," wrote Sherman, "the whole army is burning with an insatiable desire to wreak vengeance upon South Carolina. I almost tremble for her fate, but feel that she deserves all that seems to be in store for her." One soldier declared: "Here is where treason began and, by God, here is where it shall end!" A South Carolina woman whose house was plundered recalled that the soldiers "would sometimes stop to tell me they were sorry for the women and children, but South Carolina must be *destroyed*." Not many buildings remained standing in some villages after the army marched through. The same was true of the countryside. "In Georgia few houses were burned," wrote an officer; "here few escaped." A soldier felt confident that South Carolina "will never want to secede again. . . . I think she has her 'rights' now."

Slicing straight north through the middle of the state, Sherman's army cut the railroad to Charleston without going near the city, compelling the Confederate forces that had defended Charleston so effectively for four years to evacuate it on February 18. By that date much of the state capital of Columbia lay in smoking ruins, for Sherman's army did not skip that city.

—*James M. McPherson*

THE END
IN THE CAROLINAS

Burning Columbia by Robert L. Crewdson
The South's Last Gasp by James M. McPherson
Bentonville by Jay Luvaas

Burning Columbia
by Robert L. Crewdson

"**Not a sound but** the solemn echoes of my horse's hoofs broke the profound silence. Around me was a city of the dead, a sea of ashes, out of which loomed up from ghostly ruins hundreds of blackened chimneys." Such was the scene presented to an ex-Confederate soldier passing through Columbia, South Carolina, one night late in 1865. He rode through a city that once had been one of the most picturesque communities in America. But on the night of February 17 all that had been changed by fire.

Columbia came into the hands of a Federal army commanded by General William Tecumseh Sherman on February 17, 1865. Its conquest was another important gain in Sherman's drive through the heart of the Confederacy; a drive that had begun at Atlanta in mid-November and had faced negligible opposition on its course to Savannah, Georgia. That opposition had been the Confederate army under Lieutenant General John B. Hood, which had confronted Sherman in the Atlanta campaign—the same men that had swung around his flank into Tennessee in a desperate attempt to draw him out of Georgia. But Sherman had simply contained Hood and his men and started on a military picnic in the eastern part of the state.

By the time Sherman captured Savannah in late December, he had earned an infamous reputation throughout the South. By deciding not to maintain supply lines, lines vulnerable to attack by Hood, his Federal army had made the choice to live off the countryside. His foragers, unsupervised for the most part, were certainly not strictly disciplined. They were part of Sherman's theory of total war—that the women and children of the South should feel "the hard hand of war," and lose their will to resist. And as the Federals cut a swath of destruction sixty miles wide from Atlanta to Savannah, the work of that hard hand could be seen in the commonplace plundering and needless destruction that whirled about the army. But as some Union soldiers intimated to the people of Georgia, the state of South Carolina—

General William T. Sherman's triumphant entry into Columbia—South Carolina's proud capital since 1786. Much controversy has surrounded both Confederate and Union actions in Columbia on February 17, 1865. (Harper's Weekly, April 1, 1865)

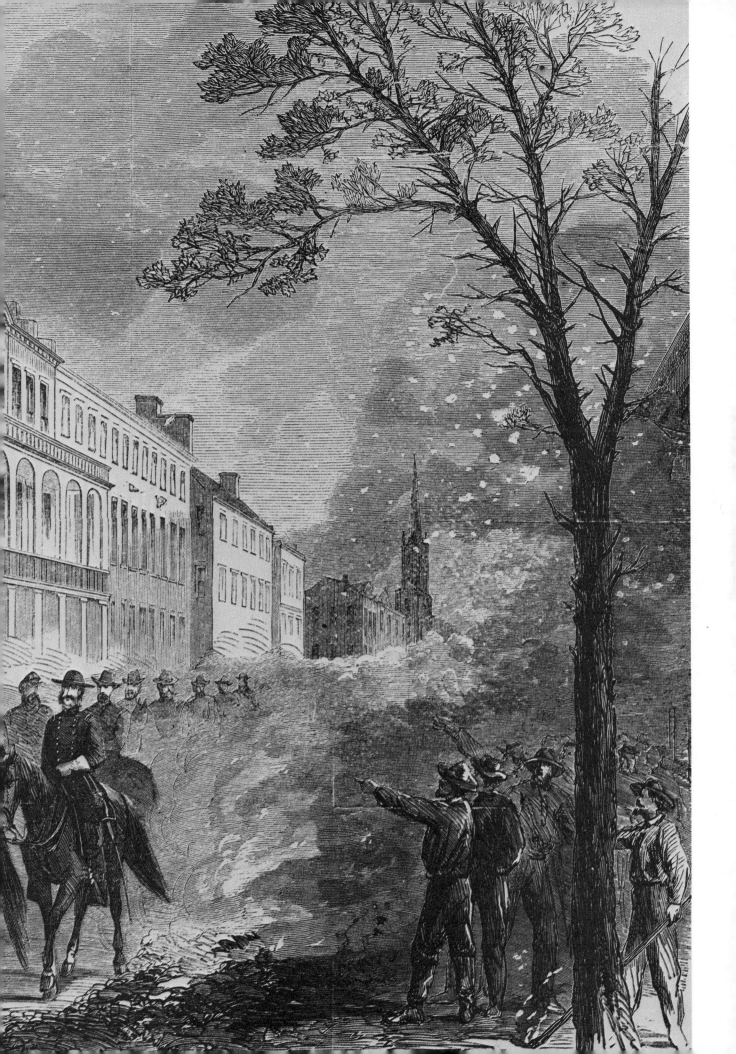

the "hotbed of secession"—was in store for much worse.

After capturing Savannah, Sherman rested his army and gained General in Chief Ulysses S. Grant's approval of his plan for an invasion of the Carolinas. And on February 1 his Union army started northward into South Carolina. To confuse the enemy as to his intentions, Sherman split his army into two columns, each with seemingly different objectives. In order to defend both Charleston and Augusta, the Confederates divided their small forces and, consequently, were unable to hinder the Federal advance.

As the Yankee host advanced into the Palmetto State the, by then, characteristic columns of smoke from burning plantations forewarned terrified Carolinians. The looting and destruction would continue. A Federal officer admitted that the villages of Barnwell and Orangeburg were utterly destroyed without provocation. And the letter of a Union officer to his wife gave specifics: "Valuables procured are estimated by companies . . . one-fifth and first choice falls to the Commander-in-Chief and staff, one-fifth to corps commander and staff, one-fifth to field officers, two-fifths to the company."

Along with the destruction came hints of what Columbia, the capital of South Carolina, could expect. One woman recalled that Sherman had told her, "As to . . . Columbia . . . I shall lay it in ashes." And another testified that two of Sherman's staff officers had told her that Columbia was to be burned. But these statements were probably examples of the bombastic rhetoric used by the Federals from time to time, rather than the result of definite plans to burn the city. However, they showed the animosity felt by the Federals toward that symbolic city.

While Sherman billeted in Savannah, Major General Henry W. Halleck, chief of staff in Washington, sent him a wire: "Should you capture Charleston, I hope that by some accident the place may be destroyed." Sherman's reply was equally amazing: "I will bear in mind your hint as to Charleston . . . the Fifteenth Corps will be on the right wing . . . their position will bring them naturally into Charleston and if you have watched the history of that corps . . . they do their work up pretty well . . . I look upon Columbia as quite as bad as Charleston."

The Union army neared Columbia, a city in panic, on February 15 and advanced to within four miles of the city. For several days, Columbians had been removing possessions from the city to prevent their capture by the Federals. This chaotic traffic turned efforts by Confederate authorities to remove impor-

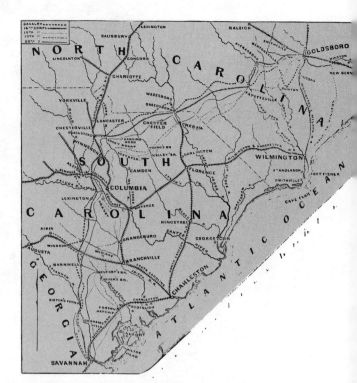

Map showing conquered Carolina cities along the route taken by Sherman's army. Sherman had two purposes: to destroy war resources and to come up on Lee's rear. (Benson J. Lossing)

tant military stores into havoc. And the Federal advance had been so rapid that there had been no time to prepare for the evacuation of the city.

Amidst this destruction and removal of supplies, much of the city's cotton was moved into the streets. General P.G.T. Beauregard, commanding all forces opposing Sherman, intended to fire the bales to prevent their falling into Federal hands. But Lieutenant General Wade Hampton, in command of the Confederate cavalry and a native South Carolinian, urged Beauregard not to burn the cotton as it would endanger the city. Beauregard agreed and the cavalry commander had a staff officer draw up the appropriate orders on the night of the 16th. Unfortunately, the orders could not be issued until the next morning— too late to be of much service.

During the early morning hours of the 17th, Confederate troops withdrew in a bizarre scene of looting and destruction. Military supplies still remaining in Columbia were thrown open to the public, and the ensuing rush for goods rounded out the picture of anarchy. Some exposed cotton was ignited, probably by Confederate troops unaware of Hampton's contrary orders. And then, at about nine o'clock that morning, Mayor Goodwyn and several aldermen rode out through the pandemonium to surrender the city to the Federals. Facing this madhouse scene Colonel George Stone, in command of the vanguard of the Federal XV Corps, accepted the surrender and assured the mayor that the city would not be harmed.

Then a Federal officer described what the Union army saw upon entering Columbia. "On every side were evidences of disorder, bales of cotton scattered here and there, articles . . . of furniture cast pell mell in every direction." And even though he did not mention burning cotton, other Northerners noticed it immediately. However, retreating soldiers and citizens swore there was no cotton on fire when the Federals entered the city. But it is likely that there were small numbers of bales afire and that it did not attract the attention of the refugees in the panic.

During that long day Federal soldiers broke into homes and robbed them of silver, jewelry, and other valuables. Citizens walking along the street would be asked the time of day, and if they unwittingly complied with the request, were relieved of their watches by the soldiers. The Federals also warned the people of what was going to take place that night. W.H. Orchard was told "before morning this damned town will be in ashes . . . you will see three signal rockets go up soon . . . you will see hell." One soldier told Mrs. Ravenel, a prominent resident, that a regiment had sworn to burn the city and that they were going to do it.

Sherman's troops raise the Union flag over the capitol building at Columbia. Although some Union soldiers helped to burn Columbia, far more Union soldiers—including Sherman himself—worked through the night to douse the fires. (Harper's Weekly, April 8, 1865)

Union foragers return to camp at night and display some of their plunder from Columbia, including an admired pocket watch. (Harper's Weekly, April 1, 1865)

To compound the already perilous situation, many of the Union soldiers had become intoxicated. Some white and black citizens injudiciously offered liquor to the Federals upon their arrival, expecting kind treatment in return. But larger quantities of liquor were "confiscated" from the cellars of wealthy Columbians. And, unfortunately, Columbia had more than its share of liquor since Charleston was considered unsafe storage for the vast quantities it received through the blockade.

The biggest concentration of flammable cotton in the streets was located on Richardson and Sumter streets near the heart of the city. But isolated fires broke out at several different places during the day. They were immediately extinguished by the fire companies, with help from Union soldiers. And citizen after citizen later testified that the only cotton they saw burning that day was immediately put out. Brigadier General William B. Hazen of the Federal XV Corps described the cotton fires as so completely extinguished that "a dozen men with tin cups could have managed it." But at about 8:00 p.m. that eve-

ning the conflagration that was to destroy over one-third of the capital city began. It was spread quickly by a strong northwesterly wind, vengeful Federal soldiers, and escaped convicts, and assisted by some Negro servants.

One woman recalled that terrifying night. "At nine precisely my mother called to me . . . she called 'four rockets have gone up' . . . I don't think that it was ten minutes before there came . . . pounding on the doors . . . we opened them . . . street filled with a throng of men, drunken, dancing . . . everyone bearing a tin torch." And fellow Columbian Emma Le-Conte recorded the scene in her diary:

Imagine night turning into noonday, only with a blazing, scorching glare that was horrible—a copper colored sky across which swept columns of black rolling smoke glittering with sparks and flying embers, while all around us were falling thickly showers of burning flakes. Everywhere the palpitating blaze walling the streets with solid masses of flames as far as the eye could reach—filling the sky with its terrible roar.

The College buildings caught . . . All the physicians

and nurses were on the roof trying to save the buildings, and the poor wounded inmates left to themselves, such as could crawled out while those who could not move waited to be burned to death. The Common opposite the gate was crowded with homeless women and children, a few wrapped in blankets and many shivering in the night air. Such a scene as this with the drunken fiendish soldiery in their dark uniforms, infuriated, cursing, screaming, exulting in their work, came nearer the material ideal of hell then anything I ever expect to see again.

William G. Simms watched the owner of a burning house, "standing woebegone, aghast, gazing at his tumbling dwelling." He remembered a "dumb agony" on his face that was "inexpressibly touching." And Mrs. Agnes Law, age 71, was told to get out of her home or be burned alive by soldiers who were already setting her curtains on fire. As the fire engulfed their homes, families scattered to the parks and churches for shelter, but even these places were not spared by the torch-bearing rioters. Many people managed to save only the clothes they wore.

Apparently, small groups of soldiers and convicts watched army rockets (possibly used by the force at night to confirm the location of the several corps) as their private signal to begin the destruction. Edwin J.

The burning of Columbia. Only the abatement of the gale-force winds prevented more of the city from being destroyed. Drawing by William Waud. (Harper's Weekly, April 8, 1865)

Columbia destroyed: A view from the capitol grounds after its occupation by Sherman's army shows the widespread damage caused by the fire of the night of February 17-18. This photograph was taken by George N. Barnard, a New York photographer who followed General Sherman on his march through Georgia and the Carolinas. (Library of Congress)

Scott, a venerable and respected citizen, witnessed this very event: ". . . three rockets were seen to ascend . . . a few minutes elapsed before fires in quick sucession [sic] broke out at intervals so distant that they could not have been communicated from one to the other."

General Sherman, who noticed the blaze at headquarters soon after it began, assisted some of his subordinate officers in trying to save homes and property. A Union officer described the irony of that scene: "General Sherman, Howard and others were out giving instructions for putting out a fire in one place, while a hundred fires were lighting all around [them]." Yet, none of the generals immediately called in any fresh troops to clear out the rioters and arsonists, Sherman stating later that he chose to try to contain the blaze rather than give up and clear the streets.

Not only was the fire spread by drunken soldiers and convicts, but also by flying pieces of shingle and cotton which the wind carried long distances. And citizens remembered seeing perfectly sober soldiers, as well as officers, engaged in the destruction of buildings and property. For them, the help of a high wind was not enough. Then shortly after midnight, a brigade under Brigadier General John M. Oliver was finally called in to restore order. It entered the city at about 2:00 a.m. and three hours later the streets were clear and the fire checked. But it had been too late to limit the damage—265 residences and 193 businesses or public structures had been destroyed.

For the next two days, the Federal army assisted city officials in providing food and shelter for the homeless. But, when they left on the 20th, there remained an undying bitterness and hatred.

The question of who burned Columbia has been a plague since the fateful night in 1865. Columbians had no doubt as to the cause of the fire that destroyed their city. And in 1866, a committee organized by Chancellor J.P. Carroll collected testimony concerning the conflagration. Their evidence placed the blame overwhelmingly on the Union army for starting and spreading the blaze, while some of the citizens even claimed that Sherman had ordered the city burned. However, no written or verbal orders were ever discovered that implied that Sherman had ordered the city destroyed. The general defended himself and his army by attributing the blame to Hampton for rolling the cotton into the streets and firing it. And immediately after the fire, and at subsequent times, Sherman also blamed Columbians for giving liquor to his men.

In 1871, a "Mixed Commission on British and American Claims" investigated the incident to determine if the United States, through the actions of Sherman's army, was liable for British property destroyed in that fire. The committee, in a most diplomatic gesture, stated that neither the Federal nor Confederate authorities were responsible for the blaze.

The cotton played a major role in the controversy over what started the fire. Sherman's assertion that the smoldering cotton began the conflagration did not stand up well in the light of the testimony. It was unlikely that the cotton fires, which were under control all day, could have begun blazes in many different places at the same time. And though cotton was a major factor in spreading the flames, it could not have begun them. A Mr. Scott testified to this fact: "The wind blew from the West, but the fires at night broke out West of Main [Richardson] and Sumter streets, where the cotton bales were, and instead of burning the houses was probably burnt by them."

But the most important figure of the tragedy was the Union soldier. It was stated that the soldiers of Sherman's army had been permitted to destroy at will. But it would have been erroneous to say that the Union army lacked discipline. At Milledgeville, Georgia, Sherman issued strict orders that private

A Columbia church razed by the fire, which destroyed a total of 265 residences and 193 businesses or public structures. Photograph by George N. Barnard. (Library of Congress)

Ruins of Columbia's Washington Street jail. Rebuilding of Columbia following the Civil War was a slow process. (South Carolina Library, University of South Carolina)

property was to be left alone—and it was. So Sherman himself would have seemed to be the crucial figure that night, and a convincing argument could be made to place full responsibility for the fire on him.

The general must have known—he intimated it many times—that his men wanted to destroy Columbia. In order for the city to be preserved, Sherman only had to issue orders similar to those at Milledgeville, but he did not. By putting restraints on his men, Sherman might have let Columbia escape "the hard hand of war." Instead, he gave in to the inevitable. Columbia provided the physical circumstances and war provided the psychological ones; the result was a certainty.

The South's Last Gasp
by James M. McPherson

Leaving much of Columbia in ashes, Sherman's veterans headed for North Carolina while Confederate officials scrambled to scrape together some kind of army to stop them. So far, the Yankees had met little opposition other than cavalry, which they easily brushed aside. Their most formidable enemies during the six weeks after they left Savannah were weather and terrain. These obstacles made Sherman's march through the Carolinas a much harder enterprise than the march through Georgia. That march of 285 miles had taken place in mostly dry fall weather along routes parallel to the principal rivers. The campaign through the Carolinas covered 425 miles and crossed numerous deep rivers and swamps in the midst of an unusually wet winter. "The march to the sea," said Sherman after the war, "seems to have captured [the attention of] everybody, whereas it was child's play compared with the other."

Indeed, the logistical achievements of the Carolinas campaign were astonishing. The Yankees averaged nearly ten miles a day for forty-five days. Rain fell during twenty-eight of those days. Soldiers corduroyed miles of flooded roads and built scores of bridges across rivers and swamps. The ground was so wet that troops—Sherman included—sometimes had to roost in trees for the night. Confederate leaders counted on these conditions to stop Sherman's juggernaut. "My engineers," said General Joseph E. Johnston, "reported that it was absolutely impossible for an army to march across the lower portions of [South Carolina] in winter." Confederate General William Hardee declared that "the Salk [Salkahatchie River and swamps] is impassable." But the Yankees built miles of bridges and crossed it. "I wouldn't have believed it if I hadn't seen it," admitted Hardee. Johnston was equally dumfounded. "When I learned," he wrote, "that Sherman's army was marching through the Salk swamps, making its own corduroy roads at the rate of a dozen miles a day, I made up my mind that there had been no such army in existence since the days of Julius Caesar."

The weather failing to stop Sherman, Johnston earned the dubious privilege of trying to do it. Robert E. Lee prevailed on a reluctant Jefferson Davis to

The end of the war in Fayetteville, North Carolina. Upper drawing: The arsenal. Lower: Sherman's troops drive the Confederate forces out of Fayetteville. (CWTI Collection)

get Johnston reassigned to his old command of the Army of Tennessee. But it was no longer the same army. It consisted of fragments of Hood's army that had survived the disastrous retreat after the battle of Nashville in December, plus the garrisons that had evacuated Savannah and Charleston along with odds and ends from elsewhere. In all, Johnston could muster a bare 20,000 effective troops. With these he hoped to blunt Sherman's advance in North Carolina long enough so that his own small force could unite with Lee's Army of Northern Virginia somewhere near the North Carolina-Virginia border. These combined armies could then strike Sherman and Grant in turn, winning additional time for the Confederacy and perhaps winning the war.

It was a forlorn hope born of desperation. At best the combined Confederate forces would number 70,000 ragged, starving soldiers of shaky morale against Grant's and Sherman's combined force of 210,000 confident, well-fed veterans eager to finish the war here and now. At Bentonville, North Carolina, on March 19 Johnston launched his attack on part of Sherman's army. It was virtually the Confederacy's last gasp.

Bentonville
by Jay Luvass

BENTONVILLE SCENE—From the April 22, 1865 "Frank Leslie's Illustrated Newspaper," this drawing by J. E. Taylor shows "Major-Gen. Mower, commanding 1st Division, 17th Corps, turning the Rebel left half a mile from Bentonville, March 20." This really happened March 21.

WILLIAM J. HARDEE—His two divisions played an important role in Confederate plans. (From "Battles & Leaders.")

T O THE weary troops of Joseph E. Johnston's command, occupying the fresh breastworks in the woods south of the hamlet of Bentonville, it must have seemed an eternity waiting for Sherman's army to enter the trap. Soon, to judge from the sounds of approaching firing, the dismounted cavalry would break off the skirmish in the ravine ahead and pass through the line of battle to reform on the flanks. Then, when the Union infantry hit the works that blocked the Goldsboro road, the real scrap would begin. Alert eyes scanned the woods at the far side of the field for signs of movement; anxious glances over the shoulder surveyed the rear for signs that William J. Hardee's two divisions would arrive in time.

Hardee's men had been in almost daily contact with the enemy for nearly two weeks, but most of those present on this Sunday morning were new to the command. Survivors from Hood's Army of Tennessee which had been destroyed at Nashville, Robert F. Hoke's division fresh from Virginia, artillery regiments grown stale from garrison duty, and even a youthful brigade of North Carolina Junior Reserves, "the seed corn of the Confederacy," were assembled at Bentonville in this last desperate attempt to block Sherman's northward sweep through the Carolinas. Ten days ago they had been scattered all the way from Kinston to Charlotte; never before had they fought together as a unit.

In addition to obvious weaknesses in organization, this makeshift aggregation of about 20,000 was top-heavy in command. Johnston, who on February 23 had been assigned the task of stemming Sherman's invasion, was assisted by D. H. Hill, a brilliant but truculent combat officer; Braxton Bragg, who had been relieved from command of the Army of Tennessee after the fiasco atop Missionary Ridge in November, 1863; Lafayette McLaws and Hoke, both of whom had received their training under Lee; and Stephen D. Lee,

A. P. Stewart, Benjamin F. Cheatham, and William J. Hardee, all capable corps commanders who had fought against Sherman in the West. The cavalry was in the aggressive hands of Wade Hampton, Jeb Stuart's successor, and Joseph Wheeler. Famous names, these, but many had not worked together before and several were conspicuous for previous failures.

PROSPECTS for victory seemed dreary. Sherman commanded a veteran force of some 60,000, which he had divided into two permanent wings to attain greater mobility. The Left Wing, comprising the XIV and XX Corps, under H. W. Slocum, was now approaching from the west; the Right Wing, led by O. O. Howard, was known to be some distance to the south and east, in the direction of Goldsboro. Faulty maps exaggerated the distance separating the two and led Johnston to believe that he could overwhelm the Left Wing before the other could come to its assistance. If Sherman's army were permitted to reach Goldsboro, it would there be joined by two additional corps under A. H. Terry and J. M. Schofield, marching inland from the coast, and Sherman would then have 100,000 men to add to Grant's beleaguering army at Petersburg. This must be prevented at all costs; to delay would be to forfeit the campaign.

Under the protective cover of Hampton's skirmishers Johnston made his dispositions. Bragg, nominally in charge of Hoke's division, was given the Confederate left, straddling the Goldsboro road. Hardee, as soon as his divisions reached the scene, was to take up position *en echelon* to the right, with Stewart's corps prolonging the line still farther until it ran virtually parallel to the

Goldsboro road. The Confederate line thus resembled a sickle, with the cutting edge poised to slash away at the Left Wing as it marched along the road to Goldsboro. But the dense woods and thickets hindered deployment and all troops had not reached their assigned positions when Hoke's pickets were driven back by advance units of the XIV Corps. Soon hundreds of blue-clad infantry could be seen moving across the fields of Cole's plantation, totally unaware that between them and Goldsboro lay Johnston's entire army.

Sherman anticipated no attack and in fact had left Slocum's wing early that morning to be with the Right Wing when it reached Goldsboro. He had ridden only a short distance when he heard artillery fire, but a message from Slocum convinced him that it was only stubborn cavalry resistance. The Right Wing continued to press toward Goldsboro.

FOR THE men in Slocum's command March 19 began like any other day. At daybreak they were roused and by 7 a.m. the leading regiments of William P. Carlin's division, XIV Corps, had consumed their usual fare of hardtack and coffee and begun their march. For the first

BENTONVILLE BATTLEFIELD—This aerial photograph, supplied through the courtesy of the Raleigh (N.C.) Times, shows the terrain over which the Battle of Bentonville was fought on March 19, 1865, the first day. Arrows "A" and "B" indicate the first attack of the Confederates; "C" and "D" their follow-up after initial success. "E" marks the route which Hardee's men followed in supporting the Confederate left; "F" the route of Cogswell's brigade which arrived just in time to relieve Confederate pressure on the rear of Morgan's troops who held the Union right. The Federals finally stabilized their lines in the wooded area in the foreground. Public interest in the Bentonville Battlefield was greatly stimulated by an article which appeared in the Raleigh Times in 1957. This attention led to improved marking of the battlefield.

time in weeks they were blessed with a beautiful day. With the worst of the weather and swamps behind them, and the peach trees in full bloom, the soldiers, warmed by the spring sun, stepped out "vigorously and cheerfully" in anticipation of a rest and fresh supplies at Goldsboro. "I would like to see [the Confederates] whaled," one of the men wrote "but would like to wait till we refit. You see that too much of a good thing gets *old,* and one don't enjoy even campaigning after fifty or sixty days of it . . ."

They had moved but a short distance when they encountered Hampton's dismounted cavalry. When these "didn't drive worth a damn," Slocum ordered Carlin to deploy and clear the road, and Carlin's leading regiments worked their way forward for five miles until, at 10 a.m., they encountered Hoke's infantry posted behind rail works. Of course they had no inkling yet that in the woods stretching off to their left the Confederates were to be found in even greater numbers.

As soon as Carlin's troops reached Cole's house, Hoke's artillery opened fire. Quickly the first two brigades took shelter in a wooded ravine a few yards in front of the house. The third brigade deployed south of the Goldsboro road. Still under the impression that the force blocking the road "consisted only of cavalry with a few pieces of artillery," Slocum sent his first message to Sherman, advising him that no help would be necessary. Meanwhile Carlin's division prepared to advance.

The men plunged into the woods. A few minutes passed, then a furious discharge of shots broke out on the left, where G. P. Buell's brigade had stumbled into a hornets' nest. One of Buell's officers candidly described the scene:

> The Rebs held their fire untill we were within 3 rods of the works when they opened fire from all sides and gave us an awful volley. We went for them with a yell and got within 5 paces of their works. . . . I tell you it was a tight place. . . . Men pelted each other with Ramrods and butts of muskets and [we] were finally compeled to fall back. . . . [We] stood as long as man could stand and when that was no longer a possibility we run like the deuce. . . .

Quickly the brigades reformed in the ravine east of the Cole house and set about improvising a defense line. South of the Goldsboro road Carlin's third brigade was joined by Morgan's division, with two brigades posted behind "good log works" and a third in reserve. Soon the leading brigade of Williams' XX Corps arrived and took up position in a small ravine behind the one sheltering Carlin's division. Thus two divisions plus a stray brigade, scarcely 10,000 men, found themselves facing a force of unknown strength (estimates ran as high as 40,000 and it was even rumored that Robert E. Lee was present to direct operations) and defending a line that was neither continuous nor well adapted to the terrain. Slocum sent another messenger after Sherman, this time pleading for reinforcements.

THE INITIATIVE now passed to the Confederates. Johnston had hoped to attack sooner, but Carlin's reconnaissance-in-force, though easily repulsed, had upset his timetable. Bragg felt sufficiently hard pressed to call for reinforcements and Johnston ordered Hardee, whose troops were just arriving upon the field, to send one of his two divisions to support Bragg. McLaws' division not only arrived too late to be of any real assistance to Bragg, but his absence was felt on the Confederate right, where Hardee and Stewart were preparing their counterstroke. This weakened the right—the cutting edge—and delayed the Confederate attack.

By 2:45 Hardee's troops were in position and the order was given to advance. Forming in two extended lines, the Confederates moved across the 600 yards that separated the two armies. It was a stirring sight, but to those watching anxiously from Bragg's trenches it was painful to see

WILLIAM P. CARLIN—His division bore the brunt of the Confederate attack on March 19.

ROBERT F. HOKE—His division, fresh from Virginia, held a position across the Goldsboro road. It was his force that a Federal reconnaissance-in-force encountered to touch off the Confederate surprise attack.

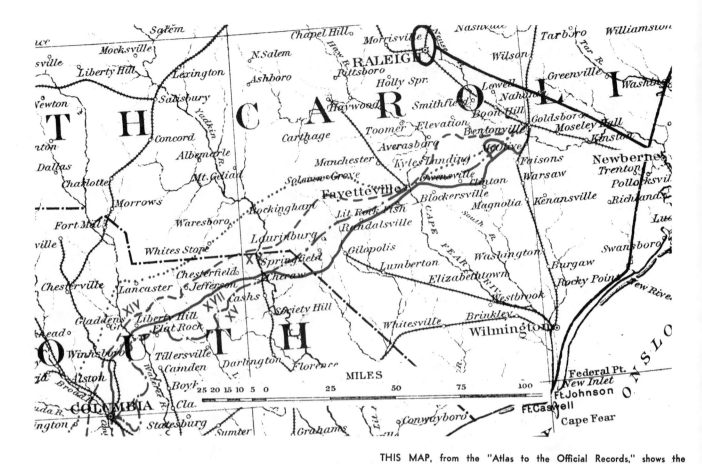

how close together the battle flags were: Some regiments were scarcely larger than companies, and one division had shrunk to a pitiful 500 men!

Though they easily brushed aside the Union pickets, the gray lines staggered as they hit Carlin's unfinished breastworks. Within minutes, however, a gap between the two blue brigades had been uncovered and, pouring through, the troops of Hardee, Stewart, and Hill overran the second Union line some 300 yards beyond. "We lay behind our incomplete works and gave them fits," Buell's candid lieutenant reported to his family.

> We checked them and held them to it untill they turned the left of the 1st Brigade and of course that was forced to retreat. . . . Our Brigade had to "follow suit." . . . When the Rebs got around us so as to fire into our rear [Carlin] turned to the boys: "No use boys," and started back. The Regt. followed and . . . it was the best thing we ever did. For falling back we met a line of Rebs marching straight for our rear and in 15 minutes more we would have been between two lines of the buggers. . . . We showed . . . some of the best running ever did. . . .

THE ENTIRE Union left was crushed by this well-executed blow and was driven back in confusion upon the XX Corps, then moving into position a mile to the rear. Carlin's third brigade was driven into the lines of Morgan's division south of the Goldsboro road. Viewing the scene, one Union soldier was reminded of the confusion after Stonewall Jackson hit the XI Corps at Chancellorsville. Another, a staff officer, saw:

> . . . masses of men slowly and doggedly falling back along the Goldsboro road and through the fields and open woods on the left. . . . Minie balls were whizzing in every direction. . . . Checking my horse, I saw the rebel regiments in front in full view, stretching through the fields to the left as far as the eye could reach, advancing rapidly, and firing as they came. . . . The onward sweep of the rebel lines was like the waves of the ocean, relentless. . . .

Jeff Davis, commanding the XIV Corps, ordered Morgan to shift his reserve brigade to the left in order to plug the expanding gap. "Give them the best you've got and we'll whip them yet." Catching up the words "we'll whip them yet," the men of Benjamin Fearing's brigade moved swiftly to the Goldsboro road and charged into the left flank of the Confederates pursuing remnants of Carlin's division. Taken in flank by additional Confederates coming down the Goldsboro road, the brigade then retreated 300 yards and threw up a new line. Here the fighting gradually "dwindled off to an extended skirmish."

The Confederates next concentrated against Morgan's division. Fearing's withdrawal had created a gap that could not be plugged before three brigades from Hill's corps smashed through and assaulted Morgan's breastworks from the rear. Hoke wanted to exploit this break-

JOSEPH A. MOWER—On March 21, he got his division around the Confederate left but was thrown back by Confederate reserves. (From "Battles & Leaders.")

of artillery fire. Five times they tried to drive a wedge into the Union line; five times they withered before a storm of canister and bullets. The Union guns were especially devastating as "the raging leaden hailstorm of grape and canister literally barked the trees, cutting off the limbs as if cut by hand." One Confederate division lost an estimated 25 per cent. A survivor from the ranks, writing years after the battle, confessed: "If there was a place [at] . . . Gettysburg as hot as that spot, I never saw it."

The final attack came at sundown. Gradually the firing died away as dusk faded into darkness and night separated the weary combatants. Hastily burying their dead, the Confederates withdrew to the positions they had occupied in the morning, but for Sherman's troops the night of March 19 was one of sustained activity. It was late in the evening before Slocum's appeal for help finally reached Sherman. Standing "in a bed of ashes up to his ankles, chewing impatiently the stump of a cigar, with his hands clasped behind him, and with nothing on but a red flannel undershirt and a pair of drawers," Sherman issued orders setting the Right Wing in motion towards Bentonville. Marching by the shortest route, the Right Wing approached the battlefield from the direction of Goldsboro, *behind* Hoke's line of breastworks. By noon on the 20th Hoke had been forced to evacuate these and take up a new position parallel to the Goldsboro road and near enough to command it. By late afternoon Sherman's army was united and by nightfall Howard's troops were firmly intrenched.

through by throwing the weight of his division into the breach, but Bragg restrained him and ordered a frontal attack instead. For the next few minutes the fighting was desperate as men clubbed each other in dense thickets and swampy woods. Some Confederate officers claimed "it was the hottest infantry fight they had ever been in except Cold Harbor," and at one point Morgan's soldiers, completely surrounded, were forced to fight simultaneously from both sides of their breastworks. Indeed, had it not been for the chance arrival of another brigade from the XX Corps the day most certainly would have been lost. As it happened, Cogswell's brigade emerged from a tangled swamp behind Hill's men as they assaulted Morgan's rear lines. With a yell the brigade went at them and managed to push the Confederates back to the Goldsboro road, where a battle line ultimately was stabilized.

THE THIRD and final Confederate attack was directed against the XX Corps, now in position a mile behind Carlin's first line. Here Carlin's division found refuge, and with Kilpatrick's cavalry guarding the exposed flank, a formidable line of trenches erected by the 1st Michigan Engineers, and powerful artillery in support of fresh infantry, the XX Corps was ready and waiting.

The Confederate attack was delayed by Fearing's threat to the left flank and the need to reorganize after the fight with Carlin's division, so it was 5 p.m. before the gray lines emerged from the pine woods in front of the XX Corps. They were promptly greeted by a deadly barrage

THERE WAS no heavy fighting on the 20th, only "sharp skirmishing" along the entire front. The Confederate position now resembled a V and in effect was an enlarged bridgehead covering Bentonville and the only bridge crossing the swollen waters of Mill Creek. The Union line roughly corresponded to the Confederate position except for the XX Corps, which remained where it had fought on the previous day. Johnston, now on the defensive, remained in his trenches, hoping to induce Sherman to attack, but Sherman had other plans. He was anxious to open communication with Schofield and Terry at Goldsboro and had no desire to bring on a general engagement until this had been accomplished. At dusk a heavy rain set in, lasting until morning. The Confederates, anticipating orders to fall back across Mill Creek, spent a sleepless night. Sherman himself expected and in fact hoped that Johnston would slip away during

THIS MAP, prepared by the author, shows the positions of the two armies on March 20-21, 1865. With the two wings of his army united, Sherman had 60,000 men to Johnston's 20,000. The Roman numerals indicate Federal corps. Mower's movement around the Confederate left is shown by an arrow. Johnston retreated on the night of March 21 to Smithfield, clearing the way for Sherman to join Schofield at Goldsboro.

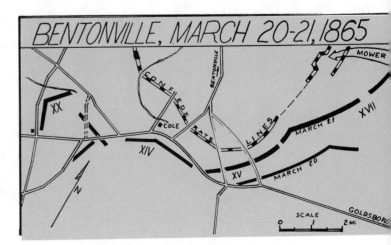

BENTONVILLE, MARCH 20-21, 1865

the night, as he had done so frequently during the recent campaign for Atlanta. At daybreak, however, his old antagonist was still there and the fighting flared up anew.

Throughout the 21st steady pressure was maintained against the Confederates. Union sharpshooters, lodged in the buildings of Cole's plantation, annoyed the men opposite in Hill's trenches. Farther to the right the XV Corps wrenched an advanced line of rifle pits from Hoke and McLaws. The most serious fighting developed on the extreme Union right where J. A. Mower succeeded in working two brigades from the XVII Corps around the Confederate left flank. By 4 p.m. these had seized two lines of rifle pits and were advancing toward the bridge that spanned Mill Creek—Johnston's only line of retreat. But in his eagerness Mower had outdistanced the rest of the corps, with the result that he now found himself isolated and three-quarters of a mile in advance of the nearest supporting troops.

To meet this sudden thrust the Confederates mounted a series of spirited counterattacks. Cumming's Georgia brigade, which had already been ordered to bolster the left, arrived just in time to meet Mower head-on as he neared the Smithfield road. Simultaneously Hardee, in command of the Confederate left, appeared at the head of the 8th Texas Cavalry and promptly charged Mower's left flank while Wheeler's cavalry, moving up on the right of Hardee, drove a wedge between Mower's brigades and the rest of the XVII Corps. Hampton assisted in the repulse of Mower by attacking the exposed right flank with another brigade of cavalry.

Forced to retreat from this nest of angry hornets, Mower fell back to the shelter of a ravine some distance to the rear, and when the fire slackened he again withdrew, this time to his original position. He had reformed his lines and was about to renew the assault when orders arrived from Sherman to remain where he was and dig in. With this order all offensive action ceased for the day.

AGAIN both armies spent a wet, miserable night huddled in trenches and rude shelters, exposed to a driving rain that denied them even the comforts of a camp fire. Occasionally the flash of gun fire would illuminate the sky and reveal the position of the Union batteries which lobbed shells into the Confederate lines with cruel persistence. During the night Johnston learned that Schofield and Terry had reached Goldsboro and were within a day's march of the battlefield. With nothing to gain and everything to lose by remaining cooped up at Bentonville he ordered an immediate withdrawal. When Sherman's skirmishers probed cautiously forward the next morning they found only vacant works before them. A gesture was made to follow the retreating Confederates a few miles north of Mill Creek, but after burying the dead and removing the wounded Sherman's army went into camp near Goldsboro, "there to rest and receive the clothing and supplies of which they stood in need." Later they moved on to Raleigh, and at the Bennett House, a few miles west of Durham's Station, Johnston on April 26 surrendered the remnants of his army.

Bentonville was the climax of Sherman's Carolina campaign. By Civil War standards it was not a large battle, for compared with the slaughter at Shiloh, Antietam, Gettysburg, or Chickamauga the casualties seem slight. Sherman lost 1,527, most of them in the Left Wing, while Johnston suffered 2,606 casualties, a large number of whom were prisoners. Neither army won a clear-cut victory and public attention soon focused on the more dramatic events that led to the surrender of Lee's army at Appomattox.

BELOW, from the April 15, 1865 edition of "Harper's Weekly," is a drawing by William Waud showing the "Fifteenth Corps engaged on the right" at Bentonville March 20. Bentonville attracted little attention because it was followed so soon by Lee's surrender at Appomattox.

AFTER THE BATTLE—This is how a part of the Bentonville battle-field looked after March 21 when Johnston withdrew. The battlefield is much the same today.

STRATEGICALLY the battle failed to prevent or even seriously to delay the fulfillment of Sherman's objective—the occupation of Goldsboro, the consolidation of his forces there, and the establishment of a new line of communications based upon the railroad to New Bern. Sherman's main concern was supplies; he had nothing to fear from Johnston's army unless the latter could catch one of his columns and defeat it in detail.

But was this likely, or even possible? By 1865 the American soldiers had become so adept in constructing fieldworks that it was a rare occasion when either side achieved a decisive victory. At Bentonville the Left Wing outnumbered Johnston's whole army by some 10,000, and Slocum had only to dig in and hold on until help arrived. True, Carlin's division was dispersed and Morgan's division might well have been destroyed but for the timely intervention of Cogswell's brigade, but even with these two

divisions routed, there remained the XX Corps plus four brigades which had been left to guard the wagon trains. It is inconceivable that this corps, posted behind strong earthworks and supported by both cavalry and artillery, could not have maintained its position until reinforced the following morning. One is forced to agree with Gen. Jacob D. Cox who, when informed by "rebel citizens" that Slocum had been whipped, noted in his journal: "We suspect that his advance guard may have received a rap, but know the strength of his army too well to believe that Johnston can whip him." And even if the Left Wing were crippled as a fighting force, it would not have prevented Sherman from concentrating over 60,000 troops at Goldsboro, and there was no way in which Johnston could have stopped this force from marching northward into Virginia.

Bentonville was a battle of subordinates. Sherman was not even present on the 19th. Slocum handled his reserves with skill, but the credit for stopping Johnston's attacks properly belongs to Fearing, Cogswell, and Morgan. Had it not been for the faulty judgment of another subordinate, Carlin, in selecting a defensive position in front of instead of behind a swampy watercourse, there might have been no cause for a retreat at all. Among the Confederates, Hampton and Hardee seem to have been the guiding spirits; Hampton selected the site and suggested the plan of battle, Hardee personally organized and led the Confederate charge on the 19th, and both were responsible for driving back Mower on the 21st. Bragg figured in two unfortunate decisions. By calling for reinforcements which were not needed he must bear the responsibility for delaying the Confederate attack against Carlin as well as for weakening it at its most decisive point, and by restraining Hoke from exploiting Hill's breakthrough behind Morgan's lines he may also have jeopardized the success of this attack.

As for the rival commanders, both are open to criticism. Johnston's strategy was sound enough but he lacked the numbers necessary for a decisive victory. Why he remained at Bentonville after Sherman's army was united, however, is a mystery. He claimed that it was to evacuate the wounded, but this is scarcely a valid justification for the likely sacrifice of one of the few Confederate armies that remained intact. Yet he lingered with no apparent plan, no hope of reinforcements, and no right to assume that Sherman would repeat the mistake he made at Kenesaw Mountain. Perhaps he sensed that his mission was futile. Whatever his reason, Johnston maintained his position with his usual skill and his withdrawal was as masterly as any in his career.

TO APPRECIATE Sherman's conduct one must understand his method of waging war. Sherman was essentially a strategist, a master of maneuver and logistics. With him strategic considerations always came first and in this instance Goldsboro and not the enemy army was his primary objective. He wished to shun a general engagement on the 20th because he was unwilling "to lose men in a direct attack when it can be avoided." He has been criticized for recalling Mower and it is probably true that had he supported his impulsive subordinate he would have won a great victory. But his opportunity was not as golden as it often is made to appear. Mower had actually retreated *before* receiving the order to withdraw, and had he been permitted to advance a second time he would have found the Confederates heavily reinforced in his front. Sherman did not realize the extent of Mower's penetration until the next day, when bodies of Union soldiers were found within 50 yards of Johnston's headquarters. By counterattacking promptly with all available troops, the Confederates had created an illusion of strength. That it was not altogether illusory, however, is suggested by the Union casualty returns. Mower lost 149 men in this action—more than the entire XX Corps in the first day's fighting.

THE CAMPAIGN
TO APPOMATTOX

by William C. Davis

"To Close the War Right Here"

In the early evening of April 1, 1865, Colonel Horace Porter mounted his horse and rode toward the headquarters of the Army of the Potomac at Dabney's Mills, seven miles southwest of Petersburg, Virginia. As he and his orderly passed groups of men, the aide called out to them the news of a great victory over the Confederates at Five Forks, five miles to the west. But some of the soldiers were unimpressed by the news. "No you don't," one called back while thumbing his nose, "April fool!"

All Fools' Day it was, and as Porter came wildly riding into Dabney's Mills, yelling his good news from the moment he sighted headquarters, not a few onlookers took him to be either overwrought with the spirit of the day, or else just drunk. Porter was neither. He approached the tent of General in Chief U.S. Grant to find him and his staff sitting around a blazing fire. Finally Porter's hearers began taking his shouted reports of a triumph seriously. "In a moment," he later wrote, "all but the imperturbable general-in-chief were on their feet giving vent to boisterous demonstrations of joy . . . Dignity was thrown to the winds."

Porter rushed to Grant and started vigorously slapping him on the back in congratulation before he remembered himself. Grant, cigar in mouth, exasperatingly calm, only asked how many prisoners had been taken. Then, after hearing from Porter a full account of the victory, and writing a few dispatches in his tent, Grant came out again. He had written to the President and to his subordinates. He had sent out orders that he had waited almost a year to give, directives that meant the final, speedy demise of the Confederate army before him, and of the enemy capital at Richmond. Calmly, almost as if talking about the weather, he told his staff that "I have ordered a general assault along the lines." Grant was on his way to Appomattox.

For over nine months the Federal Army of the Potomac led by Major General George G. Meade and the Army of the James recently placed under Major General E. O. C. Ord had faced General Robert E. Lee's Army of Northern Virginia and other Confederate commands along an ever-lengthening line of entrenchments and fortifications extending from Richmond twenty miles south, past Bermuda Hundred on the James River, to Petersburg on the south side of the Appomattox River. Encircling the city, the lines of defense had gradually crept to the southwest over the months, stretching Lee's thin ranks of men even thinner as Grant, exercising over-all command of both Federal armies, sought continually to get around the Confederate right flank and cut off Lee's routes of escape. Aside from several severe battles such as The Crater, Globe Tavern, Poplar Springs Church, and Hatcher's Run, there was little to break the seemingly endless tension and monotony of siege life.

As the spring of 1865 approached, both Lee and Grant made plans. Grant's intentions were no secret to an intuitive Lee. The Federal would continue his attempts to cut the Confederates off from their lines of communications to the south, isolating them at Petersburg until surrender was inevitable. Lee, on the other hand, planned to attempt not only a break out of the siege lines but grand strategy as well, for the first and only time since his appointment as Confederate general in chief in January 1865. It was a plan born of desperation and deluded hopes.

With fewer than 50,000 men to face Grant's 112,000, Lee could hardly hope to survive where he was. But if he could join the bulk of his army with the Army of Tennessee led by General Joseph E. Johnston, now facing a much superior army under Major General William T. Sherman in North Carolina, then the two of them combined might perhaps defeat Sherman and be ready to meet Grant soon thereafter. At the same time, however, Lee must be able to leave a force in Virginia strong enough to keep Grant at arm's length while all this was taking place. It is indeed remarkable that a man of Lee's genius would even consider so patently hopeless a plan. But then, there was little else he could do.

As a prelude to his movement, Lee would have Major General John B. Gordon lead an attack on Fort Stedman in the Federal line east of Petersburg. A devastating surprise victory here would draw men away from Grant's left flank off to the west, thereby

Grant and his staff at City Point, Virginia, shortly before the opening of the Appomattox Campaign. (Library of Congress)

Sheridan and his generals at Dinwiddie Court House, reconnoitering before the attack at Five Forks.
(Rossiter Johnson, Campfires and Battlefields)

opening the way for Lee to move south to join Johnston. But Gordon's attack failed, costing Lee 5,000 casualties in the process.

What was worse, it alerted an equally intuitive Grant to Lee's next move. It had been assumed for some time that the Confederates would attempt a linkup with Johnston. Grant had closed off all rail routes out of the city but one, the South Side Railroad that led west to Burkeville. There Lee could hope to take the Richmond & Danville into North Carolina. Obviously, now that Gordon's attack had failed, Lee's only remaining move was to escape via the South Side before Grant captured it, too.

Lee sent his nephew, Major General Fitzhugh Lee, commanding the army's cavalry, off to Five Forks with his entire command. Three brigades of the infantry division of Major General George E. Pickett went with him, along with two other brigades, their mission being to hold Five Forks, a major intersection through which Grant would have to pass in taking the South Side. By advancing from there toward Dinwiddie Court House, Lee hoped to push Grant's left back and away from the railroad.

This same day, March 29, Grant sent the newly arrived cavalry corps of Major General Philip H. Sheridan to Dinwiddie with instructions to take Five Forks, assisted by Meade's V Corps under Major General Gouverneur K. Warren, and pass on to destroy part of the South Side Railroad. The night before, Grant had told Sheridan that he "intended to close the war right here, with this movement."

Pickett, exercising over-all command of the forces at Five Forks, moved south and advanced on Dinwiddie Court House on March 31, a hopeless attack of 10,000 Confederates against at least 12,000 cavalry and Warren's approaching 16,000 infantry. He made surprising progress before night fell, and then came the news that Warren was moving toward Pickett's rear, heading to get between him and the railroad. At 5 a.m. the next morning, April 1, Pickett pulled his command back toward Five Forks, deploying it rather carelessly in the expectation that a diversion from the main Confederate line would prevent Sheridan's advancing against him that day. Then too, though there were better positions available a mile north, he had just received a dispatch from Lee. "Hold Five Forks at all hazards," it said.

Sheridan, meanwhile, despite muddy roads, followed Pickett, "sure that he would not give up the Five Forks crossroads without a fight." As he approached the intersection, Sheridan formulated his plan of attack, intending to assault the whole Confederate front with two of his cavalry divisions led by Brigadier General Wesley Merritt, fake an attempt to turn Pickett's right flank, and send Warren's V Corps around the Confederate left to cut him off from Lee.

The attack was a crushing success, in part because both Pickett and Fitzhugh Lee were absent from the field at a fish fry. Fighting on foot, Sheridan's cavalry held the Confederates at their entrenchments. Then at about 4 p.m., after some apparent delay, Warren moved, at first missed finding Pickett's unprotected flank, but with Sheridan's aid finally found it. Sheridan, ruthless, ambitious, easily moved to resentment, did not like Warren, who lacked the jugular instinct that characterized "Little Phil." Now at the height of the battle, even as Pickett's command was being crushed, Sheridan relieved Warren of his command. Though later exonerated of the charges Sheridan placed against him, Warren was scarred for life.

So was Pickett. At first skeptical when word of the Federal advance interrupted his fish fry, he finally believed it only when he saw his couriers actually being captured before his eyes by Sheridan's cavalry pickets. Running a terrible gantlet of enemy fire, he rode back to his shattered command, only to join it as all but a few regiments were in full retreat. Fitzhugh Lee was entirely unable to rejoin his command. Instead, the rout went on, Sheridan capturing in all nearly 4,000 Confederates, Five Forks, and a sure path to the South Side Railroad.

Pickett never fully lived down the disgrace of his defeat—though R. E. Lee's specific orders to hold Five Forks prevented him from taking better ground elsewhere—and Lee never forgave him. Curiously enough, however, Lee seems to have uttered no reproach of his nephew, though Fitzhugh Lee was just as culpable as Pickett.

Before the fighting was entirely done, couriers in blue and gray were riding east, one of them, Colonel Porter, jubilantly proclaiming the success to all hearers. The news that went to Lee was just the opposite. Already he had advised President Jefferson Davis that to save his army, and perhaps the cause, he would have to leave his present lines soon. Word of

The Battle of Five Forks, sketched on the spot by Alfred R. Waud. (Library of Congress)

Pickett's disaster, received late in the afternoon, confirmed his advice. Quickly he sent three brigades of Lieutenant General Richard H. Anderson's small command to the right of his line. They would help Fitzhugh Lee's remaining cavalry in an attempt to hold the railroad. By doing so, however, Lee virtually had to abandon three miles of his line near Hatcher's Run—tacit admission to all in the army that evacuation was imminent. At the same time, Lee ordered Lieutenant General James Longstreet, commanding the First Corps in the fortifications around Richmond, to bring Major General Charles Field's division down to reinforce his sparsely manned line. Sending his men by foot, then train, Longstreet and staff rode through the night on horseback. "Our noble beasts peered through the loaded air," wrote Longstreet of the night ride, "and sniffed the coming battle." "The cause," he said, "was lost."

"This is a Sad Business"

Before dawn the next morning Lee knew this was his last day in Petersburg. "I see no prospect of doing more than holding our position here till night," he wired Secretary of War John C. Breckinridge. "I am not certain that I can do that." He hoped to withdraw his army across the Appomattox and then move west to the Richmond & Danville Railroad near Amelia Court House, thirty-six miles west of Petersburg. There Lee's Petersburg command, Major General William Mahone's division of Longstreet's corps, still facing part of the Federal Army of the James at Bermuda Hundred, and Lieutenant General

Grant's supply vessels line the bank of the Appomattox River near Petersburg. (U.S. Army Military History Institute)

A Federal pontoon bridge spans the Appomattox River west of Petersburg. (U.S. Army Military History Institute)

Richard S. Ewell's troops east of Richmond could all rendezvous for the movement to join Johnston. Orders went out accordingly. "It will be a difficult operation," Lee confided to Breckinridge.

Just how difficult was largely up to Grant, and as April 2 dawned, his "general assault along the lines" bid fair to prevent Lee from making the move at all. The Federal lines advanced before dawn all across the Petersburg front. They emerged from the thick morning fog to crush almost everything before them. By noon all of the western portion of Lee's line had crumbled, except for an outstanding resistance at Fort Gregg. This alone kept Meade's II, VI, and XXIV Corps from rolling up Lee's right into the city of Petersburg itself. Gordon held the city proper against the Union IX Corps. Meanwhile, Lieutenant General A.P. Hill, commanding Lee's Third Corps, had been killed in a chance encounter with two Federal soldiers, and the newly arrived Longstreet assumed temporary command of what remained of Hill's troops.

Cut off from Lee by the Federal breakthrough were the remnants of Pickett's division of Longstreet's corps; the division of Major General Bushrod Johnson, comprising the whole of Lieutenant General Anderson's corps; Major General Henry Heth's division and part of the Light Division of Hill's corps; and Lee's cavalry corps. They would have to cross the Appomattox at Bevill's Bridge several miles to the

After Lee was forced to evacuate the city of Petersburg on April 2, elements of the Army of the Potomac began moving into the Confederate stronghold. (Library of Congress)

west in order to reach Amelia Court House, if at all. To an officer near him, as the orders for the evacuation were being executed, a weary Robert E. Lee confessed that "this is a sad business."

By 8 p.m. the movement was under way, though Anderson and the other isolated commands with him had started west some hours before, pursued by Federal cavalry. Lee's artillery went first: heavy, slow wagons and gun carriages, always in bad condition, and now struggling through the mud and darkness. Yet all but ten guns of the mobile artillery were gotten out, and those that remained were spiked or otherwise disabled. Field's division of Longstreet's corps followed, along with Major General Cadmus Wilcox's division of Hill's command, now under Longstreet. Under "Old Pete" Longstreet these divisions crossed the Appomattox and turned west. After them came the rear guard, Gordon's Second Corps, which took a road north of Longstreet's route, and parallel to it.

Even later that night, and on into the early hours of April 3, Ewell's two divisions left Richmond after Davis and the government escaped on a train that would take them to Danville, 125 miles to the southwest, on the Virginia-North Carolina border. Meanwhile, Mahone's division of Hill's corps, the only remaining troops facing the Army of the James at Bermuda Hundred, pulled out of the fortifications there and marched west. Behind them Richmond was in flames, her people in a panic, and the Federals preparing to occupy the prize they had sought for nearly four years.

No march in the history of the Army of Northern Virginia had been as sad as this one. Defeat, utter and final defeat, weighed heavily on almost every mind. The enemy was behind them and surely pushing west on the south side of the Appomattox, hoping to cut off their retreat to North Carolina. Their gallant Capital, symbol of Confederate resistance and strength against a host of enemy campaigns, had fallen. Ahead lay only the night, gloom, and uncertainty.

Longstreet marched his tired command sixteen miles through the mud before he halted for rest. He, Lee, and a number of other generals took dinner at a plantation house, where their hosts bravely asserted that ultimate victory would still be theirs. Lee was not so sure, and Longstreet ignored the comment entirely as he hacked at his meat with his one good arm. "Whatever happens," said Lee, "know this, that no men ever fought better than those who have stood by me."

For Gordon this night march was even sadder. Behind him in Petersburg he had had to leave his wife. "As the last broken file of that matchless army stepped from the bridge and my pioneer corps lighted the flames that consumed it, there came to me a vivid and depressing realization of the meaning of the appalling tragedy of the last two days," Gordon wrote. "The breaking of Lee's power had shattered the last hope of Southern independence."

The men with Ewell, members of one of Longstreet's veteran divisions commanded by Major General Joseph B. Kershaw, and a largely untested division led by an equally untried major general, George Washington Custis Lee, son of R. E. Lee, marched through the night with the explosions and blazing glow of the Capital behind them. In their path were thousands of refugees from Richmond fleeing to escape Grant. They so clogged the road that young Lee's small command was fragmented into a score of small groups, its organization entirely gone.

Daylight on April 3 brought no cessation of the marching. These men, especially those from the lines at Petersburg, were tired, worn from a hunger that had not been fully satisfied in months. The miles came hard to many stiff, blistered, often unshod feet, torturing the muscles of legs for which nine months of normally sedentary siege life had made fast marching a dim memory. Where they could they stopped to rest, to cook what pitiful rations they had brought with them, or to forage the already stripped land for what food could be found. Many of the men and officers alike were sustained by the knowledge—just how it came to them is hard to say—that ahead of them at Amelia Court House supplies would be waiting. Before the evacuation Lee had asked that rations be sent there from Richmond. His men would need them desperately if they were to continue on.

By evening on April 3 Lee had made surprising progress considering the state of his men. Anderson and his fleeing remnant were nearly to Bevill's Bridge and had been joined at last by Pickett himself with a few followers. His whereabouts had been unknown to the rest of the army for two days. Heth and his men, traveling a different route, had finally crossed the river and rejoined the main army. "We moved on in disorder," wrote one of Heth's men, "keeping no regular column, no regular pace." Few spoke, and

Major General John B. Gordon. His attack at Fort Stedman was Lee's last major assault of the war. (Library of Congress.)

Lieutenant General James Longstreet. His corps led the advance of Lee's retreat. (Battles and Leaders of the Civil War)

those who did said little. "An indescribable sadness weighed upon us."

Longstreet, reaching Goode's Bridge on the Appomattox by nightfall, crossed Field and Wilcox. They had intended originally to cross at Bevill's Bridge, to meet the waiting Anderson, but high water made the crossing impossible. In all, Longstreet's men had marched over twenty-five miles since leaving the lines at Petersburg. Singly and in groups they collapsed into troubled sleep, burdened with the weariness of years of their lives now seemingly spent for nothing.

Yet already Lee and his army had achieved something remarkable in the retreat. With these tired, hungry men he had brought off successfully a withdrawal that was one of the most difficult coordinated movements in the war. Longstreet—joined by Heth—and Anderson had met west of Goode's Bridge, holding that crossing while Gordon followed. When Gordon reached the bridge he, in turn, would hold it until Mahone arrived, and Mahone would hold it for Ewell. Each detachment, in turn, helped ensure the crossing of the next, making it possible for what had been five different commands spread over nearly forty miles on April 2 to come together at Amelia Court House two days later, to move as an army once more.

Of course, it helped that Grant was little in evidence on April 3. Instead of directly pursuing Lee, he sent Sheridan west toward Jetersville, ten miles southwest of Amelia Court House, on the Richmond & Danville Railroad. If the Federal horse could reach it before Lee arrived at Amelia, then the Confederates' best avenue of escape to Johnston would be cut off. Lee would have no choice but to keep marching west toward Lynchburg and then try to turn south and reach Johnston on foot. (No trains were running on the Danville line, but Lee did not know it.) The longer and farther Lee marched, the weaker he would become, and the less fight there would be left in him. There was more than just strategy in Grant's plans. There was humanity. When he took Petersburg immediately upon Lee's evacuation, Grant was in the city while hundreds of Confederates were still crossing the bridge over the Appomattox. He could have opened on them with his cannon, disrupting their retreat severely. But he did not. "I had not the heart to turn the artillery upon such a mass of defeated and fleeing men," he said, especially since "I hoped to capture them soon." If at all possible now, he would bag Lee by maneuver, not by pitched battle.

After securing his position in Petersburg on April 3, Grant met with President Lincoln, who had come up from City Point on the James River. Meanwhile,

Richmond was being occupied, and jubilation coursed through the Army of the Potomac which had so long sought, and so long been denied, these prizes. But time for elation was short, for Grant sent Meade's II, V, and VI Corps off to the west to follow Sheridan and directed three divisions of Ord's Army of the James, with Meade's IX Corps, to parallel Sheridan several miles to the south, heading toward Burkeville. Should Lee somehow get past Sheridan, Ord would still have the Danville line cut.

When April 4 dawned, despite losses at Fort Stedman and Five Forks, and isolated commands unable to join him, Lee faced the prospect of soon having almost 30,000 men concentrated at Amelia Court House, 30,000 hungry men. Yet they set out with a will, anxious to reach their destination, and their expected rations. Their pace quickened somewhat at the sound of firing off to the south. It meant that Sheridan was there. Longstreet skirmished with him throughout the day, but no real fighting took place and Lee was not much worried by the Federal cavalry's presence. He felt that he could overcome it in a fight if he must. It was Grant's infantry that he hoped to avoid. As for Sheridan, his only object at this point was to slightly harass and delay Lee while the infantry corps were marching ever west toward Jetersville.

Spirits were high enough among the Confederates that Lee could mildly scold a young officer who appeared with his uniform carelessly put on that morning. The young man took the reprimand in silence and was about to leave, when the general called him back to explain. "I meant only to caution you as to the duty of officers, especially those who are near high commanders," said Lee. "You must avoid anything that might look like demoralization while we are retreating."

Riding with Longstreet's advance, Lee reached Amelia Court House at about 8:30 a.m. What he found was heartbreaking. Despite an abundance of ammunition and ordnance stores, not a single ration was there awaiting his famished troops. He had ordered 350,000 rations sent out from a reserve accumulated in Richmond. The Danville line was still open between the Capital and Amelia on April 2–3—Davis and his cabinet had passed by this same route on their way to Danville—and the supplies could have made it. But there was confusion in the War Department as Richmond prepared for evacuation, and a request for clarification sent to Lee at Petersburg never reached him. The breakdown of the communications systems, not supply, had conspired against him. Where the fault lay, though, seemed immaterial.

His men would have nothing to eat now but their daydreams of food, fantasies that could hardly fill empty bellies.

"No face wore a heavier shadow than that of General Lee," wrote an officer standing near him now. "The failure of the supply of rations completely paralyzed him. An anxious and haggard expression came to his face." There was nothing to do but send his wagons out into the countryside to forage for whatever they could find. At the same time, he issued a proclamation calling upon the people of Amelia County to give whatever they could to his quartermasters when they called. Meanwhile, he sent an urgent message off to Danville to ship him 200,000 rations from the stores collected at that place.

Hour after hour the famished regiments marched into Amelia Court House, only to find nothing to eat. Wilcox came in just after noon, followed sometime later by Heth. Gordon halted back about five miles to await Mahone, who was at Goode's Bridge holding it for Ewell, from whom nothing had been heard. Anderson and Fitzhugh Lee, who had been skirmishing much of the day with Sheridan and advance elements of the Federal V Corps, were not far away.

Finding their hopes of food destroyed had varying effects on the weary Confederates. Some, seeing nothing unusual in the situation, took it calmly. Others, already disheartened, began to melt away into the woods. They had given all but their last ounce of devotion to a cause that could not feed them. What little they had left might better be used to salvage some semblance of life from the war's wreckage. A few simply became delirious, lost their mental balance, and raved about or muttered quietly to themselves. For them, the workings of the yet unexplored mysteries of the mind had mercifully ended their war.

But still the men could cheer, and they proved it by hurrahing Lee more than once. And late in the day heartening news did come. Finally word arrived from Ewell that he would shortly cross the Appomattox by a railroad bridge that was closer to his route of march than Goode's. By 9 p.m. his troops would almost all be over the river safely. This now meant that Mahone could destroy Goode's Bridge and march in to the main army.

Thus, by the next day Lee was assured of completing the concentration of his army. Unhappily, though, this also meant more hungry mouths to feed. His forage wagons would not be due back in his camps until the next morning. He had hoped to be on his way out of Amelia Court House within a few hours of his arrival. Now he could not expect to leave before late on the morning of April 5 at best. These were precious hours lost, hours when the Federal

Confederate officers, from left: Lieutenant General Richard S. Ewell, who commanded the Richmond defenses, leaving on the night of April 2-3; Commander John R. Tucker, who led his seamen-turned infantry out of Richmond to join Lee; and Major General William Mahone, often offensively egotistical but still one of Lee's best fighting generals. (LC, USAMI, LC).

infantry was steadily catching up, closing the gap between themselves and the Confederates, cutting ever shorter Lee's chances of escape.

The night passed without giving rest. Light showers and winds whipped through and around the headquarters tents, where lights burned well into the morning. Lee tried to set his alternatives with the variables of his situation. If only he could get rations on the morrow, he could then march his army down the railroad toward Danville and the supplies known to be there. If, as he hoped, rations were going to be sent up the road to him from that place pursuant to his order, then they would reach him all the sooner. Well-fed and rested, he knew his army could out-march the Federals to join Johnston, though all he now knew of the enemy was that Sheridan had broken off skirmishing at nightfall and that Meade's infantry was still several miles southeast of him. All through the night anxious ears listened amidst fitful sleep for the sound of a train coming from the south, a train bringing rations from Danville. It did not come. All they heard was the hollow patter of the rain on the tents.

For Mahone it had not been a difficult march. By midafternoon of April 3 his command had reached Chesterfield Court House, midway between Bermuda Hundred and Goode's Bridge. All along the way he encountered refugees, scattered and straggling soldiers, and a host of wagons of all description. Once at Chesterfield, he organized the wagons and stray soldiers. Soon after arriving, Mahone saw 2,000 sailors and Marines led by Commodore John R. Tucker marching in, having abandoned their naval batteries

Left: Major General Henry Heth, though cut off after Five Forks, rejoined the Confederate Army as it marched toward Appomattox. (USAMHI) Right: Major General Cadmus M. Wilcox, whose division had been under A.P. Hill's command. (LC)

along the right bank of the James above Bermuda Hundred. They came, said Mahone, "armed with cutlass' and navy revolvers, every man over six feet and [the] picture of perfect physical development." Henceforward, Tucker's men would march with Mahone's, and that night they all set out again. By the evening of April 4 they had reached Goode's Bridge, where Mahone received Lee's order to come on to Amelia the next morning.

On the morning of April 5, amid a constant rainy drizzle, Mahone marched to Amelia Court House. What he found was depressing. The commissary wagons sent out the day before had come back. They brought almost nothing. The countryside had been giving bountifully to feed the army for four years. Now it had nothing more to give.

Passing through ranks of unhappy, grumbling, disheartened soldiers, Mahone made his way to report in person to Lee. He found the general seated with Longstreet at the edge of a barren oat field near the court house. Longstreet arose and gave Mahone his seat, then left. "The chat with Genl Lee was pleasant," Mahone recalled. As they talked, however, he noticed Lee was in his full dress uniform, wearing his gold spurs and the famed "Maryland Sword" given him in better days by an anonymous Marylander. "He wore all his best clothes," wrote Mahone. "It impressed me that he anticipated some accident to himself and desired to be found in that dress."

If Lee had a premonition of death, he never spoke of it, but it required no prescience whatever to know what was in store for his army now. The day spent at Amelia Court House had been wasted and his precious lead over the Federals was all but vanished. He must move down the railroad quickly to meet the supplies hopefully coming from Danville. The men were ordered to form ranks. In order to allow the infantry to make the best time possible, the slow wagon train was ordered to move south toward Danville on a separate, parallel road.

Mahone later wrote that while he and Lee were still talking, the other division commanders of the old Third Corps, Heth and Wilcox, came up and asked to whom they should now report. Almost as if he did not hear them, Lee pointed to their staff wagons, asked whose they were, and ordered that they be sent with the rest of the main wagon and artillery train. "Depend on your haversacks as I shall do," Lee told them. Then, almost as an afterthought, he told them to report to Longstreet, at the same time warning that he intended to reorganize the army to reduce the number of corps and division commanders. According to Mahone, even amid chaos, Lee was still thinking of efficiency in his command.

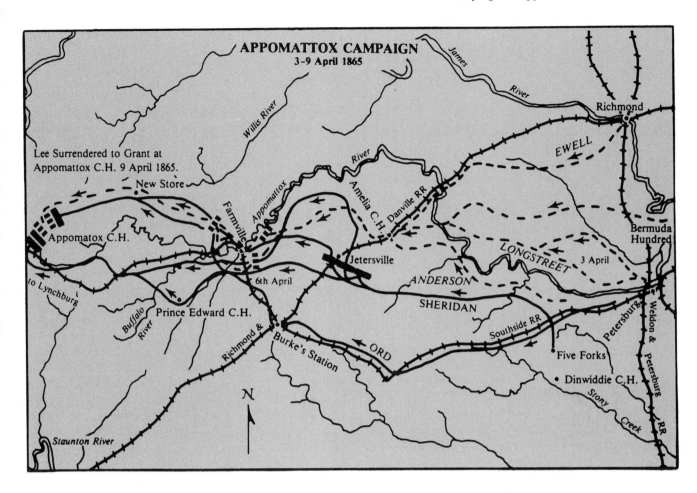

While everything that could not be taken with the army was put to the torch, Lee marched his columns off southwest along the Richmond & Danville tracks toward Jetersville. Longstreet took the advance, followed by Mahone, who accidentally got on the wrong road and ran into the wagon train after a mile or two. Retracing his steps, he found that the enemy cavalry stood between him and Longstreet, but he drove them away easily and united his column with Old Pete's. Behind Mahone came Anderson's corps and, later in the day, Ewell finally came up to the army with Custis Lee and Kershaw.

While the troops marched, Lee remained behind at the courthouse, gathering intelligence and generally overseeing the movement. Longstreet was there with him. Disturbing news came in that the wagon train had been attacked by enemy cavalry, and now they could hear the sounds of skirmishing as the gray columns moved toward Jetersville. Shortly after 1 p.m., Lee and Longstreet themselves rode south to find out the situation. They passed through Jetersville, eight miles from Amelia Court House, and then came upon Sheridan's dismounted cavalry be-

hind earthworks placed squarely across their line of march. Enemy infantry was nearby and coming up quickly. Unless Lee could push his way through these Federals, there would be no rations and no escape to Johnston by this route.

Lee's immediate problem was whether or not to fight. On the one hand his men were tired and, worse, starving. There might not be enough fight in them. On the other hand, his only alternative was to go on fifteen miles west to Farmville, on the Appomattox. There he would rejoin the South Side Railroad, which ran back southeast to Burkeville, crossing the Danville line at Burke's Station. Unless the enemy cut off that route, too, he could then march south along the tracks, hoping that he could outdistance Grant and still join Johnston somewhere south of the Roanoke River.

While the men rested, Lee alone studied his maps and the enemy line. Curiously, he seems not to have consulted with Longstreet over the decision to be made, but instead called in Mahone—or so claimed "Little Billy." Perhaps it was not so curious after all, however, for Mahone's were the freshest troops in the

The fighting near Amelia Court House. (Library of Congress)

command, and among the hardest fighters as well. Mahone's advice on what he could do in an attack now should be valuable. On the porch of a little farm house the two generals met, pouring over Lee's charts. By this time it was nearly sundown, and Mahone argued that it was too late for an attack. Besides, the army was not sufficiently concentrated on this line to hit with full force. Move off to the right, advised Little Billy, concentrate the army, and then turn and hit the Federals in flank on the morrow.

When Lee ordered the army to move off toward Farmville, Mahone thought the commanding general had taken his advice in toto. In fact, Lee was taking the second of the alternatives that he had considered even before consulting Mahone. Risking a fight on the morrow without food, as Mahone suggested, would be even worse than risking it today. He must avoid battling with the enemy, at least until his men had eaten. He sent couriers to order supplies to be sent to Farmville from Lynchburg, forty miles west. He hoped they would be there when he arrived.

"A Race for Life or Death"

Having lost his lead over the Federals, Lee now had to push his men through every hour of daylight left and well into the night. Mahone and Field took the advance, then came the remnants of Heth's and Wilcox's divisions, behind them Anderson's tiny corps, then Ewell, and finally Gordon's rear guard. It was the worst march the Army of Northern Virginia ever suffered. Forced to go on the same road with the wagon and artillery train now, the men stumbled

among the vehicles. Hundreds lost their grasp on reality, mumbled incoherently, wandered off into the woods to fall down in a stupor, or panicked at the slightest provocation.

Several times firing broke out as the men shot at shadows or, worse, each other. Many were killed, left where they fell by comrades who had not the strength or the time to bury them. The wounded had to do what they could for themselves. Men and officers who had held up under the greatest trials of the war now broke down. When Mahone came to Flat Creek he found that the bridge over it had collapsed. He let his men rest in ranks while his engineers repaired it. When the work was done, Colonel Charles Marshall of Lee's staff, one of the finest officers in the army, ordered Mahone's lead brigade under Brigadier General Nathaniel H. Harris to cross over and resume the march.

Under the strain, Marshall was drinking from a bottle of "pine top" whiskey—distilled from pine boughs in the absence of corn mash—and irresponsibly giving orders without consulting Mahone. As a result, Mahone's command was soon spread out along the road, its marching formation lost for the first time in the war. When the general, dining at a nearby farm house, discovered what had happened

"Fighting Against Fate," Rufus Zogbaum's drawing of Confederates vainly resisting Grant's advance in the last days of the war in Virginia. (Harper's New Monthly Magazine, April 1898)

and why, he too gave way to the anguish and frustration of this terrible night and informed Lee in blunt terms that if Marshall ever again interfered with his command "Genl Lee would be short a staff officer." The strain was getting to them all, for what was at stake was their very existence. One of the soldiers in the ranks found time to note in his diary that "it is now a race for life or death."

In the end, this night march helped doom the army. Mahone, after re-forming his straggling division, continued on in good order behind the advance under Field. The rear led by Gordon was in equally good order. But in between the two the disorganized commands of Anderson and Ewell plodded wearily, straggling, struggling to keep up. The weakest point of the army now was at its very center. In this condition, once the sun appeared on April 6, the army would have to cross Sayler's Creek.

This Alfred R. Waud drawing shows the capture and destruction of a Confederate wagon train near Paineville on April 5, by Davies' brigade. (Battles and Leaders of the Civil War)

The night marches were hard on the Federals, too, but their feet moved swiftly with the exhilarating assurance that these days of marching were numbered. Tomorrow, the next day, within a week, the war in Virginia would be over; the army that had so long kept them at bay would at last be vanquished. Following a day of little or no fighting on April 3, Sheridan rode hard on the fourth, sending the cavalry division of Brigadier General George Crook riding fast for Jetersville. "Our cavalry were untiring," wrote Crook. "We scarcely rested, but were going day and night . . . We all felt that the end of the war was near at hand."

Crook reached Jetersville that same day, followed shortly by Sheridan himself, who set up a line somewhat south of the town. Elements of the V Corps under Brigadier General Charles Griffin, Warren's successor, marched in late in the afternoon. Sheridan entrenched the command across the road to Burkeville, hoping that Lee could be forced to surrender at Amelia Court House. The next afternoon Major General A. A. Humphreys' II Corps and Major General Horatio Wright's VI Corps arrived, and Sheridan placed them on either side of Griffin. Meade was present now as well but, feeling very ill, he asked Sheridan to direct the troops.

Grant, meanwhile, had stayed several miles in the rear, giving over-all direction to the pursuit. On the evening of April 5, however, he finally set out for the front after receiving a message from Sheridan that intimated that Meade might not press Lee hard enough, thus jeopardizing their chances of capturing the army. This could not be allowed to happen. The hard-luck Army of the Potomac had finally won a decisive victory at Petersburg. "That is all it ever

wanted to make it as good an army as ever fought a battle," said Grant. Now it must follow that victory with a final triumph. His determination was enhanced by a captured letter that Sheridan sent to him. It had been written earlier that day by Colonel Walter H. Taylor of Lee's staff. "Dear Mamma," he wrote, "Our army is ruined, I fear."

Meade wanted to attack Amelia Court House with the full Army of the Potomac on the morning of April 6. Sheridan, however, argued that Lee would not be there then. Correctly reading Lee's intentions, he claimed on the basis of his intelligence that the Confederates were on their way west again. Still, Grant agreed to Meade's attack, but Sheridan's cavalry was not to be included in it. This would allow "Little Phil" to move toward Farmville to keep up with Lee if he was actually moving in that direction. "If we press on," Sheridan told Grant, "we will no doubt get the whole army."

"My God Has This Army Disolved?"

On the morning of April 6, Meade advanced his army toward Amelia Court House, only to discover that Lee, indeed, was not there. Instead, part of the Confederate army could be seen off to the west. Meade turned his corps to the left to follow. For hours they pestered Lee's rear, Humphreys doing most of the work, while Sheridan's column paralleled Lee's line of march and harassed his flanks throughout the morning, in addition sending a detachment ahead to attack Lee's wagon trains. The fatal delay at Amelia

Court House was now agonizingly evident. Lee must run for his life from a confident enemy whose relentless legions were within his very sight.

At 4 a.m., April 6, Lee ordered Gordon to destroy the Flat Creek bridge as soon as he crossed it. The rest of the army would soon pass through Deatonsville, taking the road to Rice's Station, about twelve miles away. From Rice's it would be only an hour or two to Farmville. Lee himself just now was at Amelia Springs, and he had good news. Commissary General Isaac M. St. John had come in to headquarters, having escaped from Richmond with a wagon train of rations that he had unsuccessfully tried to bring to Lee. Now, though he came empty handed, he did tell the general that 80,000 rations were waiting at Farmville. At last Lee's men would eat.

But they must get there first. As if the harrowing night march had not already strained them enough, now the Confederates felt the constant harassment of Sheridan and Humphreys. Time and again the men had to fall out of ranks to the left to form a line for meeting the Federal skirmishers. It was exhausting work to hungry men, especially to those in the center of the column under Anderson and Ewell. The command structure there had broken down almost completely, the officers exercising no control over the men at all. They straggled, stretching the line out even farther along the road, holding up Gordon in the rear.

Longstreet with the advance marched well, crossing Sayler's Creek and moving on to Rice's by shortly after noon. Mahone followed. There was word that Federal cavalry was ahead of them going toward Farmville. Longstreet sent part of Fitzhugh Lee's horsemen after them, while putting his own infantry in line facing south to meet an enemy infantry force reported a few miles below.

But by this time Lee was already worried about something much more serious. A gap had opened between Mahone and Anderson. What had happened was confusing but understandable considering the state of the men and officers by now. The wagons that were moving between Ewell and Gordon were being frequently attacked by Federal skirmishers. To protect them, and to keep the attacks on them from delaying Gordon, Ewell—senior officer with the center and rear of the army—ordered his own and Anderson's troops to halt to let the wagons move past them. He did so without consulting Lee or notifying him, with the result that as Mahone moved on unawares, a gap gradually opened. The wagons that passed Ewell moved on ahead into the gap, virtually unprotected as they crossed over Sayler's Creek.

Here was an opportunity that Sheridan would not pass by. Finding no openings to do real harm to the enemy trains when Gordon was guarding them, Sheridan had taken the bulk of his cavalry forward. He had just crossed the creek himself when he saw the unprotected wagons moving ahead of Ewell toward Rice's. At once he sent Crook and Merritt with their divisions to attack. The wagons never had a chance. Hundreds were captured and set ablaze, and with them he took sixteen pieces of artillery and several prisoners. But best of all, he now had two divisions astride the Confederate line of retreat, standing between Lee and Longstreet and the rest of their army.

When Anderson found what had happened in his front he tried to resume his march, only to discover

Among the Union officers who played prominent roles in the Appomattox Campaign were, from left: Major General Horatio G. Wright, who helped cut off Lee's escape down the Richmond & Danville Railroad line; Brigadier General Charles Griffin, who took over Warren's V Corps for the pursuit of Lee; Major General Alexander A. Humphreys, whose corps played a major part in the final entrapment of Lee; Brigadier General George Crook, whose cavalry division was the first to cut the Richmond & Danville line at Jetersville. (All photos: USAMHI)

Crook placed squarely across his path. As he halted, wondering what to do, a message came forward from Gordon saying that he was being attacked and urging that the advance continue. And now mistake followed hard upon mistake. Without orders, one of Anderson's brigades attacked Crook with some success but, since no one had ordered it, no arrangements had been made to send reinforcements to capitalize upon the initial advantage. The brigade fell back with the rest of the corps.

Meanwhile, to the rear, Ewell received news of what was happening in front and now took measures to save what remained of the wagon train behind him. The wagons were just then near a fork in the road. The lower fork, the one taken by the army, led on to Rice's. The upper fork paralleled the lower at a distance of about three miles. Ewell directed that the wagons take this upper fork to avoid the Yankee cavalry. It was a sound move. But just as no one had notified Mahone that Anderson was halting to let the wagons pass, now Ewell failed to send word to Gordon of the change in route. Since Gordon had been following these wagons for hours now, when they took the upper fork he naturally assumed that he was to follow. Thereby Anderson and Ewell effectively isolated themselves from any support for their front or rear. Lee and Longstreet could not reach them, and Gordon, who might have, was marching away from them.

Ewell and Anderson, leaders who had served competently in days gone by, stood bewildered, too tired to think clearly or to understand what had happened to them. For the moment, they debated whether to attack Crook and Merritt—now being joined by more divisions of Federal cavalry—and try to break out, or to move off to their right, to the north, in hope of striking the road that Gordon and the wagons were traveling. Ewell preferred the latter course, but could not make the decision, passing it to Anderson. That officer, too confused to see the wisdom of Ewell's choice, could think of nothing to do but to attack.

They were hardly in a good position for defense, much less offense. Both were on the south side of Little Sayler's Creek. To their front lay several hundred yards of timbered bottom land, on the other side of which ran another branch, Sayler's Creek. The ground was largely wooded, with clearings not more than two or three hundred yards wide spotted here and there. Behind them, north of Little Sayler's, a low ridge ran up past the Hillsman House and back to the fork in the road where Gordon had turned off. The Confederates had no artillery—it had all been sent ahead several miles for protection—and only about 7,000 men with whom to face Sheridan, whose troopers were well placed midway between the creeks.

Anderson directed the formation for the attack, but the men responded sluggishly, many only partially aware of what they were being asked to do. Meanwhile, Ewell began leading his command up the road to support Anderson when word came to him that Wright's VI Corps had come up behind him, where Gordon should have been, and was preparing to attack. They were facing the enemy now in front and rear.

Fighting back panic, Anderson sent Ewell around to hold off Wright while he attacked the cavalry in his front. But when he gave the order to advance, he found that his men acted "wholly broken down and disheartened." They made what he called a "feeble effort" and then broke up in confusion, falling back, surrendering, or simply dropping in exhaustion where they stood. One brigade, Brigadier General Henry Wise's, fought stubbornly, however, and managed to break its way out. Reaching the road on the other side of the enemy cavalry, they hurried on to join Lee at Rice's. Behind them lay men whose war would end before nightfall.

With the failure of his attack, Anderson took position behind hasty breastworks and prepared to meet Sheridan's counterattack. Meanwhile, Ewell, facing Wright, had taken a position on the crest of a hill about 300 yards back from Little Sayler's Creek. He placed Custis Lee's little command on his left, and on Lee's right rear assigned Tucker's naval battalion. Kershaw's division of three brigades held the right of the line. They all faced across the creek, toward positions now occupied by two divisions of Wright's corps.

Within a few minutes the Federals placed artillery near the Hillsman House and opened fire on the Confederates. In the bombardment that ensued, Ewell, lacking any artillery, could do nothing but crouch behind the crest of his hill and sit it out. As the cannonade went on, perhaps thinking that nothing was imminent on his front, the general rode back to Anderson's position. As he did so, Wright's divisions finally launched their assault, racing down their hill, splashing through the creek, and running

on up the slope to the waiting Confederates. Confused though the gray line was, the men stood firm in their places. Tucker was shouting orders to his men in naval cant. "To the starboard, march," he cried. "Aye, aye," his web-footed "infantry" called back. Men were cut in two by the enemy's shells. One man, nearly severed by a shot, was thrown up in the air, his arms flailing and nearly slapping a comrade in the face as he flew past.

As the Federals closed to within yards, a strange silence was felt by many in the lines. They could see some of the Yankee officers holding white handkerchiefs, calling on them to surrender. Then a crushing volley from the gray line tore into the Federals and sent them reeling back. Lee's men and Tucker's battalion, not realizing that this was only a temporary repulse, leaped up and followed the Yankees to the creek, where the artillery fire began once more and cut them to pieces. "Quicker than I can tell it," wrote Confederate Major Robert Stiles, "the battle degenerated into a butchery and a confused melee of brutal personal conflicts." Bayonets and rifle butts crushed and pierced. Others who had lost their weapons used their teeth to bite noses and ears in the terrible scuffle. They were hopelessly outnumbered. Almost suddenly, the fight stopped for Lee and Tucker. Surrounded by much superior numbers, they surren-

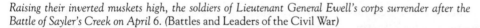

Raising their inverted muskets high, the soldiers of Lieutenant General Ewell's corps surrender after the Battle of Sayler's Creek on April 6. (Battles and Leaders of the Civil War)

dered or were captured in attempting to escape. "I was not sorry to end it thus, in red-hot battle," wrote Major Stiles.

Kershaw had kept better rein on his disciplined troops. He knew that when the first Federal advance was repulsed, another would come soon enough. And so it did. The right of Wright's line, the division of Brigadier General Truman Seymour, occupied itself with Lee and Tucker. Wright's left, Brigadier General Frank Wheaton's division—Wheaton was the son-in-law of the Confederacy's senior general, Samuel Cooper—faced Kershaw's front. Now to assist it, the cavalry brigade of Colonel Peter Stagg came up on Wheaton's left. As a result, in their advance the Federals faced Kershaw all along his front and overlapped his right flank.

Before Stagg came up, Wheaton advanced, and Kershaw fought like a tiger to hold him off. Word had come back from Anderson that he needed more time to break out, and Kershaw was determined to give it to him. As he frantically tried to hold off Wheaton, he suddenly saw Stagg's cavalry ride up and into his rear. In an instant Kershaw's right melted away in retreat, followed by the rest of his line. After futile attempts to bring some order out of this chaos, Kershaw allowed his men to try to save themselves as best they could. In minutes he and his entire command were surrounded and forced to surrender.

Kershaw did not then know that the remainder of Anderson's command, as well as Ewell, were prisoners by now, too. They never really recovered from the feeble attempt to attack, and a single advance by Sheridan's cavalrymen captured all but the brigade already escaped, and Anderson, Pickett, Bushrod Johnson, and a handful of followers who managed to ride off toward Rice's Station. In all, nearly 6,000 Confederates and nine generals had been captured in the disaster along Sayler's Creek and Little Sayler's.

Meanwhile, to the north, Humphreys' II Corps had come up to the rear of Gordon's corps and attacked him repeatedly. When Gordon himself tried to cross Sayler's Creek, the Federals hit again and cut off 1,700 men of his command before the rest got away. And up ahead at Rice's Station, Ord's Army of the James was approaching while his cavalry, sent ahead earlier, threatened the Confederates' crossing points over the Appomattox at High Bridge and at Farmville a few miles away. Only spirited fighting preserved these structures for the retreating Army of Northern Virginia.

Lee, at Rice's Station, received little news of what was happening in his rear until word came that the wagon train had been captured. "Where is Ewell and where is Anderson?" he said to Mahone. "It is strange I cannot hear from them." He rode with Mahone's division back toward the scene of the fight until they topped a crest overlooking the battleground in the distance. "Here the scene beggars description," wrote Mahone. Lee, watching the debacle before him, straightened in his saddle, "looking more of the soldier if possible, then ever." Mahone heard him say, as if to himself, "My god has this army disolved?" At once Little Billy replied. "No Genl," he said, "here is a division ready to do its duty." "Yes Genl," said Lee, "there are some true men left." Lee asked him to keep "those people"—the Federals who had captured Ewell and the others—back. Mahone quickly went into line of battle, but by now dark was approaching and he knew the enemy would not press him.

Lee, meanwhile, was surrounded by the fleeing fugitives from Anderson's corps, and soon Anderson himself approached. Losing his equanimity for once, Lee refused even to look at Anderson, but only jerked his arm toward the rear disdainfully and told Anderson to take command of the stragglers and get them out of the way. Shortly afterwards Lee relieved Anderson, Pickett, and Johnson of command.

What to do now with only half an army left, and much of that disorganized, presented the greatest problem that Lee had yet faced since the evacuation of Petersburg. He had to get his command across the Appomattox above Farmville and burn the bridges behind him. Only then might he get some rest. He ordered Longstreet to proceed from Rice's on to Farmville to cross there, while Mahone and the remnants from the Sayler's Creek disaster would march north to High Bridge, where Gordon would be crossing that night.

For Longstreet the march was hard, but he made it to Farmville, crossing the river the next morning. And here, at last, his men found the rations St. John had promised, their first in five days. Gordon, meanwhile, crossed at High Bridge without difficulty, and Mahone followed. On the other side Mahone sought out Gordon, the slender, combative Georgian, and found him talking with Anderson. They were talking of surrender, and Mahone agreed with their views. It was decided that Anderson would approach Longstreet with the proposal, leaving it to Old Pete to take it up with Lee. Apparently, though, nothing was done. Mahone claimed that he left only after getting an assurance from Gordon that the latter would see to burning of the rail and wagon bridges at High Bridge before morning, a task which Gordon failed to do. The wagon bridge was left intact.

Dawn of April 7 brought a ray of hope for the

Confederates as the rations were doled out to Longstreet's men. They began cooking their corn pone and what meat was to be had, only to learn that the Federals were crossing at High Bridge. Lee was furious—Mahone would always get the blame, though Gordon may deserve a share—and saw his hopes of gaining some time on the enemy dashed. Even before many of the regiments had received their longed-for rations, the rail cars had to be closed and sent off towards Lynchburg. Hopefully Lee could meet them somewhere down the line and finish feeding his men. For now, they started off once more. Longstreet marched north toward Cumberland Church, four miles away. Here Mahone and Gordon would rendezvous with him.

Before leaving Farmville, Lee closeted himself for discussions with Secretary of War Breckinridge, who himself led a narrow escape from Richmond and tried to bring a wagon train of supplies to Lee. When he emerged from the talk, Breckinridge sent President Davis a brief dispatch. "The situation," he said, "is not favorable."

At Cumberland Church a stiff rearguard action had to be fought against Humphreys while Lee turned west toward New Store, about ten miles distant. They would march on well into the morning of April 8 to reach it. Still Lee headed west, ever in the hope of reaching supplies from Lynchburg and of outrunning the enemy so that he might turn south toward Johnston, who was now near Smithfield, North Carolina.

It was not long after the Confederates left Farmville that Grant, accompanying Wright's corps, rode into the small but important railroad town. He sent Meade with Wright on north to join Humphreys in the pursuit of Lee, while ordering Major General John Gibbon and Ord to move with Sheridan as he sought to outdistance Lee on the south. During the day Sheridan had learned that a trainload of rations was waiting for Lee at Appomattox Station, twenty-two miles west of Farmville, and now he meant to get them.

Grant, sitting on a porch in Farmville, reflected upon the military situation, and remarked to Gibbon, "I have a great mind to summon Lee to surrender." Taking pen and paper, he addressed a letter to the Confederate general.

Headquarters Armies of the United States
April 7, 1865—5 P.M.

General R. E. Lee,
    Commanding C.S. Army:

    General: The results of the last week must convince you of the hopelessness of further resistance on the part of the Army of Northern Virginia in this struggle. I feel that it is so, and regard it as my duty to shift from myself the responsibility of any further effusion of blood, by asking of you the surrender of that portion of the C.S. army known as the Army of Northern Virginia.

    Very respectfully, your obedient servant,
        U.S. GRANT,
        Lieutenant-General,
    Commanding Armies of the United States.

At once Grant sent the letter off toward Lee by flag of truce, but it did not reach him until several hours later, when Lee and Longstreet were nearly ready to go to sleep as Mahone continued to hold at Cumberland Church. Lee read the note without any comment, then handed it to Longstreet. Old Pete's response was quick and to the point. "Not yet," he said emphatically. Lee agreed, but still there might be a

finally the entreaty that Gordon, Anderson, and Mahone had discussed two nights before. Major General William Pendleton, a man often mistaken for Lee himself, approached the general and suggested that it was time to capitulate. Lee would have none of it, and Pendleton went away embarrassed.

By nightfall the advance under Gordon and Longstreet's rear guard had come to a halt about two miles from Appomattox Court House. Appomattox Station and the supplies that should be awaiting them there were only three miles beyond the little courthouse village. Word had come of Sheridan's advance toward that place, but as yet Lee had every reason to believe that he could reach the station first.

Now came another letter from Grant. His terms for surrender were simple. "Peace being my great desire," he said, his only condition was that the men surrendered take their parole and return to their homes, not to bear arms again until properly exchanged. Lee's response was that "I do not think the emergency has arisen to call for the surrender of this Army," but that, in a general way, he would be glad to discuss "the restoration of peace." What this implied was their coming to terms for all of the Confederate armies, in effect, the negotiation of a peace. This Grant was not empowered to do. Despite the fact that Lee had proposed that they meet between the picket lines on the following morning, Grant saw no choice but to decline the meeting.

Lee did not receive Grant's reply until the morning of April 9, but by that time something had happened to change his mind. About 9 p.m., April 8, he heard cannon off to the southwest. Not long afterward the dark skies in that direction turned a soft red on the horizon, reflecting the glow of thousands of camp-

chance in this overture from Grant to arrange for a peace on some basis short of surrender. Lee replied immediately. His situation was not so hopeless, he said, but he, too, wished to stop the bloodshed. What terms would Grant offer should he, Lee, consider surrender?

Meanwhile, Lee's column moved steadily onward into the night. Since Longstreet's troops were still fairly fresh, he had them trade places with Gordon's much battered rear guard. And on they marched, past dawn, and on through the bright, warm sunshine of April 8. As on April 3 the presence of the enemy was little felt by the Confederates. They were allowed to march almost undisturbed. But still the knowledge of the ever-present enemy and the rumors in the command that notes had been passed between Lee and Grant emboldened Lee's generals to make

At nightfall on Saturday, April 8, Confederates destroy the railroad from Appomattox toward Lynchburg while artillerymen destroy gun carriages. (Battles and Leaders of the Civil War)

Appomattox Station, where Sheridan captured Lee's last long-hoped-for supplies. Sheridan, who had outdistanced his own supply trains, could use those rations. (Library of Congress)

fires. Then reports came in. Sheridan had won the race. He stood squarely between the Confederates and Appomattox Station. Lee's last route of escape to North Carolina was closed, and behind him to the northeast Longstreet's rear guard faced two Federal infantry corps. He was trapped.

Sheridan had ridden hard that day, anxious to reach the Appomattox Station supplies before Lee did. And he knew something about those supplies that Lee did not. On April 4 Sheridan had captured one of Lee's couriers carrying orders for the supplies to be sent there from Lynchburg. Yet Sheridan himself directed that the message be carried through by one of his own scouts. He had far outdistanced his own supply trains, and could use those rations. He sent part of the division of brevet Major General George A. Custer around behind Appomattox Station to break up the track and prevent the trains from retreating, while the remainder of Custer's command

rode into the depot and captured the supplies. Meanwhile, Sheridan also took much of the artillery that Lee had sent ahead of his army. Soon thereafter, the Confederate cavalry in advance of Lee's march came in sight and attacked, but Sheridan held. There was no sleep for him or his generals that night. He anxiously waited for Ord's infantry to arrive, and with it Griffin's V Corps. If they were in position with him by morning, Lee would be trapped, and "all knew that the rebellion would be ended on the morrow."

With the sound of those cannon at Appomattox Station, Lee knew it too. He called Fitzhugh Lee, Gordon, and Longstreet to him for what would be their last council of war. What should be done? Gordon and the younger Lee thought that the Federals had only cavalry at the station. If so, then they might attack and break through, out of the trap they were in between Sheridan on their front and Wright and Humphreys at their rear. But if Sheridan had infantry with him, then all was lost. Surrender would be the only alternative. It was agreed. Gordon and Lee would try the breakout, during the night if possible, by daylight for sure. Lee then retired to his tent and dressed himself yet again in his finest uniform. "I have probably to be General Grant's prisoner," he told Pendleton. "I must make my best appearance."

"I Would Rather Die a Thousand Deaths"

The attack was made shortly after 5 a.m., April 9, Palm Sunday. Gordon hit Sheridan first, who allowed himself to be pushed back slowly while Ord's infantry was taking position. When Gordon found that Ord was there and that Fitzhugh Lee's cavalry had been driven back on his right, he had no choice but to stop the attack. "I have fought my corps to a frazzle," he told the commanding general. Without support he could do nothing, but the only support was Longstreet, then engaged in holding back Meade and Humphreys. Hearing the report of Gordon's situa-

tion, Lee said sadly that, "then there is nothing left for me to do but to go and see General Grant, and I would rather die a thousand deaths." A little later, overwrought, Lee remarked that he was tempted to ride along his front line and expose himself to the enemy's bullets. "How easily I could be rid of this," he said. Then he regained control. "But it is our duty to live."

There was another conference with Longstreet and with Mahone as well. Both advised capitulation. "It is your duty to surrender," said Mahone. Longstreet would only say that "I agree with Mahone." By now it was 8:30 a.m., a clear, sunny, spring day. Lee mounted his horse Traveller. Accompanied by Marshall, Taylor, and Sergeant G. W. Tucker, he rode to the rear toward the meeting place he had proposed for the anticipated meeting with Grant at 10 o'clock. Strangely, he forgot to make any arrangements for a truce or temporary cease-fire in order to protect himself and Grant as they conferred.

At first the oversight seemed not to matter. Just as Lee reached the works of his rear guard, Lieutenant Colonel Charles Whittier rode up under a white flag and presented Lee with Grant's letter declining the

Their last council of war: Lee confers with Gordon, Longstreet, and Fitzhugh Lee late on April 8 to decide what must be done. (Appomattox Court House National Historical Park)

proposed meeting. Now Lee had no choice but to ask for an interview to speak specifically of the surrender of his army. As he was writing, word came from Fitzhugh Lee that he had found a way out. Lee did not credit the report and ignored it, though in fact Fitzhugh Lee did break away with his cavalry.

An anxious three hours ensued. The sound of firing on Gordon's front reminded Lee that he had neglected to instruct his corps commanders to send out truce flags to halt the firing. The orders now went out. Then Whittier came back with a message from Humphreys saying that he had orders to attack Lee and could not find Grant to authorize a change in those orders. He had no choice but to advance. Lee was bitterly disappointed. He wanted no more lives lost, and now, as he read Humphrey's note, he tore it into tiny pieces and angrily stamped them into the ground. Soon the Federal line approached. Humphreys, wanting also to avert bloodshed, suggested that Longstreet withdraw slowly before him.

This map indicates the relative positions of Confederate (hollow rectangles) and Union (solid rectangles) troops at approximately 11 a.m. on April 9. At the upper right, Humphreys' corps is advancing against one division and scattered remnants led by Longstreet. Just above Appomattox Court House, Gordon's corps and other remnants with W.H.F. Lee's cavalry division face elements of Griffin's V Corps and Ord's Army of the James. Two of Sheridan's cavalry divisions close off any possibility of escape to the south, while another Federal horse division chases Fitzhugh Lee's cavalry toward the west. Obviously trapped, General Robert E. Lee has little choice but to surrender. (Official Records, Atlas)

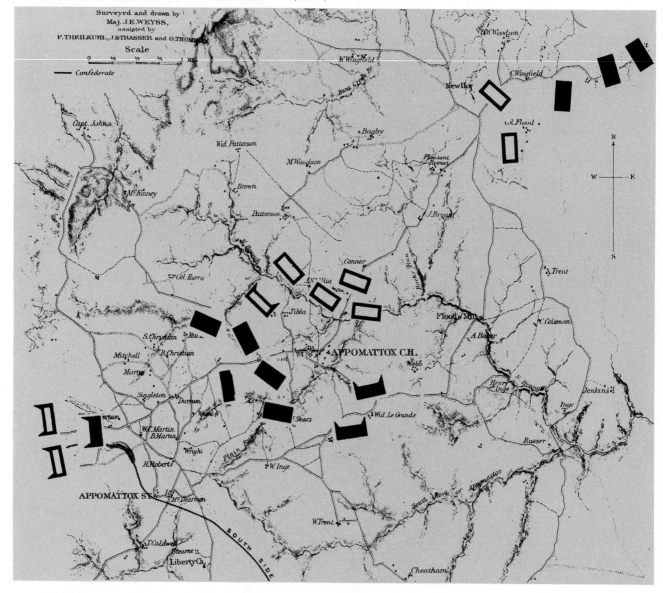

Appomattox Court House, sketched at the time of the surrender. A tiny hamlet, it consisted of about a dozen houses, one or two stores, and the courthouse of Appomattox County. McLean's house is at right, the courthouse in the center. (Battles and Leaders of the Civil War)

Finally, with the Federals only 100 yards away, Lee mounted and rode back to safety to rejoin Longstreet. Then a note came from Meade agreeing to an hour's truce. Lee sent another copy of his last letter in the hope of its reaching Grant, and learned that Gordon had fallen back on Longstreet northeast of Appomattox Court House and that his army now was almost entirely surrounded. He was tired, fearful that Grant would exact humiliating terms. Longstreet, who had known Grant well in better days, assured Lee that such would not be the case. Lee lay down on a hastily made bed of blankets thrown over fence rails beneath an apple tree. For all the rest it afforded his tortured mind and heart, it might as well have been a bed of nails.

"This Will Have a Very Happy Effect"

At a quarter past noon the reply from Grant finally came. He had only just received Lee's note sent by Whittier. He would meet Lee wherever he chose and was leaving immediately to come toward the front. The note came by Grant's aide Colonel Orville Babcock, and in company with him, Marshall, and Sergeant Tucker, Lee rode toward Appomattox Court House, between Sheridan's and Gordon's lines, the most likely place for the coming meeting. On the way

he asked Colonel Marshall to go ahead of them to find a suitable place for the interview.

Into Appomattox Court House rode the bespectacled Marshall, accompanied by Tucker. It was a tiny hamlet, no more than a dozen houses, a store or two, and the courthouse of Appomattox County. A quiet village, untouched by war until now. "I rode forward and asked the first citizen I met to direct me to a house suitable for the purpose," wrote Marshall. As inscrutable chance would have it, the citizen that Marshall first met was Wilmer McLean.

Few stories of the war present more sad irony than

Wilmer McLean's house, with members of the family sitting on the porch, not long after General Lee's surrender. (USAMHI)

Wilmer McLean's house became the surrender site because it was more comfortable than the Clover Hill Tavern, the initial choice. (Harper's Pictorial History of the Great Rebellion)

that of this farmer-turned-businessman. At 47 too old to take arms at the war's outset, still McLean was an earnest, if not rabid, proponent of the Confederate cause. In 1861 he was living on a small plantation called "Yorkshire" near Manassas Junction, Virginia. There the peaceful life of the farmer was interrupted that summer by the first hostile movements of the same two armies that now were come to Appomattox. In June 1861 McLean helped General P.G.T. Beauregard inspect the area, and that same month a Confederate signal station was placed near the plantation home. In anticipation that there would be a battle soon, the Confederate army rented Yorkshire and its buildings to use as a hospital. The army occupied the buildings on July 17, McLean and his family already having departed for safer climes. The next day, at about noon, Beauregard was making his headquarters at McLean's house when a Federal battery 1,500 yards away came into sight and fired three shots. One plowed into the ground. Another struck a piece of farm machinery. The third tore into McLean's kitchen building. They were by all accounts the first hostile shots fired between the two major armies of the East.

Following the Battle of First Manassas, McLean returned to Yorkshire to work without compensation for the Confederate quartermaster. But slowly his support for the cause began fading into disillusionment. He saw inefficiency and incompetence in the Rebel supply system. While he was donating his time, being paid only for traveling expenses, he saw other businessmen gaining great profits from the war through speculation. Perhaps worst of all, he saw his beloved Yorkshire mistreated and abused by the soldiers. Eventually, McLean, too, began charging higher prices for the commodities he sold to the Confederates, hoping to recoup the losses suffered by his property. By March 1862 he would remain no longer.

Thereafter, McLean speculated with some success in the sugar market, traveling widely from Richmond to the Mississippi. By the fall of 1863, however, he was ready to find another home for his family. He found it at Appomattox, a quiet village in south central Virginia where, he said, he hoped he might never see another soldier. In fact, he bought a substantial dwelling there, the Charles Raine house, sometime in 1862, and the McLeans settled in. He did not take up farming again, though, for little land had come with the house. Instead, he continued his financial maneuvers in the sugar trade, probably working out of nearby Lynchburg. And here he was in April 1865, when fate once more brought the armies to his door.

McLean took Marshall to an empty brick house, unoccupied and unfurnished, but the Confederate complained, "Isn't there another place?" Giving in, McLean—remembering the ravages at Yorkshire—reluctantly took Marshall to his own home, just a few hundred feet from the courthouse. It was a comfortable house, well furnished, its lawn and outbuildings shaded by locust trees. Entering the house, Marshall found the parlor on the left of the hallway to his liking and sent Tucker back to bring Lee and Babcock. When they arrived, Tucker took Traveller while the two officers joined Marshall inside. Lee walked to a small square-topped table and sat down beside it. Marshall and Babcock also took seats. For the next half hour, as they awaited the coming of Grant, the officers talked in what Marshall called "the most friendly and affable way." Exhausted, Lee may have dozed briefly. Then they heard hoofbeats on the road outside, followed by the pounding of Grant's boots upon McLean's porch.

Grant had awaked that morning with a terrible headache. One might have thought that the certain knowledge that Lee's days were almost done would have driven the pain from him, but it did not. At 4 a.m. Colonel Porter found the general pacing back and forth in the yard outside his quarters, his hands held to his head as if to pull out the pain. Coffee seemed to help some, and then he wrote to Lee, declining the proposed meeting and advising him that he could treat only with the surrender of the Army of Northern Virginia.

Riding to the front, Grant found Meade advancing against Longstreet with little difficulty. At once he decided to ride around the armies, to the south, to see how Sheridan was doing. After riding a few miles, he was approached by an officer bearing Lee's final request for an interview to discuss surrender. Grant's headache was still with him, "but the instant I saw the contents of the note," he wrote, "I was cured." He sent Babcock with his reply to Lee.

The ride to Appomattox Court House took Grant through Sheridan's lines and, just outside the village, he found Sheridan, Ord, and a number of other generals and staff officers. Sheridan was furious at the cease-fire. His were the instincts of a tiger. With the enemy mortally wounded, now was the time to pounce upon him for the glorious kill, not to talk terms. Grant would have none of it. "Is Lee over there," he asked, pointing to the village. "Yes," a disgruntled Sheridan replied, "he is in that brick house, waiting to surrender to you."

"Well, then," said Grant, "we'll go over."

Upon walking into the McLean parlor, Grant saw Lee arise. The two exchanged greetings, shook hands, and then Lee resumed his seat while Grant took a chair in the middle of the room and had a table moved over to him. Sheridan, Ord, and the others took seats or stood along the walls. Marshall stood beside Lee's chair.

"What General Lee's feelings were I do not know," Grant would recall, "but my own feelings, which had been quite jubilant on the receipt of his letter, were sad and depressed. I felt like anything rather than rejoicing at the downfall of a foe who had fought so long and valiantly, and had suffered so much." Grant, who had so often known humiliation in the years before the war, now felt embarrassed at the possible humiliation these proceedings might inflict upon Lee.

He hardly knew how to start. Reluctant to speak of the subject at hand, Grant mentioned that they had met once during the Mexican War, and that Grant remembered Lee well. Lee, too, recalled they had met. Glad to put off speaking of the surrender, Grant went on in this fashion for several minutes before Lee reminded him of why they were there. What were Grant's terms?

All he asked, said Grant, was that Lee lay down his arms and not pick them up again until and unless exchanged. All arms, ordnance, and supplies were to be surrendered. Lee assured Grant that he understood the terms as outlined, whereupon the Federal turned the conversation to other subjects once more, nearly as embarrassed by victory as Lee was by defeat.

Once again Lee brought them back to the subject. "Do I understand you to accept my terms?" asked Grant.

"I do," Lee replied, and then suggested that Grant write out the proposal formally in order that it might be put into effect. At once Grant took his order book from one of his staff, lit a cigar and puffed while trying to collect his thoughts, and then began to write with a pencil. Amid perfect silence, broken only by the scratching of the dull pencil across the rough paper, he spelled out the last of Lee's once magnificent army. Grant's mind moved faster than his fingers at the work, as he accidentally omitted words, hastily crossed out others, and wrote a verb in the wrong tense. When nearly finished, after providing for the surrender of the arms and artillery, he paused, glancing at Lee's beautiful Maryland sword. Once again he worried about humiliating this remarkably self-controlled man sitting before him. On he wrote: "This will not embrace the side arms of the officers, nor their private horses or baggage." Then a final sentence promising that the men would not be molested by the Federal Government so long as they observed their paroles, and Grant was done. He signed it "very respectfully."

Now it was Lee's turn to postpone the inevitable. Just as Grant had delayed by talking of other, better days, now, as he took the copy of the surrender terms, Lee performed a succession of studied, drawn-out motions. He set the order book carefully upon the marble-topped table beside him. From his vest pocket he withdrew his spectacles. From another pocket he took a handkerchief and wiped the lenses meticulously, perhaps seeing in every speck of dust on the glasses a moment more of life for his army before he agreed to its contract for death. He crossed his legs,

deliberately placed his spectacles over his eyes, and picked up the book once more. He read as slowly as possible.

As he read, Lee, after asking Grant's permission, corrected one of Grant's errors, and then visibly showed his reaction when he read the part about the government not persecuting his men after the surrender. He had feared prison or even worse for them. "This will have a very happy effect on my army," he told Grant.

Grant proposed that he have a copy made in ink for signing. Before this was done, though, Lee observed that in his army the artillerymen and cavalrymen owned their own horses. Might they take them with them? No, said Grant, the terms did not provide for that. Reading over the paper again, Lee said that "I see the terms do not allow it; that is clear."

Whether or not Lee meant his observation as a gentle hint he never said, but Grant read in it a wish

Resplendent in his dress uniform, General Robert E. Lee surrenders his Army of Northern Virginia to Lieutenant General Ulysses S. Grant, shown seated in the center. Lee's secretary, Lieutenant Colonel Charles Marshall, stands nearby, at left. (U.S. Army)

The parole signed by Lee and his staff at Appomattox. (National Archives)

that he was immediately prepared to fulfill. The Confederates would need their horses when they returned to their farms for the spring planting. He expected that this would be the last action of the war—he certainly hoped so—and he saw no reason why the men should not take their horses with them. He knew it would be a generous measure to start North and South on the long road to reconciliation. All those who claimed a horse would be allowed to take it.

"This will have the best possible effect upon the men," Lee said with relief. "It will be very gratifying and will do much toward conciliating our people."

Sometime either before or after the terms were discussed, Grant introduced Lee to the other officers in the room. Lee remarked that he had a number of Federal prisoners whom he could not feed and that, indeed, he could not feed his own troops. Grant asked if 25,000 rations would feed Lee's men. This

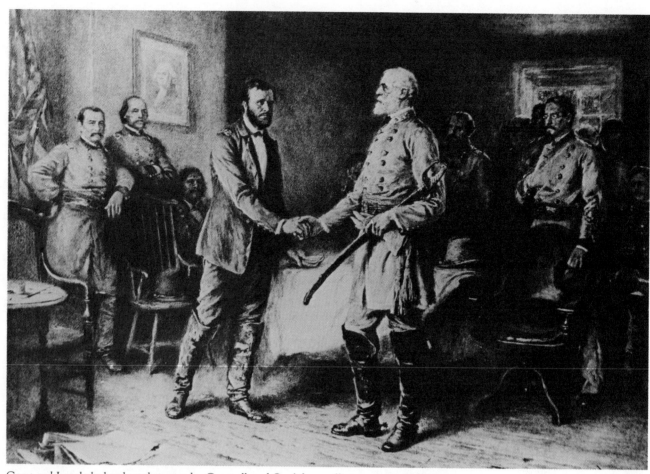

Grant and Lee shake hands at the surrender. Grant allowed Confederate officers to retain their side arms and horses. And, in tribute to his gallant adversary, Grant did not require that Lee give up his sword as a symbol of surrender. (CWTI Collection)

would be ample, he replied, and Grant sent out immediate orders. Interestingly enough, many of the rations sent to Lee were from those same trains he had so desperately tried to reach at Appomattox Station.

Once the documents were completed, Grant signed the terms and gave them to Lee. Lee signed his letter of acceptance and gave it to Grant. The Army of Northern Virginia was officially surrendered.

Grant's mind was seemingly on other things. Still worried lest he embarrass Lee in the least, he now explained why he was dressed in a muddy field uniform and minus his sword. There had been no time to have his saber and dress uniform brought up from his baggage wagon some distance away. Lee understood. A little more conversation, more hand shak-

Lee rides away from the McLean's house after the surrender negotiations, to break the sad news to the soldiers he had so long commanded. (Battles and Leaders of the Civil War)

ing, and sometime before 4 p.m. Lee and Marshall prepared to leave. The officers on the porch stood to attention when Lee stepped out. Deliberately he put on his hat, returned their salute, and then walked down into the yard, absent-mindedly smacking his gloved hands together several times. He seemed somewhere else at that moment, but quickly he returned to the present, called for his horse, and mounted. Just then Grant stepped out on the porch. Silently they raised their hats to each other. And then Lee rode back to tell his army that they were going home.

The ride back was agony for Lee. His soldiers had a fair idea of what had happened. "Are we surrendered?" they cried. "Blow, Gabriel, blow," shouted another, unwilling to outlive his army. They wept, they shouted. Officers drove their sabers into the ground and then broke the blades. Men bashed their rifles against trees. Proud, old banners that had gone through so many fights were torn to pieces that the men might have some memento to keep. Around Lee they gathered, uplifting their hands to touch him, to clasp his hands, to whisper or cry their assurances of devotion undimmed, their willingness to fight on to

the death. Lee's eyes watered with tears, his iron self-control tested to the fullest to keep him from breaking down with the emotions he felt. When finally he dismounted with his staff, he could not stand still, but paced back and forth by himself. Later, when he rode back to his headquarters, it all happened again, and then he must stand in his tent and receive the throngs who came to make their farewells.

As for Grant, the depression he felt was almost as great as Lee's. As they watched the Confederate chieftain ride away from McLean's, one of Grant's staff members, Adam Badeau, commented that "this will live in history." Grant did not respond but only kept watching Lee. "I am sure the idea had not occurred to him until I uttered it," recalled Badeau. "The effect upon his fame, upon history, was not what he was considering." Then, in a final gesture to save the pride of his fallen foe, he sent members of his staff to the various commands to stop the firing of muskets and cannon which had begun when word of the surrender spread among the ranks. "The war is over," he told them. "The Rebels are our countrymen again."

As for poor Wilmer McLean, who had tried so

The Confederates when the surrender was announced. (Harper's History of the Great Rebellion)

Head-Quarters, *Appomattox C. H. Va.*

Apl. 9th 1865, 4.30 o'clock, *p* M.

Hon. E. M. Stanton, Sec. of War Washington
Gen. Lee surrendered the Army
of Northern Va this afternoon on
terms proposed by myself. The
accompanying additional cor-
respondence will show the
conditions fully.

U. S. Grant
Lt. Gen

By Command of

Following the meeting with Lee, and while riding back to his head-
quarters, Grant was reminded that he had forgotten to notify the War
Department in Washington of Lee's surrender. He dismounted by the
roadside and wrote out a hasty dispatch (above) to Secretary of War
Stanton. Drawing below by Rufus Zogbaum. (Above: Appomattox
Court House National Historical Park. Below: Harper's New
Monthly Magazine, April 1898)

desperately to escape the destruction of war at Manassas, the ravages of peace proved even worse. He
was besieged by Federal officers wanting to buy this
and that piece of furniture from the parlor. Ord
bought one of the tables, Sheridan bought or took
another. Men shoved money in McLean's hands despite his angry protestations that he was running no
auction here. Soon his furnishings were simply
looted, many of them broken into tiny bits as sou-
venirs. Even at Grant's headquarters, the officers
bartered among themselves for mementoes of the
surrender, while Grant himself sat down in his tent,
surrounded by interested generals and staff who
hoped to hear him tell the details of the meeting with
Lee. Instead, as though nothing had happened, he
began again to reminisce about the Mexican War.

The working out of the actual details of the surrender was left to a commission to consist of three
officers of each army. Lee appointed Longstreet, Gordon, and Pendleton; Grant sent Griffin, Merritt, and
Gibbon, commanding the XXIV Corps of Ord's
army. The next day, April 10, while Lee's men were
enjoying the rations sent them by Grant the previous
day, the commission met first in the Clover Hill
Tavern, but found it cold and cheerless, and soon
moved to the surrender room in McLean's house. As
Longstreet came into the house to meet with the
commission that morning, he passed a room that
Grant was using as temporary headquarters. Grant
looked up as Old Pete passed, "recognized me," said
Longstreet, "rose, and with his old-time cheerful
greeting gave me his hand." He also gave him a cigar.

While the commission deliberated over just which
troops were included in the surrender—all those present? all within a twenty-mile radius? all those present
when negotiations began on April 8? etc.—the officers of the two armies began to seek out old friends
from before the war. Sheridan and two other generals
asked Lee's permission to bring Wilcox, Longstreet,
and Heth out to see Grant at his headquarters and
asked Marshall to compose a farewell address to the
army. Heth had served with him in Mexico. "We
chatted for half an hour about old times, kissing the
beautiful girls in the army, about Mexico," wrote
Heth. They spoke not at all about the war which for
them was ended, though the Confederates did express
their gratitude for the generous surrender terms.
Meanwhile, Meade went to Lee's headquarters to
renew an old acquaintance. "What are you doing
with all that gray in your beard?" asked Lee. Meade
replied that "You have to answer for most of it!"

Now that the Army of Northern Virginia was
surrendered, Grant and Lee did meet once more.

Appomattox Court House, photographed during the Federal occupation that followed the Army of Northern Virginia's surrender. (Library of Congress)

Among other things they incidentally discussed the other armies of the Confederacy, but since the President and his fleeing government were still free, Lee did not feel that he could make any terms for Johnston and others without first consulting Davis. This ended the matter. Grant left for Washington that same day, unwilling to witness the final surrender ceremonies. Lee went back to his headquarters and asked Marshall to compose a farewell address to the army. Marshall, who usually acted as Lee's ghost writer when more than military prose was needed, presented him with a rough draft of General Order Number 9.

As Lee read it, he found that Marshall had included a paragraph that showed his own bitterness, words not well calculated to heal the country's wounds. Lee struck it out. The rest was beautiful. "After four years of arduous service, marked by unsurpassed courage and fortitude, the Army of Northern Virginia has been compelled to yield to overwhelming numbers and resources." Lee had no choice, it said, but to surrender or else waste more of those lives that were more precious to him than his own. The terms were generous, and he prayed that "a Merciful God" would show them the same generosity in the days to come. "With an unceasing admiration

of your constancy and devotion to your Country," it concluded, "and a grateful remembrance of your kind and generous consideration of myself, I bid you an affectionate farewell."

"The Passing of the Dead"

According to the agreement of the commissioners, that last farewell would take place on April 12. Actual paroling had begun two days before, but on this last day the Confederates were to go through the physical motions of surrender, stacking arms and turning over their flags. Brigadier General Joshua L. Chamberlain was given the honor of formally receiving the surrender. That morning he formed his command on either side of the Richmond-Lynchburg road, which led from the Confederate camps, across the North Branch of the Appomattox, and up a slope past the courthouse. "Great memories arose," he recalled, as they prepared to receive "the last remnant of the arms and colors of that great army which ours had been created to confront for all that death can do for life."

The Confederates formed, too, silently, some sullenly. Lee would not take part in this, but stayed back

General Lee bids an affectionate farewell to his soldiers. (CWTI Collection)

The surrender of the Army of Northern Virginia at Appomattox on April 12, 1865. This painting by Ken Riley originally was reproduced in Life magazine. (West Point Museum Collection)

in his tent. The other generals were here, though, Gordon's corps in the lead, followed by what remained of Anderson's men, then Heth's, and finally Longstreet's. Without drums or fifes they marched forward in the measured tread that had become a part of their souls. When they came in sight of the Federals, they presented a vision that made many gasp. With the ranks of most of the regiments thinned to the size of companies, the scores of battle-flags that waved above them made it appear that "the whole column seemed crowned with red."

As Gordon approached, Chamberlain spoke to an aide and soon a bugle called the Federals to stiff attention, shifting them from "order arms" to "carry arms" as Gordon's men passed. It was, said Chamberlain, the marching salute. "Gordon at the head of the column, riding with heavy spirit and downcast face, catches the sound of shifting arms, looks up, and, taking the meaning, wheels superbly, making with himself and his horse one uplifted figure, with profound salutation as he drops the point of his sword to the boot toe; then facing to his own command, gives word for his successive brigades to pass us with the same position of the manual,—honor answering honor."

And so it went. Few eyes were dry on either side as the ragged yet proud Confederates passed, made their salutes, then dropped their rifles, bayonets, cartridge boxes, and flags in heaps beyond in a "triangle" formed just east of the courthouse by the main road and two private lanes. The sight woke "memories that bound us together as no other bond . . . What visions thronged as we looked into each other's eyes!" Finally they were all past, their actual number uncertain, but when all the stragglers had come in, and when all the wounded were found, 26,672 were paroled. In addition, Fitzhugh Lee and 1,559 cavalry finally surrendered in bits and pieces. But now no one thought of numbers, or of victory. "On our part," wrote Chamberlain of the ceremony, "not a sound of trumpet more, nor roll of drum; not a cheer, nor word nor whisper of vain-glorying, nor motion of man standing again at the order, but an awed stillness rather, and breath-holding, as if it were the passing of the dead!"

It was done. And now Lee and those who had followed him for so long must travel their separate roads to find what was left of the old life and make what they could of the new. Grant had generously given orders that the paroled soldiers should be al-

Brothers once again: Their fighting done, Federal soldiers share their rations with starving Confederate soldiers. Drawing by Alfred R. Waud. (Battles and Leaders of the Civil War)

lowed free passage on all government transportation in order to reach their homes. Many, accustomed to no other mode of travel but the march, walked.

Several days after the surrender, Colonel Robert McAllister, commanding a brigade in Humphreys' corps, was walking down the road between Burkeville and Farmville with a companion. They came upon a young paroled artilleryman resting under the shade of a tree. He had been captured by Sheridan the night before the surrender and took his parole with the rest. Now he joined McAllister, and as they walked he told the story of his and his army's last days. Barely 19, he showed a maturity brought by war, not by years. For a long time they walked and talked, the young man seeming reluctant to part with McAllister. He had known only the company and life of the soldier for years. Now, facing the uncertainties ahead, he clung to this last association with a man whose life and ways he understood, even if that man wore the blue. But finally he had to make his farewell and walk the road alone.

"Well, sir, where are you going?" McAllister had asked him.

"Home, sir," the boy replied.

"Home . . ."

Lee, his son Custis at left, and his adjutant Lieutenant Colonel Walter Taylor, taken by Mathew Brady at Lee's home in Richmond shortly after the surrender. (Library of Congress)

"The Last Speech
He Will Ever Make"

As news of Lee's surrender spread through the Union camps around Appomattox, northern soldiers began a wild celebration. Bands played and cannons boomed out salutes until Grant sent word to stop it. But even these orders could not prevent soldiers from cavorting and yelling. "The air is black with hats and boots, coats, knapsacks, shirts and cartridge boxes," wrote one veteran who described the scene.

Celebrating the war's end: The Army of the Potomac marches along Pennsylvania Avenue in the nation's capital. The fall of Richmond merited a nine-hundred gun salute in Washington; the surrender of Lee produced another five hundred. (CWTI Collection)

Cherokee Chief Stand Watie, who attained the rank of Brigadier General in the Confederate Army, was the last Confederate general to surrender. (Oklahoma Historical Society)

"They fall on each others' necks and laugh and cry by turns. Huge, lumbering men embrace and kiss like schoolgirls, then dance and sing and shout, stand on their heads and play leapfrog with each other." It was like all the Fourths of July in history rolled into one.

And the celebrations in the army paled by comparison with those back home. The rejoicing had begun with the news of Richmond's fall on April 3. In Washington a 900-gun salute proclaimed the capture of the rebel capital. "From one end of Pennsylvania Avenue to the other the air seemed to burn with the bright hues of the flag," wrote a reporter. "Men embraced one another, 'treated' one another, made up old quarrels, renewed old friendships, marched arm-in-arm singing." The North barely recovered from this jubilee when news of Lee's surrender started it all over again. On Wall Street in New York "men embraced each other and hugged each other, *kissed* each other, retreated into doorways to dry their eyes and came out again to flourish their hats and hurrah," wrote a participant. "They sang 'Old Hundred,' the 'Doxology,' 'John Brown' and 'The Star-Spangled Banner' over and over." Such intensity of feeling was "founded on memories of years of failure, all but hopeless, and the consciousness that national victory was at last secured."

In Washington large groups of people went from house to house of prominent officials serenading them and calling for speeches. Lincoln was ready for the crowd that came to the White House on April 11. The president spoke from a prepared text on the problem of reconstructing the Union in a manner that would bind up the nation's wounds but at the same time insure justice for freed slaves, including the right to vote for those who were qualified. At least one listener, an embittered Confederate sympathizer, did not like this talk. "That means nigger citizenship," snarled John Wilkes Booth to a companion. "Now, by God, I'll put him through. That is the last speech he will ever make."

—James M. McPherson

THE ASSASSINATION OF ABRAHAM LINCOLN

The Tragedy at Ford's Theater
by Robert H. Fowler
The Search for Booth by Robert H. Fowler

Ford's Theater was built on a site originally occupied by the First Baptist Church. In 1861 John T. Ford leased it as a theater causing one church member to predict a dreadful fate for the building. Ford renovated the building and reopened it March 19, 1862 as Ford's Atheneum. The theater was highly successful until December 30 of that year when a defective gas meter started a fire that gutted the building. Ford immediately built a new and larger building with a capacity of 1,700 that opened on August 27, 1863. By April 14, 1865 there had been 495 performances, eight of which were seen by Lincoln. On November 9, 1863 Lincoln saw John Wilkes Booth star in The Marble Heart. *(LC)*

The Tragedy at Ford's Theater
by Robert H. Fowler

ABRAHAM LINCOLN arose about 7 a.m. on April 14, 1865, dressed, and went directly to his desk for an hour of paper work. It was Good Friday on the church calendar and he had every reason to believe it would be a good Friday for him in the secular sense.

Five days before, at Appomattox, Robert E. Lee had surrendered his once seemingly invincible Army of Northern Virginia. With this bulwark of the Confederacy gone, the four-year civil war that had cost the Nation more than 600,000 lives was practically over and Lincoln could relax for a while.

During four years of constant anxiety, the President had lost twenty pounds. But his haggard face glowed with the festive spirit that prevailed in Washington. The streets were hung with flags and bunting. The night before, people from other cities had crowded into the capital to march in impromptu torchlight parades and to gather on street corners for band concerts. They thronged to stare at and cheer General U.S. Grant, just back from receiving Lee's surrender. The Lincolns themselves rejoiced at the return of their oldest son, Robert, who had been on Grant's staff.

The President would soon face problems in ways more formidable than winning the war. What to do with the leaders of the "Rebellion?" How to re-establish loyal governments in the eleven seceded states? How to demobilize the vast Union armies and graduate three million newly freed slaves into citizenship? How to effect reunion without retribution when Radical members of his own party thirsted for revenge? But he had three years and ten months of his second term to work out these problems. He had earned a rest.

About 8 a.m. Lincoln sat down to breakfast with Mrs. Lincoln, Robert, and twelve-year-old "Tad," his father's pet. Portraits of Lee already were being hawked in Washington. Robert showed one to his father who studied it and remarked: "It is a good face. I am glad the war is over at last."

The President's schedule called for a full but not strenuous day. He was to grant interviews until 11 a.m. when he would meet with his Cabinet and General Grant. There would be more interviews after lunch and then a drive with Mrs. Lincoln. He might drop by the War Department's telegraph room. Later some old political friends from Illinois were coming to chat. In the early evening he would eat dinner and conduct a little more business. Then he would go to the theater with Mrs. Lincoln. At the Cabinet meeting he would ask Grant to attend Ford's Theater with him and Mrs. Lincoln.

The managers of the two chief theaters in town had invited Lincoln to occupy the "State Box" that night, and suggested he bring Grant, thus ensuring a sellout on what traditionally is a poor night for show business—Good Friday. He accepted both invitations but decided to send Tad with some of his friends to Grover's Theater where "Aladdin and His Wonderful Lamp" was playing.

At least twice that day, Lincoln said he was going to the theater to please his wife. Yet the play was his type of broad comedy, Tom Taylor's "Our American Cousin," a farce about how an English family, upon settling an estate, discovers an American cousin who is entitled to a large share. They conspire to get him to England and cheat him out of his inheritance, but he turns out to be a

A rare picture of John Wilkes Booth at eighteen (above). Booth was the family "pet" and was given to grandiose dreams. (RC)

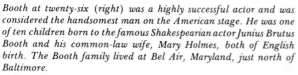

Booth at twenty-six (right) was a highly successful actor and was considered the handsomest man on the American stage. He was one of ten children born to the famous Shakespearian actor Junius Brutus Booth and his common-law wife, Mary Holmes, both of English birth. The Booth family lived at Bel Air, Maryland, just north of Baltimore.

"J. Wilkes Booth," as he usually signed himself, was a ladies' man. He made little effort to conceal his ardent sympathies for the South. Evidently he was under some emotional strain during the last year of the war, being engaged in several altercations for little reason. Also during this period Booth invested heavily in oil stocks and, it came out later, brought together a gang for the purpose of kidnapping President Lincoln. (LC)

shrewd down-east Yankee who outwits them at their own game.

This would be the 1,000th performance of one of the stars, Laura Keene, and the show would be a benefit for her, meaning she would get the proceeds above house expenses. When the Lincolns attended Ford's Theater the manager brought down comfortable chairs from his adjoining apartment. A partition between the two boxes was taken out, thus turning them into a single "Presidential box."

ABOUT 11:30 on the morning of April 14, James R. Ford, business manager and brother of the owner, received a note from the White House saying that the Lincolns would attend that night, bringing General and Mrs. Grant. This was good news for the Fords. Laura Keene's fans would help swell the crowd but it would help more to have it known the Lincolns and Grants were coming. Ford quickly prepared notices for the afternoon editions of the *Evening Star* and the *National Intelligencer*. New handbills were got up for the many soldiers in town.

In that day actors used a certain theater in each town as a mailing address. John Wilkes Booth's address was Ford's. Shortly before noon, Booth, who was staying at the National Hotel, came into the theater office and got from Harry Clay Ford, the theater treasurer, "a couple of letters" which he read while sitting on the office doorsill. Ford knew that Booth, a native of Bel Air, Maryland, was a strong Southern sympathizer, and to twit him he solemnly announced that Grant would occupy one box in the theater that night and Lee the opposite box. At this, Booth's face clouded and he snapped back that "General Lee is too fine a gentleman to be paraded as the Romans did their captives."

Ford told him he was only joshing about Lee but that, sure enough, Lincoln was coming with Grant. At that Booth wadded the letters in his pocket and strode away, in Ford's words, "as a man with an idea."

THE 26-year-old, strikingly handsome Booth had been "a man with an idea" for several months. That idea was to capture Abraham Lincoln and rush him to the Confederate Capital in Richmond. The previous spring, when he became Commander in Chief of all the Union armies, Grant had halted prisoner exchanges with the South. The Confederates could not replace their losses. Booth thought that Lincoln could be exchanged for many thousands of Confederate prisoners of war.

Whether this scheme had the blessing of the Confederate Government is not known. It appears, however, to have had the approval of Confederate agents in Canada and to have been well financed.

Booth was quite a "ladies' man," but he also had the ability to charm men, especially men not as intelligent as he or as sophisticated. He collected a motley group of conspirators consisting mostly of boyhood friends and ne'er-do-wells but also including two persons of special ability: John H. Surratt, a young Confederate courier who carried messages between Richmond and Montreal, and Lewis Thornton Powell, alias Lewis Paine, a giant Floridian who had been captured at Gettysburg, escaped, and after brief service with Mosby's partisans, had taken the oath of allegiance at Alexandria, Virginia, on New Year's Day of that year. Paine, 20, had the strength it would take to subdue the 6-foot 4-inch Lincoln.

In addition, there were 28-year-old Samuel Arnold and 27-year-old Michael O'Laughlin, both old school chums and former Confederate soldiers; George Atzerodt, 33, a stupid little German immigrant who ferried Southern couriers and spies across the Potomac near his home at Port Tobacco, Maryland; and David Herold, 23, an inoffensive drug clerk who, as an avid small-game hunter, knew intimately the back trails of southern Maryland.

THIS ASSORTED CREW met several times at the home of John Surratt's widowed mother, Mrs. Mary E. Surratt, 45, in Washington, where she had opened a boardinghouse after leasing the family home at Surrattsville, Maryland. She knew her son John Harrison was engaged in dangerous undertakings for the Confederacy, but she may not have known he was in the plot to capture the President. Mrs. Surratt's 17-year-old daughter, Anna, also lived at the boardinghouse.

The gang considered three different plans. Booth proposed seizing Lincoln in a theater but his fellow conspirators balked. Another idea was to pounce on the President while he visited an army hospital across the Anacostia River. This would solve the problem of one river barrier, but there were likely to be Federal soldiers about.

The most workable scheme seemed to be to lie in wait along a deserted stretch of the road Lincoln followed on visits to the Soldiers' Home on 7th Street. The plan was to halt his carriage, either chloroform or gag and bind Lincoln, then with companions mounted on the box of the distinctive carriage, and others as "outriders" disguised in blue uniforms, rush him out of the city into the secessionist countryside southeast of Washington.

Late in 1864, Booth visited this area, to work out routes and arrange for boat passage of the lower Potomac. During the war, mail, newspapers, and contraband such as medicine flowed between well-established clandestine signal stations and relay points. Some time late in the war, word was passed to op-

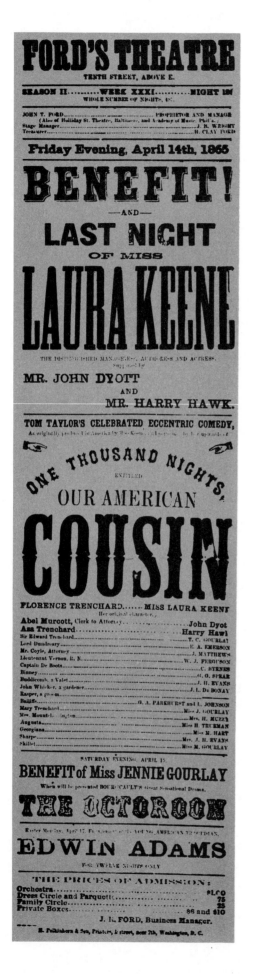

Thomas T. Eckert (right), head of the telegraph office in the War Department, refused to act as bodyguard for Lincoln on the night of April 14, 1865. (KA)

Playbill of the performance is at left.

Congressman George Ashmun of Massachusetts wished to talk to Lincoln at length but it was time for the theater. Lincoln wrote a pass so Ashmun could return for an interview the next morning. (Lloyd Ostendorf Collection)

Allow Mr. Ashmun & friend to come in at 9. A.M. to morrow—

A Lincoln

April 14. 1865.

When he was shot, Lincoln was sitting in this upholstered walnut rocker brought down from the apartment of Harry Ford, theater treasurer. (LC)

eratives along this route to be ready to help move a captured high official quickly to the South.

There was at least one other gang with plans similar to Booth's in this period. Just which one alerted the chain of Confederate spies is not clear.

The weather was against the kidnapping plot early in the year but Booth and his cronies had numerous opportunities to shoot Lincoln. Enlarged sections of a photograph taken at the second Lincoln inaugural ceremonies on March 4, 1865 show Booth and other conspirators standing within easy revolver range of the President.

ON MARCH 17, 1865, with time fast running out for the Confederacy, the gang heard that Lincoln had been invited to Campbell General Hospital at 7th Street and Boundary (now Florida) Avenue for an entertainment for invalid servicemen. With an hour's notice, according to John Surratt, the gang raced out and waited until they saw a carriage approach. Riding alongside, they saw the man in the vehicle was not Lincoln. It may have been Salmon P. Chase, the Chief Justice of the Supreme Court, who did attend the show. Lincoln at the last minute had decided to review a veteran Indiana regiment newly arrived from the front. At any rate Booth and his friends, infuriated and discouraged, drifted apart after this.

One man on the fringe of the gang, Louis J. Weichmann, a friend of Surratt's and a boarder at Mrs. Surratt's house, tipped off the War Department about the kidnap plot. Some time after April 14, it was disclosed that the War Department had been warned of such a scheme. It is significant that the first persons to be arrested in the assassination conspiracy were those who had been involved in the plot to capture the President. Possibly, with the end of the war, the responsible persons felt the danger had passed.

SO, Lincoln went about his business that day guarded only by William H. Crook, a former Washington policeman. The Cabinet meeting with Grant was uneventful. Secretary of State Seward was absent, having suffered a broken jaw and collar bone in a carriage accident. Secretary of War Stanton came in late with a report that Sherman was about to start negotiating in North Carolina with Johnston for the inevitable surrender of the last large Confederate army.

Lincoln told about having the same dream the previous night he had had before every great event of the war. In it he was in some great vessel on the water moving rapidly toward a vague shoreline. "We shall, judging from the past, have great news very soon," he predicted.

In discussing how to establish law and order in the South, Lincoln said he had no intention of taking

Booth's gang met several times at the boardinghouse operated by Mrs. Surratt at 604 H Street, N.W., in Washington. The widow's son, John Harrison Surratt, was a Confederate courier who plotted with Booth to kidnap Lincoln. While Lincoln lay dying early on the morning of April 15, detectives called at the house for young Surratt but left when told he was in Canada. How the detectives knew of his connection with Booth so early has never been explained. (RC)

part "in hanging or killing these men (Confederate leaders), even the worst of them." The best course, he said, was to allow them to escape the country. "Enough lives have been sacrificed; we must extinguish our resentments if we expect harmony and union."

Secretary Stanton then proposed that the military governments of Virginia and North Carolina be combined and the two states administered as a unit. Two other cabinet members objected to this plan and Lincoln sided with them, directing Stanton to set up a separate and temporary military government for each state. He did not wish to destroy the autonomy or individuality of any state.

After the meeting broke up, Lincoln invited Grant and his wife to attend the theater that night. Grant accepted. He and his wife planned to take an early morning train to visit their two daughters in school at Burlington, New Jersey but they had no other plans.

Booth could have shot Lincoln on several occasions before April 14. In fact he stood only a few feet away from the President during the second Lincoln inaugural on March 4, 1865. The large photograph (left) was taken as Lincoln delivered his memorable address. Above is an enlarged section of this photograph. The blurred figure at the lower right is Lincoln. Wearing a stovepipe hat and standing above and behind him (indicated by arrow) is Booth. The bearded man beneath Booth is believed to be John T. Ford, owner of the theater. (Photographs from Lloyd Ostendorf Collection, as reproduced in Lincoln in Photographs.*)*

THE REST of the day was busy, but pleasant. During their drive, the President talked to Mrs. Lincoln about returning to his law practice in Springfield some day and buying a farm nearby.

"I never felt so happy in my life," he remarked.

Mrs. Lincoln was devoted to her husband but she had a morbid, often disagreeable nature. "Don't you remember feeling just so before our little boy died?" she asked. She had never recovered from the death of their middle son, 13-year-old Willie, in early 1862.

Mrs. Lincoln's wet-blanket remark may account for something the President said later that day to his bodyguard as they walked to the War Department.

"Crook, do you know, I believe there are men who want to take my life? And I have no doubt they will do so."

"Why do you think so, Mr. President?"

"Other men have been assassinated."

"I hope you are mistaken, Mr. President," Crook said. To which Lincoln replied, "I have perfect confidence in those who are around me—in every one of your men. I know no one could do it and escape alive. But if it is to be done, it is impossible to prevent it."

At the War Department, after talking to Secretary Stanton, Lincoln asked that Major Thomas T. Eckert, head of the Telegraph Office, be assigned as his bodyguard that evening. Eckert was a powerful man whom Lincoln had seen demonstrate his strength by breaking cheap cast-iron pokers over his arm.

Stanton refused, saying that he had important work for Eckert to do that night. In spite of this, Lincoln went into Eckert's office and asked him directly. Eckert also declined, pleading hard work that could not be put off.

SINCE Crook would be off duty, who would guard the President that night? On April 3, while Lincoln was visiting Grant's headquarter's in Virginia, the chief of the Washington Metropolitan Police Force received a note from the Executive Mansion, which read:

> This is to certify John F. Parker, a member of the Metropolitan Police Force, has been detailed for duty at the Executive Mansion.

It was signed, "By order of Mrs. Lincoln."

So Parker was to be the guard that night. Parker, 35, was a notoriously unreliable, even an unsavory policeman. He had been tried fourteen times by the police board for violation of orders, inattention to duty, and other infractions. A married man, he once spent a week in a Washington bawdy house, later explaining that he was there to protect the place. No light has ever been shed on why Mrs. Lincoln chose him as a guard.

Meanwhile, that afternoon at Ford's Theater, Harry Ford had the Presidential box flanked with

A corridor led from the dress circle of Ford's Theater to the two boxes combined as the "Presidential box" on April 14. Frank Leslie's illustration shows the doors to the two boxes. A hole bored in the door at left permitted Booth to peep in before entering to shoot the President. (KA)

two American flags on standards and a large flag draped on the balustrade. He also had a gilt-framed engraving of George Washington placed on the central pillar. Edman Spangler, an ignorant stagehand who idolized John Wilkes Booth, assisted the stage carpenter in removing the partition between the two boxes. Harry Ford had a walnut rocker brought down from his apartment and placed in a corner for the President.

Some other less innocent arrangements were made. The doors to the combined boxes opened onto a passageway which led through another door to the south aisle of the dress circle. Someone placed a piece of wood from an old music stand in the passageway and cut a notch into the plaster so that the stick could be braced against the door to prevent anyone from entering from the dress circle. Someone also bored a small peephole in one of the doors opening into the box. The locks on these doors had been broken some weeks earlier and the screws loosened. Booth may have done these things. He had access to the theater. There is no proof either way.

ABOUT 5 P.M., Lincoln returned to the White House from the War Department to find waiting for

Three people were in the box with Lincoln when he was shot.

Clara Harris (top right) was twenty and Henry Rathbone's fiancee. Her father, New York Senator Ira Harris, married Rathbone's widowed mother; the couple fell in love after their parents' marriage and themselves were married some time after Lincoln's death.

Mary Todd Lincoln sat next to the President.

Henry Rathbone, a twenty-eight-year-old major in the Army Pay Department, tried to seize Booth after the President was shot. Rathbone sustained a deep knife wound across his arm.

All three met tragic ends. Major Rathbone murdered his wife, the former Miss Harris, several years later and was put in an insane asylum. Mrs. Lincoln also spent time in an insane asylum.

Facing page: The presidential box was flanked by two American flags; on the balustrade were another large flag, an engraving of George Washington, and a Treasury flag. (LC)

Below is a floor plan of the presidential box that appeared in Harper's Weekly. O, corridor from dress circle to box. H, entrance to corridor. I, bar Booth used to secure door behind him. J, circle. M, the stage. F and G, doors into box. N, point from which Booth vaulted out of the box. (KA)

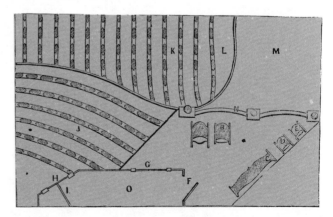

him two Illinois friends, Governor Richard J. Oglesby and General Isham N. Haynie of Springfield. Lincoln read aloud passages by humorist David R. Locke's creation, Petroleum Vesuvius Nasby, a fictitious and verbose Copperhead who indicted his cause with his pronouncements.

After dinner, Schuyler F. Colfax, Speaker of the House of Representatives, came (for the second time that day) to inquire whether Lincoln would call an extra session of Congress that summer. Lincoln said no. Downstairs, Congressman George Ashmun of Massachusetts, an early Lincoln supporter, waited. There was no time for a full interview, so Lincoln wrote a pass for Ashmun to come again first thing the next morning. Mrs. Lincoln interrupted to remind the President that it was time to go to the theater. It was then Lincoln learned that the Grants would not attend Ford's with them after all. Instead of going to Burlington the next day as planned, Mrs. Grant had decided to leave that same evening on a train that was much slower and which necessitated a long wait in Philadelphia. In fact, by leaving twelve hours earlier they would get to Burlington only two hours sooner.

Why this change of plans? One explanation is that Mrs. Grant wanted nothing to do with Mrs. Lincoln, who had greatly embarrassed her just two weeks before at City Point, Virginia. Mrs. Lincoln had become jealous because a younger woman had ridden next to her husband en route to the review field, and when Mrs. Grant tried to calm her, she had exploded with charges that Mrs. Grant was ambitious to be a president's wife. Later, at a reception, Mrs. Lincoln created another distressing scene, and the next day returned to Washington ahead of schedule. A ride on a slow train and a long layover would be preferable to another such experience.

MRS. LINCOLN told the President she had asked Robert to go with them but he wanted to "turn in early" so she had invited a popular young couple, 28-year-old Major Henry Rathbone and Miss Clara Harris, daughter of New York Senator Ira Harris. Senator Harris had married the major's widowed mother and now their children were engaged.

John Parker was waiting at Ford's Theater when the Lincolns arrived with Rathbone and Miss Harris. The play was in progress as the party walked up to the Presidential box. The audience applauded the President, many rising and cheering, and the orchestra struck up "Hail to the Chief." Lincoln bowed and sat down in the rocker; Mrs. Lincoln curtsied and sat beside him with Miss Harris in the next chair and Major Rathbone behind her, on a sofa.

It was now after 8:30 p.m. and Abraham Lincoln, who had undergone the most demanding four years

Booth shot Lincoln with a .44-caliber, single-shot, muzzleloading derringer. Booth dropped the weapon when Major Rathbone arose to grapple with him and the pistol was found on the floor of the box later. The picture at right appeared in the April 29th edition of Harper's Weekly.

of any President, at times singlehandedly holding together the Union, was to spend his little remaining time at one of his favorite pastimes, watching a diverting comedy. It was Fate's final kindness to perhaps the greatest of all Americans.

Only part of Booth's movements from the time he walked away from Ford's Theater that day can be traced. He hurried to Howard's Stable on 7th Street and left instructions for his one-eyed horse to be taken to a shed behind the theater. He then went to another stable on the Mall and reserved a mare to be saddled and ready for him at 4 p.m. Some time after 2 p.m. he appeared at the Surratt House on H Street to ask for John, who was out of town. Mrs. Surratt was about to leave for Surrattsville in a rented carriage driven by her boarder, Louis Weichmann. She later said the 24-mile round trip was an urgent legal errand. It would be charged that Booth gave her a mysterious package to deliver for him but there is considerable debate on this point.

Booth then looked up Lewis Paine at the Herndon House, 9th and F Streets, talked to him, and then asked for George A. Atzerodt at the Kirkwood House. Atzerodt was not there but a little later, after a drink in a bar, Booth returned and inquired if another resident, Vice President Andrew Johnson, was in. Told he was not, the actor did a strange thing: He scribbled on a card, "Don't wish to disturb you. Are you at home?" signed his name, and left it to be delivered to Johnson.

Whether he did this to embarrass the Vice President or whether, as was later rumored, the two had once been wenching companions in Nashville where Johnson was the wartime governor, there is no certain answer.

After slipping a note under the door to Atzerodt's room, Booth got his mare at the stable on the Mall. He tried her out for speed and then rode to Grover's Theater. There he was seen to write a letter and seal it in an envelope. He also consumed a large quantity of brandy. A little later he showed up at Ford's Theater and chatted outside with the property man. Leaving Ford's, he stopped an actor he knew and asked him to wait until next day and then deliver the letter he had just written to a newspaper editor. (The actor destroyed the letter the next day, inciden-

tally.) This actor related that as Booth started to mount, a company of soldiers herded past them a group of Confederate prisoners and Booth said, "Great God! . . . I have no longer a country."

Booth was known all over town. Dressed for riding and obviously having been drinking heavily, he waved to friends and talked to them freely about everything but what was most on his mind.

About 6 p.m. he put his hired steed with his own horse in the shed behind Ford's Theater and called for Spangler, the stagehand. Other Ford employees gathered around the popular actor and he bought them a bottle of whisky. If Booth did bore the peephole and plant the piece of wood to bar the door, this likely would have been the occasion, while the employees were distracted by the free whisky.

An hour later he was seen in the dining room of the National Hotel. On his way out, about 8 p.m., he advised the desk clerk to be at Ford's Theater that night, adding, "There'll be some fine acting there tonight."

ABOUT 9:30 P.M. Booth appeared on his hired mare in the alley to the rear of the theater and called for Spangler to hold his horse. The stagehand came out and took the horse but, after Booth entered the rear door, he summoned Joseph Burroughs, who went by the nickname of "Peanuts John," to hold the reins. Booth wanted to cross the rear of the stage but a

stagehand told him he could not because a "deep" scene was on, meaning the set extended to the back of the stage; hence he used a passageway under the stage to the adjoining Star Saloon.

Booth chatted with the bartender and others as he drank. Several times he walked from the bar into the lobby of the theater and back again. Finally, about 10:15 p.m., he walked up to the ticket taker, made a show of borrowing a chew of tobacco, and stepped inside. The drawing-room scene was on. Booth made his way to the vestibule outside the Presidential box. The guard, John Parker, had wandered away to watch the performance.

On the stage at this time "Mrs. Mountchessingson" was saying to Asa Trenchard, the wily American cousin: "I am aware, Mr. Trenchard, that you are not used to the manners of polite society, and that alone will pardon the impertinence of which you have been guilty."

With that, she flounced off the stage, leaving only comedian Harry Hawk (Asa Trenchard). As Hawk looked after her, he put his thumbs in his galluses in best Yankee style and said: "Heh, heh. Don't know the manners of good society, eh? Well, I guess I know enough to turn you inside out, old gal—you sock-dologizing old man-trap. Heh, heh, heh."

THIS rocked the audience, as Booth probably knew it would. As the laughter rang, he pushed open the

Dr. Charles A. Leale, a young Army assistant surgeon, was the first doctor to reach the wounded Lincoln. Later, Laura Keene, star of Our American Cousin, *was allowed to enter the box and hold Lincoln's head in her lap while arrangements were made to remove him from the theater.* (LC)

door into the Presidential box, and deliberately fired a .44 caliber deringer, a single-shot, muzzle-loading pocket pistol, at the back of Lincoln's head. The President slumped forward in his rocking chair. Major Rathbone looked up to see Booth standing with a smoking pistol in one hand and a hunting knife in the other. The officer sprang toward the actor, trying to get a grip on him but Booth slashed him savagely across the arm, broke away and vaulted from the box to the edge of the stage, more than ten feet below.

It would have been an easy leap for Booth except for the flag Harry Ford had draped below the box. One of the actor's spurs caught in the flag, causing him to land off balance and break the small bone in his left leg.

Arising, Booth faced the audience, shouted the motto of the Commonwealth of Virginia, "Sic semper tyrannis!" (thus always to tyrants), and hobbled rapidly across the stage.

There were more than 1,000 persons in the theater, most of them still laughing at Asa Trenchard's funny line. Some of them thought the wild-eyed man who suddenly dropped upon the stage was part of the act and laughed. Then they heard the screams of Mrs. Lincoln and the shouts of Major Rathbone, "Stop that man!"

The orchestra conductor, who stood between Booth and the door to the alley, was struck with the butt of the hunting knife and shoved out of the way. Outside, Booth mounted the mare, and when "Peanuts John" failed to release the animal promptly, struck him with the butt of the knife and kicked him away.

Sitting in the front row of the audience had been Joseph Stewart, a six-and-a-half foot tall Washington lawyer. A Union Army veteran, Stewart recognized the sound of a shot through the laughter. Within seconds after Booth had crossed the stage, the giant Stewart scrambled over the footlights and raced after Booth. He lost valuable seconds fumbling at the wrong side of the back door which Booth had slammed behind him. When he got outside, Booth was already mounted and was putting spurs to his mare.

Stewart reached out for the horse, but Booth circled to avoid him. Again the lawyer made a running grab, in vain. He was soon left behind.

BACK in the theater many of the shocked spectators stood on chairs to try to see what was going on. Dr. Charles A. Leale, a young Army assistant surgeon, pounded at the door leading to the vestibule outside the box until the faint and bleeding Rathbone removed the bar Booth had placed against it. Leale found the President slumped in the rocker with the

The cover illustration of Frank Leslie's May 6, 1865 edition showed Booth catching a spur in the Treasury flag hanging between the two boxes (above). It is more likely that he snagged the large American flag draped over the balustrade.

Alfred Waud's sketch for engravers of Harper's indicated the "spot on which the man jumped." The eleven feet, six inches from balustrade to stage that Waud notes would have been an easy leap for the athletic Booth had he not snagged his spur.

sobbing Mrs. Lincoln supporting his head. Finding no pulse, he eased the long body to the floor.

Below, another physician, Dr. Charles Taft, fought his way to the stage and was lifted high enough to get his hands on the balustrade and struggle his way into the box. They cut open Lincoln's coat and shirt, thinking he might have been stabbed. Seeing no wound on the chest, Dr. Leale ran his fingers gently through the coarse black hair until he found the bullet hole at the back of the head. He removed a clot of blood, thinking this would relieve pressure on the brain.

Dr. Leale then bent over Lincoln, and through mouth-to-mouth respiration, forced air into his lungs. He and Dr. Taft also tried to stimulate the heart, pressing against the upper stomach and pumping the arms.

"We repeated these motions a number of times before signs of recovery from the profound shock were attained," Dr. Leale later wrote. "Then a feeble action of the heart and irregular breathing followed."

WASHINGTON Mayor Richard Wallach happened to be outside the theater and Harry Ford asked him to announce from the stage that the President had been shot and request the audience to leave. While this was being done, Laura Keene, the star of the show, was allowed to enter the box and hold the President's head in her lap, as she sat on the floor.

Outside, as the news spread, cries of "Burn the theater!" went up. The street was soon jammed with the spectators and persons attracted by the hubbub.

The doctors thought it would cause a fatal hemorrhage to transport the President over the rough streets to the White House or a hospital. Accordingly they directed six soldiers to carry him across the street to a house they saw lighted there. This was the home of William Petersen, a tailor who rented rooms upstairs above his basement shop.

A light rain had started to fall. Hundreds of excited people jammed the street so that soldiers had to force a path for the President to be carried through. Soon, however, Lincoln was placed diagonally on a narrow bed in a 9½ by 17 foot room on the second floor. (Later it would be learned that Booth on one occasion, when the room was rented to a fellow actor, had taken an afternoon nap on this very bed.) At Mrs. Lincoln's request, Dr. Robert King Stone, Lincoln's personal doctor, was summoned. Soldiers were sent to get Surgeon General Joseph K. Barnes.

MANY persons had recognized Booth during his few seconds on the stage but he had got away safely, except for the leg fracture. The mischief he

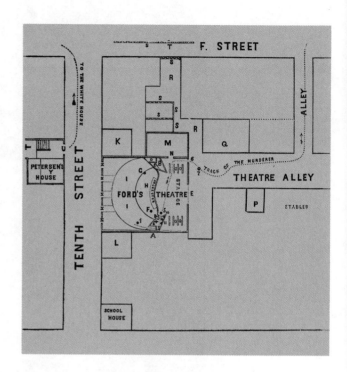

A layout for Ford's Theater and the Petersen house prepared for Leslie's shows a broken line for Booth's route from the dress circle to the alley. Several other locations are noted. A, the President's box. F, seat of Joseph Stewart, who pursued Booth. L, the Star Saloon where Booth drank while waiting for his opportunity. P, the shed where Booth had his horse brought. The number six shows the door through which Booth fled from the theater after crossing the stage. A drawing of Booth's escape behind the theater and Joseph Stewart's attempt to stop him also appeared in Leslie's. (Both KA)

had set in motion was not complete, however. At about 10 p.m., Lewis Paine, the huge former Confederate soldier, rode Booth's one-eyed horse up to the door of Secretary of State Seward's home on Lafayette Square, a stone's throw from the White House. Seward lay in an upstairs bedroom, his fractured jaw and shoulder in a metal-and-leather brace. His young daughter and a soldier-nurse were in the room with him. Elsewhere in the house were his two sons, Frederick and Augustus, and a Negro servant.

The servant answered the door when Paine rang. Told that Seward's doctor had sent medicine, the servant tried to take the package but Paine insisted on giving it to Seward personally. He finally pushed past the servant and mounted the stairs. He was stopped in the hall by Frederick Seward and after a moment's conversation he suddenly set upon the young man, beating him viciously with a heavy revolver and fracturing his skull.

Paine then burst into Seward's room and fell upon the Secretary with a knife. He cut the old man severely but the apparatus for the broken jaw prevented a fatal injury. Augustus Seward rushed into the room to see the soldier-nurse vainly trying to pull Paine away from the bed. Together the two men fought Paine to the door. Paine inflicted a long gash across

A Leslie's drawing of Booth's escape behind the theater as Joseph Stewart tried to stop him. (KA)

young Seward's scalp and stabbed the soldier in the chest and shoulders. Then, leaving behind a hysterical girl and four badly wounded persons, he ran out of the house, leaped on his horse, and rode off.

So now the President lay dying and the Secretary of State seriously wounded. Later it would be charged that Booth had assigned George Atzerodt to kill Vice President Johnson but the little German lost his nerve. Booth probably would have stabbed General Grant had he been with Lincoln.

THE PRESIDENT'S youngest son, his beloved Tad, it will be remembered, was seeing a play at Grover's Theater that night. Some thoughtless person announced from the stage that Lincoln had been shot. Sobbing, "They killed my pa; they killed my pa," Tad was taken back to the White House. Robert Lincoln first heard only that his father had been wounded. He was met at the door of the Petersen house by Dr. Stone, who told him there was no hope. Meanwhile upstairs the doctors had undressed the still-unconscious President. Finding that his feet and legs were growing cold, they covered them with hot water bottles and applied large mustard plasters to his chest and stomach. Twice the surgeons probed the wound but found the passage of the bullet

blocked by a piece of bone. There was little they could do except keep the opening free of fluid and bits of oozing brain tissue.

After Secretary of War Stanton arrived, the narrow little house on 10th Street became the headquarters of the Federal Government. Taking over another room on the second floor, the efficient, dogmatic little Stanton called for a shorthand expert. A government clerk who lived next door, James Tanner, was brought in. Stanton personally questioned witnesses and issued a stream of orders.

Tanner's shorthand notes, preserved by the Union League in Philadelphia, leave no doubt that the assassin was quickly identified as Booth.

Stanton also ordered that the theater be cordoned off. When Mrs. Lincoln grieved too loudly, he ordered her removed from the President's room. Tanner recalled her "moans and cries" throughout the night. Dozens of government officials came to the Petersen house, murmuring to themselves and bowing their heads during periods of prayer. But Stanton —the "man of steel," as Tanner called him—was firmly in charge.

LINCOLN GROANED a bit during the first part of the night but during most of the long hours until

Secretary of State William G. Seward was bedridden the night Lincoln was shot, having been injured in a carriage accident. Seward's young daughter, Fanny, was in his sickroom when Lewis Paine burst in and attacked him. Fanny was emotionally unbalanced for most of her life, some people say as a result of this episode. (NA)

early morning his only sound was labored breathing. His left upper eyelid became swollen and dark, indicating that the bullet had lodged nearby. Later the other eye became enlarged and darkened.

About 11:30 p.m. the muscles on the left side of the face twitched for about twenty minutes and the mouth became drawn.

As Dr. Taft later wrote: "The wonderful vitality exhibited by the late President was one of the most interesting and remarkable circumstances connected with the case. It was the opinion of the surgeons in charge that most patients would have died in two hours."

The end came at 7:22 a.m. with two doctors holding their fingers on his wrists and another with his hand on his chest.

The Rev. Phineas D. Gurley, a Presbyterian minister, offered a prayer. Dr. Leale "gently smoothed the President's contracted facial muscles, took two coins from my pocket, placed them over his eyelids, and drew a white sheet over the martyr's face."

It was at this point that Secretary Stanton allegedly said, "Now he belongs to the ages."

GENERAL and Mrs. Grant were among the first outside of Washington to learn of the shooting. Stanton telegraphed him to be careful, that there might be a plot against a number of prominent persons. Grant got the wire as he was about to eat in Philadelphia. Silently reading it, he handed it to his wife, who wept.

Tears and anger rolled like a tide across the North as the next day's newspapers came out. In city after city, bells tolled and citizens began to drape their doorways. At Durham Station, in North Carolina, Sherman got a telegram from Stanton telling him of the assassination. He was on his way to start surrender negotiations with Johnston. Fearful of what the Federal soldiers would do, Sherman forbade the telegrapher to tell anyone. When he told Johnston, the Confederate general broke into a sweat and commented that this was "the greatest possible calamity

Above, from Leslie's, is a drawing of the Seward house, which faced Lafayette Park near the White House. (KA)

to the South." When the news did reach Sherman's soldiers, their officers had to restrain them from burning Raleigh, the state capital. In some Northern cities, people who uttered anti-Lincoln remarks were set upon by angry mobs.

In the midst of all this turmoil, Chief Justice Chase administered the oath of office to Andrew Johnson, who became the inheritor of all the troubles of which Booth's bullet had relieved Lincoln. Booth, who had imagined himself as a great friend of the South, might as well have been its worst enemy. Within hours of Lincoln's death a caucus of Congressional Radicals decided on a "line of policy less conciliatory than that of Mr. Lincoln" and nodded agreement over the statement that "the accession of Johnson to the Presidency would prove a godsend to the country." Benjamin F. Wade, the Radical leader, supposedly told Johnson: "I thank God that you are here. Lincoln had too much of the milk of human kindness to deal with these damned rebels. Now they will be dealt with according to their deserts."

A message from Secretary of War Stanton, which told the story of the shooting succinctly, was reprinted in the New York Times *the next morning.*

After Lincoln was carried into the Petersen house, soldiers cleared the street between it and Ford's Theater. (KA)

So many people claimed to have been at Lincoln's side when he died that the nine-and-a-half-by-seventeen-foot room would have had to be many times that size to have held them all. Dozens of drawings and engravings were published showing practically every bigwig in government mourning over the form of the dying president. This drawing from the May 6, 1865 issue of Harper's Weekly is more reasonable than most. Left to right it identifies those in the room as Secretary of the Navy Gideon Welles, Secretary of War Edwin M. Stanton, an unidentified man at the foot of the bed, two unidentified men with their backs to the viewer, Postmaster General William Dennison, Senator Charles Sumner, Surgeon General Joseph K. Barnes (leaning over Lincoln), Robert Lincoln (with one hand over his eyes), General Henry Halleck, John Hay (Lincoln's secretary), and Quartermaster General Montgomery Meigs. (KA)

War Department Washington, April 20, 1865,

$100,000 REWARD

THE MURDERER

Of our late beloved President, Abraham Lincoln,

IS STILL AT LARGE.

$50,000 REWARD

Will be paid by this Department for his apprehension, in addition to any reward offered by Municipal Authorities or State Executives.

$25,000 REWARD

Will be paid for the apprehension of JOHN H. SURRATT, one of Booth's Accomplices.

$25,000 REWARD

Will be paid for the apprehension of David C. Harold, another of Booth's accomplices.

LIBERAL REWARDS will be paid for any information that shall conduce to the arrest of either of the above-named criminals, or their accomplices.

All persons harboring or secreting the said persons, or either of them, or aiding or assisting their concealment or escape, will be treated as accomplices in the murder of the President and the attempted assassination of the Secretary of State, and shall be subject to trial before a Military Commission and the punishment of DEATH.

Let the stain of innocent blood be removed from the land by the arrest and punishment of the murderers.

All good citizens are exhorted to aid public justice on this occasion. Every man should consider his own conscience charged with this solemn duty, and rest neither night nor day until it be accomplished.

EDWIN M. STANTON, Secretary of War.

DESCRIPTIONS.—BOOTH is Five Feet 7 or 8 inches high, slender build, high forehead, black hair, black eyes, and wears a heavy black moustache.

JOHN H. SURRAT is about 5 feet, 9 inches. Hair rather thin and dark; eyes rather light; no beard. Would weigh 145 or 150 pounds. Complexion rather pale and clear, with color in his cheeks. Wore light clothes of fine quality. Shoulders square; cheek bones rather prominent; chin narrow; ears projecting at the top; forehead rather low and square, but broad. Parts his hair on the right side; neck rather long. His lips are firmly set. A slim man.

HAROLD is a little chunky man, quite a youth, and wears a very thin moustache.

War Department poster. (Col. G. B. Jarrett)

The Search for Booth

by Robert H. Fowler

WHAT OF the fanatic who killed the best friend the beaten South could have asked for? Booth rode his hired mare from the theater to the so-called Navy Yard Bridge across the Anacostia. A sentry halted him and referred him to Sergeant Silas Cobb, who was under orders not to let anyone cross after 9 p.m. without the password. Booth gave his correct name, saying that he lived in Maryland and had been detained in town. Cobb let him pass.

Not long afterward, a second rider also persuaded Cobb to let him cross. This second rider was alleged to be David Herold but Cobb later could not fully identify him. (Cobb was never punished for his laxness in letting Booth pass.)

It is not clear just where or how Herold and Booth got together outside of Washington. Herold had been in the country during the day and he swore that he was returning that night when he met Booth on the road by coincidence and was persuaded to help him. The War Department tried to prove that Herold followed Booth across the bridge and overtook him — by plan. Detectives also alleged that the pair stopped first at a Surrattsville tavern to pick up a package left there for Booth by Mrs. Surratt. This allegation, intended to implicate Mrs. Surratt, was based solely on the testimony of a drunken tavernkeeper.

Whatever the truth of this, there is no doubt that about 4 a.m. on April 15, Booth and Herold knocked at the door of Dr. Samuel Mudd, a 32-year-old Southern sympathizer, near Bryantown. Booth had been in the Mudd home at least twice the previous fall, staying overnight on one occasion. In fact, Mudd had helped him buy from a neighbor the one-eyed horse Paine had ridden that night. The two men were together in Washington on December 23. Yet Dr. Mudd later swore that when the actor came to his house with Herold, he was wearing a shawl and false beard, and that he did not recognize him.

At least, Dr. Mudd did treat Booth's leg and put him to bed in the guest room. Next day, while Herold and the doctor rode into Bryantown, Booth shaved off his moustache. One theory is that he later paid Dr. Mudd $25 for two revolvers and a carbine and got directions from him on how to avoid the main road to the Potomac by taking a trail through nearby Zekiah Swamp. The pair departed about 4 p.m. leaving Dr. Mudd in more trouble than any of them imagined.

BOOTH and Herold emerged from the swamp after dark at Brice's Chapel where they were temporarily lost. The actor rested on the church steps while Herold found a Negro, Oswald Swann, who agreed to guide them to the home of "Captain" Samuel Cox, the next stop on their flight. After a whispered conversation, Cox loudly told the pair he couldn't accommodate them and please for them and Swann to leave. Booth paid Swann and made a show of going away, but Swann later told detectives he had looked back and seen "those two men returning to Captain Cox's house."

Although Cox took them in and fed them, he was afraid to let them stay. He directed them to a pine thicket nearby and sent his stepson to fetch Thomas Jones, a foster brother.

Throughout the war, Jones had operated a Confederate signal station on a bluff overlooking the Potomac. His brother-in-law, Thomas Harbin, carried out a similar function on the opposite shore.

The "Navy Yard Bridge" (above) that Booth used to cross the Anacostia River on the night of April 14. (LC) Dr. Samuel Mudd's home (below) was near Bryantown, Maryland; Booth arrived early on the morning of April 15. The inset is a picture of the room where Booth slept. (Colonel Julian E. Raymond)

They watched for Federal gunboats and indicated when the way was clear for boats to cross with couriers such as John H. Surratt. Not only had Jones risked his life for the Southern cause, he had sunk all his money in Confederate bonds and was now, of course, practically penniless.

This unusual man came about daylight on the morning of April 16 to the thicket where the two conspirators were hiding and gave a low whistle to identify himself. Jones later wrote that when he saw the handsome countenance of the suffering Booth, he resolved to do all he could to help him on his way to Virginia. For the next five days he made daily trips to bring the two men food, drink, and newspapers. Since they couldn't get the horses across the Potomac anyway and the animals' neighing might alert passing soldiers, Jones advised them that the horses be shot, and they were. Suffering from his now swollen leg, Booth wrote in a pocket diary and read newspaper accounts of the murder and search for him.

On Tuesday April 18, which was court day, Jones went to Port Tobacco, then the county seat of Charles County, to pick up news of the search for Booth. Standing at the bar in Brawner's Tavern, he was approached by a detective named Williams who told him he was authorized to pay $100,000 to anyone "who can tell me where Booth is." Jones is supposed to have commented, "That's an awful lot of money; if money will do it, that ought to be enough," and to have gone on calmly drinking.

FOR THE MOMENT Booth and Herold were safe. But while they cowered in the thicket, searchers were fanning out in all directions to scoop up anyone with the slightest possible connection with the conspiracy. Just five hours after the shooting, city officers went to Mrs. Surratt's house to ask about her son, John. She told them he had left on April 13 for Canada. She was not molested at that time.

Louis Weichmann, her boarder, could not sleep after the officers left and when another boarder saw him wandering aimlessly on the street, Weichmann told about the capture plot. The fellow boarder hauled him to the police station where he was taken into custody. Police Superintendent A. C. Richards took him in tow. At that time, for some reason, it was generally believed John Surratt had attacked Seward. Since Weichmann knew Surratt well, detectives took him along on Monday April 17 to Montreal.

ON THE NIGHT of the assassination, the telegraph lines from the War Department to the south were not working. And the War Department's search was slow getting started in the area southeast of Washington. Stanton was less slow in another regard.

The day Lincoln died, he had the Secretary of Navy order the USS *Saugus*, an ironclad monitor, to be anchored in the Anacostia River with a detachment of Marines aboard to receive prisoners and hold them against any rescue attempts. Stanton also wired Colonel Lafayette C. Baker, who was in New York on mysterious business, to return to Washington and take charge of the manhunt. Baker, head of the War Department's Bureau of Detective Police, was a ruthless individual with a good deal of experience in wholesale arrests.

And the arrests were made wholesale. Members of the cast of "Our American Cousin," the Fords (their theater was closed down, incidentally), the livery stable man who rented the mare to Booth, anyone who had been close to the actor (with a few exceptions) was hauled in for roughshod questioning. The Common Council of Washington offered a reward of $20,000 for Booth and the man who attacked Seward. To this Baker added $10,000 without saying where his share was coming from. Eventually the reward money grew to $100,000 *for all the conspirators;* Williams must have kited the figure for Booth alone in talking to Jones at Port Tobacco.

If Jones wasn't interested in the money, many others were. Letters and verbal tips, mostly invalid, flooded in. In fact, announcements of the reward muddied the water. Free lancers and cranks began snarling up the investigation.

ON MONDAY April 17, Michael O'Laughlin, the former Confederate soldier and boyhood friend of Booth's, gave himself up in Baltimore. He had been in on the plot to capture Lincoln but had had no part in the assassination, he said. Samuel Arnold, whose story was the same as O'Laughlin's, was arrested that same day at Fortress Monroe, Virginia where he was working in a sutler's store. That night, detectives went back to the Surratt house and arrested Mrs. Surratt, her daughter Anna, and some boarders. While they were waiting for the women to collect their things, who should knock at the door but a very tired and unkempt Lewis Paine. He was carrying a pick and explained that he was a laborer who was supposed to dig a ditch the next morning for Mrs. Surratt. He was just dropping by for his instructions. On his previous visits to the Surratt home, Paine had posed as a "Mr. Wood," a Baptist preacher. Mrs. Surratt, who had poor eyesight, told the officers she had never seen the man and she was glad they were there to protect her from him. They took Paine along, too, but did not identify him as Seward's assailant until later.

Also, later, Booth's one-eyed horse was found wandering about. Paine evidently hid in a woods at the

Stanton called in Col. Lafayette C. Baker, head of the War Department's Bureau of Detective Police, to direct the search for Booth and his accomplices. In this photograph Baker is seated. At left is Lieut. L. B. Baker, his cousin, and E. J. Conger, a detective, the two men who finally cornered Booth.

edge of town and came back to the Surratt house in hopes of finding a fellow conspirator there.

On April 20, officers ran down George Atzerodt near Rockville, Maryland, at the home of a cousin. They took the cousin along too, but later released him. Mrs. Surratt was placed in Old Capitol Prison. The men were confined on the monitor. The last person to be hauled in was Spangler, the hapless scene shifter who had held Booth's horse for a moment.

ABOUT noon the day Lincoln died, an autopsy was performed on his body in his bedroom at the White House. Seven medical men were present, including Surgeon General Barnes, Dr. Stone, and Dr. Taft. The body lay on two boards placed across sawhorses. When the shroud was laid back, one of the observers saw:

"A smooth, clear skin fitting cleanly over well-rounded muscles, sinewy and strong . . . at the back of the head, low down and a little to the left, a small round blackened wound."

The other doctors watched while two Army surgeons, Drs. E. J. J. Woodward and Edward Curtis, opened the skull. They found a small piece of the bullet that had sheared off. About three inches inside the path of the bullet they found a plug of bone from the skull, the obstruction that the doctors had noted the night before.

Finally they lifted out the brain and the bullet fell, as one observer put it, "With a metal mocking clatter into a basin set beneath."

The embalming was done in the same room by Charles D. Brown, who had prepared the body of Willie Lincoln for burial three years before. By order of Secretary Stanton, he was forbidden to mask the discoloration of the eyes and upper part of the cheeks caused by internal bleeding. Stanton wished this to remain "as part of the history of the event."

According to one report, Andrew Johnson came after taking the oath of office as President to observe Brown at work.

THE BODY was embalmed and ready for viewing by Tuesday April 18. Placed in the East Room of the White House, the coffin rested on a catafalque under a canopy of black silk and crepe. On that day alone, an estimated 25,000 people passed the open coffin in two steady streams. The next day, some 600 dignitaries came in a less hectic fashion for a funeral service. Robert Lincoln attended without his mother, who was in bed, wild with grief. This assembly heard the Reverend Mr. Gurley make a lengthy funeral address. In the closing invocation the chaplain of the Senate, a Baptist cleric named E. H. Gray, called for vengeance upon all traitors in general and upon the assassin in particular.

As the pallbearers carried the casket out from the White House, church bells throughout Washington, Georgetown, and Alexandria tolled and guns in the great network of forts surrounding the Capital boomed. Some 100,000 persons either walked behind the funeral coach bearing the body to the Capitol rotunda or stood along the one-mile route. Under the unfinished dome, twelve sergeants of the Veteran Reserve Corps placed the coffin on an enormous catafalque. At 10 a.m. the next morning, April 19, the doors were opened first to invalid soldiers and then to the public and by midnight 25,000 had filed past.

The next morning, one week after that tragic Good Friday, a seven-car funeral train left for Baltimore. The coffin was carried in the special Presidential car that had stood unused by Lincoln at the Alexandria railroad yards since it was delivered a year before. At the request of Mrs. Lincoln, the body of Willie was exhumed and carried in a small coffin in the same car, to be buried beside his father at Springfield.

Several prominent politicians and Lincoln's close friends rode on the train. Brown, the embalmer, and an assistant went along to keep the remains of the President presentable for display.

DURING the next twelve days, the train followed a 1,600-mile route approximating in reverse that which the untested Lincoln had followed four years and two months before in coming to Washington to save the Nation from disintegration. An estimated seven million persons either saw the funeral train go by or actually filed past the open coffin as the body lay in state at Baltimore, Harrisburg, Philadelphia, New York, Albany, Buffalo, Cleveland, Columbus, Indianapolis, and Chicago. Dozens of ceremonies were held along the route. Often the railroad tracks were strewn with flowers.

At last, on May 3, the body came to Springfield, where the Lincolns had lived and where he had spent his happiest years. Some 75,000 people viewed the body there and on May 4 it was carried out to a vault in a hillside, the kind of spot where the sometimes melancholic Lincoln just a few weeks earlier had told his wife he would like to rest.

It was here after a long and troublesome journey that perhaps the best of all possible funeral remarks were read—Lincoln's own sensitive Second Inaugural Address, those same words that John Wilkes Booth had heard without comprehending their meaning and whose kindly purpose he had so rashly thwarted:

With malice toward none, with charity for all, with firmness in the right as God gives us to see the right, let us strive on to finish the work we are in, to bind up the nation's wounds, to care for him who shall have borne the battle and for his widow and his orphan, to do all which may achieve and cherish a just and lasting peace among ourselves and with all nations.

ON THE SAME day that Lincoln's body left Washington, Thomas Jones learned that the Federal cavalry which had been riding through the area would be moved to St. Mary's County to follow up a rumor. He slipped back to the thicket and told Booth and Herold that here was what might be their last chance to get across the Potomac. Jones left and told a servant to hide his rowboat in a cove on the Potomac below Dent's meadow, giving as a reason that he was afraid the Federal troops might steal it. About 10 p.m. he returned, put Booth on his (Jones's) horse and with Herold leading it, went in front. Their three-mile route led them past Jones's house; Booth, his broken leg an agony to him, begged to go in and rest but Jones refused because his family and Negro servants were there. However, while the fugitives waited in an orchard, he did bring out warm food and drink to them.

Booth and Herold entered the rowboat below Dent's meadow. Booth had a compass and by shielded candlelight, Jones pointed out the direction to Machodoc Creek across the dark river. Booth offered to pay Jones handsomely but the man who had turned down a chance for $100,000 would take only $18, the

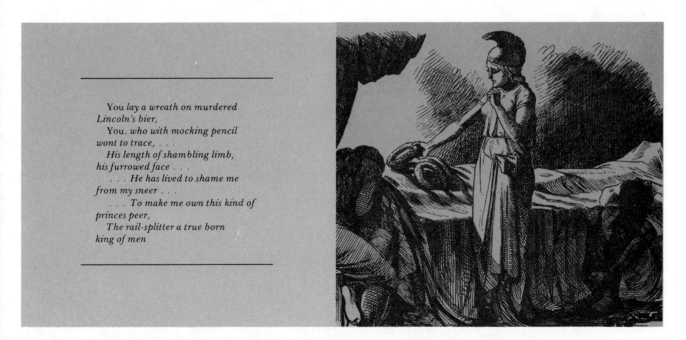

You *lay a wreath on murdered*
Lincoln's bier,
   You, *who with mocking pencil*
wont to trace, . . .
      His length of shambling limb,
his furrowed face . . .
         . . . *He has lived to shame me*
from my sneer . . .
            . . . *To make me own this kind of*
princes peer,
      The rail-splitter a true born
king of men

Throughout the war the London Punch printed a number of cruelly satirical cartoons depicting Lincoln as a sly and crude buffoon. John Tenniel, chief artist for the magazine, seized upon Lincoln's angular figure and rough-hewn features and gave them a diabolical twist. Tenniel and Punch took it all back on May 6, 1865 with a drawing entitled "Britannia Lays a Wreath on Lincoln's Bier." A poem by Tom Taylor was in the same issue.

Top: The three drawings are originals by William Waud. Woodcuts copied from them are crude by comparison. At left is a giant pavilion erected for the Lincoln coffin in a city park at Cleveland. Waud's note reads: "I have made the flags drooping; it was raining hard all day. I am afraid if you make them flying, it makes the building look too gay." At center is the reception of the body in the Cook County Courthouse at Chicago. At right is the scene on May 3 when Lincoln lay in state at Springfield.

Bottom left: Following funeral services in the White House on April 19, the body of Lincoln was borne in a vast procession — which was joined and watched by 100,000 — to the rotunda of the Capitol to lie in state for two days. (KA)

Above: A woodcut from Harper's Weekly based on a William Waud original. Lincoln's coffin is being carried from the funeral coach to a vault constructed in a hillside in Oak Ridge Cemetery outside Springfield. Final services for Lincoln were held here. He was then entombed beside the body of his son, Willie, who had died in 1862.

value he placed on the boat which he assumed he would never see again.

Herold rowed for what seemed hours until land loomed on the right and they glided into a creek. They were safe across the Potomac, they thought. But at dawn Herold discerned that they were still on the Maryland side. The incoming tide had carried them several miles *up* the river. They were in the mouth of Nanjemoy Creek. Leaving Booth in the boat, Herold went to a nearby house for water, food, and directions to Machodoc Creek. They lay in the boat all day.

THE AREA between them and Washington now fairly boiled with out-of-state detectives, L. C. Baker's agents, and men from the provost marshal's office—all working at cross purposes. The chief of police from New York City had come to join the hunt. Several thousand cavalrymen were scurrying about. During the week after Lincoln died, detectives visited Dr. Mudd's house several times. He at first said he had seen no strangers, but Negroes in the neighborhood told of seeing the doctor on the road with Herold. After he was confronted with a boot with Booth's name in it, found in his house, Dr. Mudd remembered that two strangers had come to his home and that one had a broken leg which he had treated. He was arrested and taken to Old Capitol Prison.

Meanwhile, aboard the *Saugus* and a sister ship *Montauk*, Booth's friends were being kept under painful conditions. Stanton had ordered that the prisoners "for better security against conversation, shall have a canvas bag put over the head of each and tied about the neck, with a hole for proper breathing and eating but not seeing, and that Paine be secured to prevent self-destruction." It seems that the giant youth had tried to kill himself by battering his head against the bulkhead of his cell. His hood accordingly was padded.

No formal charges were made; no lawyer or other person was allowed to see the prisoners. Stanton had a tight grip on the situation. But he had not yet landed Booth. Nor had the Federals yet apprehended Jefferson Davis and other leaders of the Confederate Government, who were at that time erroneously thought to be involved in the assassination. Davis was fleeing south with part of his Cabinet and part of the Confederate gold reserves in a vain attempt to reach safety west of the Mississippi.

ON THE NIGHT of April 21, after first making sure of the direction of the tide, Herold once again rowed Jones's boat into the Potomac. At daylight, however, they saw other boats coming out of their destination—Machodoc Creek—and so turned into nearby Gambo Creek. At last they were in Virginia.

Again Booth remained in the boat while the faithful Herold went to a nearby house to obtain food and get word to Thomas Harbin, who soon showed up to guide them to the home of an illiterate white man. This man, who did not know of Lincoln's death, led them five miles to the home of Dr. Richard Stewart, a wealthy Confederate sympathizer. Later questioned by detectives, Dr. Stewart said that two strangers had come to his door. One of them was lame, he said, but he had not treated him, as he was "not a surgeon." His house was full of sons back from the war, with their families, so he had simply sent out some food to the men. He said the next day one of his field hands had brought him an insulting note from one of the men, with money attached. He had pocketed the money and thrown away the note. His wife produced the note from a trash basket. It read:

Forgive me, but I have some little pride. I hate to blame you for your want of hospitality, you know your own affairs. I was sick and tired, with a broken leg, in need of medical advice. I would not have turned a dog away from my door in such a condition. However, you were kind enough to give me something to eat for which I thank you, and because of the manner in which it was bestowed I feel bound to pay for it. It is not the substance but the manner in which a kindness is extended that makes one happy in the acceptance thereof. The sauce to meat is ceremony—meeting were bare without it. Be kind enough to accept the enclosed $5.00, though hard to spare, for what we have received.

Yours respectfully,
Stranger

This was Booth in good style. Only he had crossed out the $5.00 and written in $2.50. The detectives were skeptical and took Dr. Stewart back to Washington for questioning.

Whatever the truth of Dr. Stewart's story, Booth arranged with William Lucas, a Negro on the place, to drive him and Herold the seven miles to Port Conway on the Rappahannock early the next day. Lucas' son hid them under straw in a mule-drawn wagon and drove the pair to Port Conway, arriving about 9 a.m. on April 24. They found the scow that served as a ferry on the other side of the 300-yard stream. The ferryman, William Rollins, was fishing on it. Rollins yelled over to them that the tide was too low. Booth tore a page from his pocket diary, wrote that aforementioned note to Dr. Stewart and gave it to young Lucas with $2.50 to deliver upon his return. He paid Lucas $10 for the wagon ride.

WHILE THEY WAITED for the ferry, three Confederate officers, William J. Jett, A. S. Bainbridge, and M. B. Ruggles, from Mosby's recently disbanded command, rode up. Herold divulged their identity, much to Booth's dismay, but the officers agreed to help. Seeing tatooed on the back of Booth's right hand the initials "J.W.B.," the men suggested he call himself "John William Boyd" and that Herold pose as his younger brother. They then ordered the ferryman to put up his fishing pole and get the scow over, tide or no tide. Once across the river, they rode to the house of Randolph Peyton, a friend of Jett's. Forgetting his pain for the moment and posing as J. W. Boyd, Booth turned on the charm for Peyton's two sisters. The girls served refreshments while Booth sat in their parlor, but the charm only went so far. Their brother Randolph was not yet home from the war, they told Jett, and they wouldn't think of letting male guests stay overnight.

Not far down the road toward Bowling Green there lived one Richard Garrett whom Jett knew as a man who couldn't say no to a Confederate soldier. So they lifted Booth onto Ruggles' horse, while the other four men paired off for the ride. At the lane leading to the Garrett house, Herold slipped down and hid while the others went to the house. Jett presented "John W. Boyd" as a paroled soldier who had been wounded at Petersburg, and the sympathetic Garrett agreed to care for him for a few days. Booth was introduced to Jack Garrett, a paroled Confederate cavalryman, another son, William, two young daughters, and Mrs. Garrett and her sister, a Miss L.K.B. Holloway, a school teacher who lived with the Garretts and tutored her young nieces.

Booth's charm worked as usual on Miss Holloway, who thought him an extremely interesting and intelligent man. Leaving Booth in this comfortable situation, the three officers picked up Herold and rode into Bowling Green. Halfway to town Herold and Bainbridge stopped off at a tavern to spend the night while the other two went on, Jett to see his sweetheart, whose father ran the Bowling Green Hotel.

THE NEXT DAY Bainbridge and Herold joined Jett and Ruggles in Bowling Green, and later that afternoon Ruggles, Bainbridge, and Herold returned to Garrett's place where Herold was introduced as "Mr. Boyd's" younger brother, Davey. That afternoon the two Confederate officers said goodbye to Booth and Herold but were back in a few minutes with the distressing news that Federal troopers were crossing the river at Port Royal. Booth and Herold fled in fear to nearby woods and heard the soldiers ride past the farm lane en route to Bowling Green.

They would have been even more fearful had they known that the soldiers had learned from the ferryman that a lame man and his companion had crossed the river with three Rebels. What's more, they knew one of the Confederates as Willie Jett and figured he would be going to Bowling Green to see his girl.

When the fugitives crept back to the house, Garrett couldn't understand why they were so afraid. Booth said he had had a run-in with Federals "on the Maryland side" and they might be looking for him. Wouldn't Mr. Garrett furnish them horses so

From a contemporary journal: Herold rowing Booth across the Potomac in Thomas Jones' boat. (RC)

The heavy line indicates the probable route taken by Lincoln's assassin from Washington, D.C. to Garrett's farmhouse in Virginia. From Ford's Theater he rode east on F Street to Massachusetts Ave., thence southeast to 11th Street and on that street to the Navy Yard Bridge; thereafter as shown here. The route has been plotted, from data furnished by Col. J. E. Raymond, on an adaptation of a modern map. Only modern roads and towns that will enable a reader to follow the route on the ground are shown. Some place names and roads have changed. For example, at the time of the assassination, the hamlet formerly known as Surrattsville was renamed Robystown. Later it was changed to Clinton. Some early accounts claim that Booth went through this town, but today some authorities doubt this. The shaded portion of Greater Washington represents the built-up portion of area as it is today.

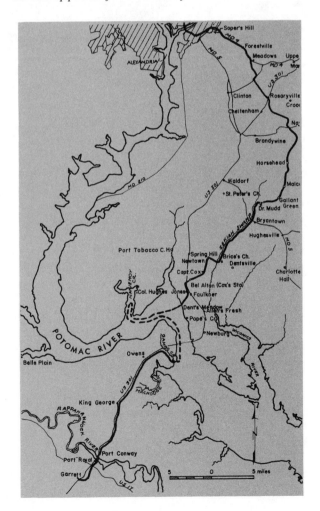

The house where Thomas Jones lived (above) near the north bank of the Potomac. The inset is a photograph of Jones in later life, when he first told the full story of the assistance he gave Booth and Herold. He was never prosecuted for helping Booth. (JC)

they could ride the eleven miles to Guinea Station and there take the train for Richmond? They would pay well. Suspicious now, Garrett refused, saying it was then too late but that he would do it in the morning. He became even more suspicious that night when Booth asked that he and his "brother" be permitted to sleep in the barn. Glad to get them out of the house, Garrett let them bed down in a former tobacco drying shed which his neighbors along the Rappahannock used for storing their furniture. Federal gunboats sometimes shelled houses along the banks.

After Booth and Herold retired, Garrett had his son snap a lock on the tobacco shed, and sleep in a nearby corn crib. He felt that the strangers might be planning to steal his horses during the night.

THE SOLDIERS who crossed the Rappahannock were twenty-six troopers of the 16th New York cavalry, led by Lt. E. P. Doherty, but under the supervision of L. B. Baker (a cousin of the notorious L. C. Baker) and E. J. Conger, both detectives. The Federal dragnet had picked up bits and pieces of Booth's

trail. Now they were ready to strike for the prize.

Forcing Rollins, the ferryman, to go with them, they rode past the Garrett farm lane fifteen miles to Bowling Green. Arriving about midnight, they surrounded the Bowling Green Hotel and the detectives found Jett in a bedroom.

"What do you want?" the Confederate asked.

"We want you," said Conger. "You took Booth across the river, and you know where he is."

When Jett denied this, Conger put a pistol to his head and Jett finally agreed to tell if they would "shield me from complicity in the whole matter."

"Yes, if we get Booth."

JETT TOLD what he knew. After a brief rest, with Jett as a prisoner, the men were on their way back to the Garrett house. After pausing to secure Rollins and Jett and leave them guarded, the force charged into the Garrett yard and surrounded the house. When Mr. Garrett came to the door, Baker put a pistol in his face and demanded Booth. When the farmer pleaded ignorance, they produced a rope and threatened to hang him on the spot.

About this time young William Garrett appeared out of the darkness. "Don't injure father," the 17-year-old said. "I will tell you all about it."

While Conger was moving the soldiers into position around the barn, Baker took William by the arm and walked toward Booth's hiding place.

Going to the shed and unlocking the door, Baker shoved the boy inside.

"Damn you, for you have betrayed me," they heard Booth say. "Get out of here."

William called to Baker, "Let me out, this man will kill me."

Baker told the boy he could not leave unless he brought the weapons from the shed but finally relented and William darted out the door.

IT TOOK half an hour to deploy the soldiers around the barn. Baker said this was because they had to tie their horses, which might have become frightened and bolted. Once the men were in place, he called out to Booth that he had fifty men and demanded that he surrender.

Booth attempted to parley: Why not give a cripple a chance and withdraw 100 yards? He would come out and shoot it out with them. Baker replied that they were there to capture him, not fight. Booth asked for five minutes to consider.

Baker again demanded that Booth surrender and the actor replied, "Captain, there is a man here who wants very much to surrender." Baker said he would have to bring his weapons out.

The soldiers could hear Booth curse Herold, calling him a "damned coward." Herold then rapped on the door and pleaded to be let out, lest Booth shoot him. Again Baker said he would have to bring his arms. At this, Booth said, according to Baker, "Captain, the arms are mine, and I shall keep them. This man is guilty of no crime."

Conger whispered to Baker that they would have one less to fight if Herold were allowed to come out. They eased open the door, Herold stumbled out, and they locked the door behind him.

THEY THEN GAVE Booth ten minutes to surrender or they would fire the barn. "Captain, I consider you a brave and honorable man; I have had half a dozen opportunities to shoot you, but I did not do it." This was true, for rather foolishly Baker had been holding a candle. He set down the candle and told Booth they were ready to fire the barn.

"All right, my brave boys. Prepare a stretcher for me. One more stain on the Old Banner."

Conger slipped around to the rear of the barn and touched a match to straw sticking between the wide cracks. Within minutes the shed was on fire.

Baker later gave this description of what happened:

I opened the door quickly, and the first I saw of Booth he was leaning against the hay mow, with a crutch under each arm and a carbine resting at his hip. He was in the act of getting up from the hay. He did get up and dropped one crutch, and started toward the fire. He got within six or eight feet of the side of the barn, and peered all about as though he should like to see who fired the barn . . . Then he seemed to give it up . . . there was a table lying there bottom side up. He turned to throw the table on the fire, but he dropped it, and turned to look around the barn. The fire was rolling over the roof. He saw the door open, and he turned and dropped the other crutch and started toward the door . . . with a kind of limping halting jump.

Baker closed the door and did not see Booth fall, but hearing a shot, he flung open the door and found the actor face down with a revolver in his right hand. Conger rushed in and they dragged Booth from the flaming barn.

He had been shot below the right ear, the ball passing out the neck on the other side. Conger said he thought he had shot himself. They began to ask the soldiers if they had fired and all denied it until they came to Sergeant Boston Corbett. He had fired the shot, he said. Why had he disobeyed orders?

"Providence directed me."

The other soldiers laughed at this remark. Corbett, a religious fanatic and self-castrated eunuch, was eccentric and they didn't believe him. He was disarmed and put under arrest.

THE SOLDIERS pitched in and tried to help Garrett remove the furniture stored in the shed, but it was no use. They carried Booth to the porch and put him on a mattress brought from the house.

Seeing that Booth wished to speak, Conger bent low and heard him whisper, "Tell Mother that I died for my country." Later, after they had loosened his collar and washed his face, Booth opened his eyes and said, "Kill me, oh, kill me."

Baker said they did not wish to kill him and that they hoped his wound would not be fatal.

Miss Holloway was allowed to bathe his face and comfort him. At one point, overhearing them mention Captain Jett, Booth asked, "Did Jett betray me?"

A little later, he murmured "Useless, useless" when his hands were held up for him to see, and about two hours after he had been shot, Booth died.

(Miss Holloway reportedly never again spoke to Jett. The former Confederate became a social outcast in the area and eventually was committed to a mental institution in Maryland.)

EVEN BEFORE Booth died, Conger started back to Washington to report. A little later, the soldiers sewed up Booth's body in a horse blanket, placed it in a wagon and set out, with Herold and Sergeant

The house owned by Richard Garrett near Port Royal, Virginia where Booth found refuge. Booth was shot in a tobacco drying shed near the house and died on the porch. The house no longer stands. The farm is now part of A. P. Hill Military Reservation. (JC)

Corbett as prisoners, for Belle Plain. There they went aboard the steamer *John S. Ide* and arrived in Washington that evening. Booth's body was transferred to the deck of the monitor *Montauk*. The next morning Surgeon General Barnes and Dr. Woodward, both of whom helped perform the autopsy on Lincoln, examined the body of Booth laid out on a carpenter's bench. They found "the third, fourth, and fifth cervical vertebrae and a portion of the spinal cord perforated by a conoidal *pistol* ball, fired at a distance of a few yards." This section of the spine was removed and given to the Army Medical Museum for preservation. A number of persons were brought aboard the *Montauk* that morning to identify Booth. Although the features were badly distorted and blackened, he could be identified by the tattooed "J.W.B." on his hand and a scar on the neck.

By personal order of Stanton, Colonel L. C.

Baker and his cousin came alongside the *Montauk* in a row boat that afternoon and took the body away, as if they meant to bury it in the Potomac. Actually they headed for the Washington Arsenal and left the body on the prison dock. That night the body, still in a gunny sack, was buried in the dirt floor of the exercise portion of the penitentiary's cell block.

THERE WAS no doubt that Booth was dead, but as to whether he shot himself or Boston Corbett shot him there is disagreement. Corbett was taken directly to Stanton, who decided that rather than punish the little soldier he would declare him a hero. The only difficulty was that Booth seemed to have been shot with a pistol whereas Corbett had been armed only with a carbine. Again by personal order of Stanton, a revolver was issued to Corbett and he thereafter gloried in being known as "the man who shot Booth."

Boston Corbett, the soldier who claimed he shot Booth, stands at left with Lieut. E. P. Doherty, the commander of the detachment from the 16th New York Cavalry which surrounded the barn where Booth and Herold hid. It has never been proved that Corbett really shot Booth. No one saw him fire; he was armed only with a carbine while Booth, according to the autopsy report, was killed by a pistol ball. (The revolver Corbett wears in this photograph was issued to him after Booth's death.) Booth had a revolver in his hand when he was dragged from the barn.

Corbett, who was a religious fanatic, moved to Kansas and had a job in the State Capitol as assistant doorkeeper until the day he went berserk and waved a revolver at fellow state employees holding a mock session of the legislature. Corbett was declared insane and put in the State Asylum. He escaped after a year and all trace of him was lost. (LC)

Booth is struck by a bullet fired outside the burning tobacco shed (above) in this version by Alfred Waud. (Illustrious Americans by Edward Everett Hale.) Soldiers drag him from the burning barn (below). (JC)

It was not revealed until 1867 that L. C. Baker and L. B. Baker buried Booth secretly in the exercise area of the Washington Arsenal Penitentiary. This drawing (above) makes it appear that the burial was in a prison cell. (KA)

An autopsy was conducted aboard the monitor Montauk *and he was positively identified. The Harper's Weekly version (below) appeared in the May 13, 1865 edition. (KA)*

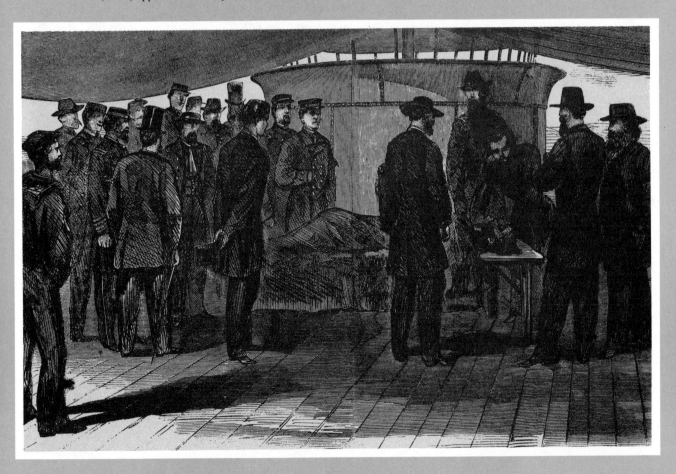

Prisoners from the Saugus were brought into the Washington Arsenal Penitentiary hooded and in irons according to this drawing by Col. James G. Benton, commandant of the penitentiary. (JC)

THE
COMMON SOLDIER
OF THE CIVIL WAR

by Bell I. Wiley

Robert **E. Lee's biographer**, the late Douglas Southall Freeman, once remarked that he regarded it a rare privilege to have lived for more than a decade in the company of such a great gentleman. In all his research, he said, he had never found evidence that Lee ever used an obscene or profane word.

To their everlasting credit, the same cannot be said about the men who served under Lee, and Grant, and all the others. They were more real, tangible, flesh and blood characters; earthy, natural people in whose natures the fear of God was mingled with a healthy interest in the attractions of the world, the flesh, and the Devil. These common soldiers were the very heart of the America over whose fields and plains they fought the most tragic of American wars.

"Johnny Reb" and "Billy Yank" were more alike than not, despite their differing accents and obviously contrasting views on government. They were mostly farmers and rural people; they spoke the same language, making it decidedly colorful thanks to a variety of words not found in General Lee's vocabulary; they cherished many of the same personal ideals and hopes; and they endured the same hardships and

perils of soldier life. They disliked regimentation, found abundant fault with their officers, complained about the food, and hoped earnestly for an end to the fighting and a speedy return home.

Many men in both armies were of foreign birth, newly come to America to escape the upheavals of Europe, only to find a greater conflict in their adopted land. Most, though, were native Americans, primarily farmers from the South, and more often city-dwellers from the North. They varied widely in age and education, but most were young, and the majority—particularly among the Federals—knew at least a few rudiments of reading and writing, though in some companies from the rural South fully one half of the men could not sign their names to the muster rolls.

Outwardly, their interests seem divergent. Better educated, Northern soldiers read more and took a greater interest in public affairs and other news, largely because political campaigning went on in the Union while it languished in the Confederacy. On the other hand, perhaps because of their deeper ties to the simple life on the land, and because theirs was

Billy Yank: A Union soldier, typical of the men on both sides who endured the perils of soldier life. (Library of Congress)

Johnny Reb: A Confederate early in the war, carrying a Springfield rifle. (Mississippi Department of Archives & History)

a cause that demanded a high degree of faith, Confederates were more devoutly religious. Great revivals swept over both the eastern and western armies of the Confederacy in the last two years of the war.

But beneath these differences, Reb and Yank were the same, bound by one great common denominator: They all sprang from the lowly ranks of American society. They were America personified in all its human facets, and now at war with itself.

In the Civil War the common folk put themselves on record to an unprecedented extent because, for the first time in the nation's history, large numbers of them were separated from their families and neighbors. Absence from home impelled them to write letters and keep diaries. Moreover, their novel and exciting experiences as soldiers aroused them to an unusual degree of expressiveness. So they wrote long and interesting accounts of their experiences and impressions, and in so doing, they revealed very much of themselves. As a rule the lowly people did not save personal documents, but because the Civil War was by far the most important episode in their humble careers, they preserved for transmission to their descendants the letters and diaries telling of their involvements in the conflict. These manuscripts, still available in great numbers in public depositories and in private possession, are a rich mine of information about the ordinary folk.

Owing to the incompleteness of Civil War records—especially on the Confederate side—and the confusion caused by re-enlistments, the number of soldier participants has to be stated in approximate terms. The same is true of casualties, deserters, and prisoners. The aggregate of men who donned the blue was about two million, while those who wore the gray were roughly half that number. On both sides those who served at one time or another as common soldiers—i.e., privates and non-commissioned officers—comprised well over nine-tenths of the fighting forces.

A study of muster and descriptive rolls indicates that about 95 percent of Confederates and 75 percent of Federals were born in the United States. Of the foreign-born soldiers, the Germans and the Irish were the most numerous, owing to the heavy immigration of those nationals in the decades immediately preceding the Civil War. Scattered through the Federal forces were about 200,000 Germans, 150,000 Irishmen, 50,000 Englishmen, 50,000 Canadians, and lesser numbers of Scandinavians, French, Italians, Hungarians, and natives of other countries. Some Union camps were a Babel of tongues. One regiment, the 39th New York, had in its ranks natives of fifteen foreign countries, and the Hungarian commander,

Colonel Frederic Utassy, gave orders in seven languages. The 15th Wisconsin regiment, made up largely of Scandinavians, had 128 men whose first name was Ole.

On the Confederate side the Irish were the most numerous of the foreign groups; their aggregate was probably between 15,000 and 20,000. The second largest alien group in the Southern armies were the Germans, who numbered several thousand. Other foreigners who had substantial representation among Confederates were Englishmen, Frenchmen, and Italians.

On both sides the foreign soldiers added color and variety to camp life. They sang their native songs, ate their native foods, and drank beverages popular in the countries of their birth. St. Patrick's Day was always a festive occasion in Irish units. The jumping contests, wrestling matches, boxing encounters and horse races that the celebrants staged were enlivened by heavy draughts of whiskey (frequently donated by the officers), and before night guard houses were filled with inebriates, many of them suffering from blackened eyes, broken noses, bruised muscles, or fractured bones. Indeed, in some Irish units, St. Patrick's Day produced as many casualties as a major battle.

In combat the foreigners generally acquitted themselves well. The 15th Wisconsin, commanded by Colonel Hans Heg, a gallant Norwegian who died at Chickamauga, had an enviable fighting record, as did the 6th Wisconsin, made up largely of Germans, and Wiedrich's Light Artillery Battery, which was also overwhelmingly German. On the Confederate side a German company, G of the 6th Louisiana, achieved distinction in battle and the same was true of the 3d Texas Cavalry, recruited from the German settlement of New Braunfels.

No foreign group on either side won greater renown in battle than the Irish. Their response to combat was reflected in a letter that one of them, Felix A. Brannigan of the 76th New York, wrote his homefolk on May 15, 1862, following the Battle of Williamsburg. "We were so close to the rebels," he said, "that some of our wounded had their faces scorched with the firing. . . . Fierce, short and decisive was the struggle. . . . As we rush on with the tide of battle, every sense of fear is swallowed up in the wild joy we feel thrilling thro every fibre of our system." A month later, with more heavy fighting in prospect, Brannigan wrote: "I was never in sounder health or better spirits in my life. There is an elasticity in the Irish temperament which enables its possessor to boldly stare Fate in the face, and laugh at all the reverses of fortune . . . and crack a joke with as much glee in the heat of battle as in the social circle by the winter fire, or among boon companions at the festive board." At Chancellorsville on May 2, 1863, Brannigan won the coveted Medal of Honor. His citation stated that he "volunteered on a dangerous mission and brought in valuable information." His ability and gallantry brought him steady promotion from private to lieutenant colonel.

A glimpse of another Irishman's reaction to combat was afforded by Lieutenant Andrew J. O'Byrne's report of an engagement near Winchester, Virginia, in September 1864. "I took particular notice of a wild looking Irishman who stood near me," he stated. "He was loading and firing as fast as he could. . . . While loading and reciting some prayers in a jumbling sort of way . . . he would shout, 'Now Jeff Davis, you son of a bitch, take that,' giving his head a twist at the same time and his eyes looking wildly in front he repeated this several times til the front line was drawing near. We then ceased firing."

One of the most famous fighting units on either side during the Civil War was the Irish Brigade, recruited largely from New York City and commanded by Brigadier General Thomas F. Meagher. (One of the regiments of this brigade, the 88th New York, was known as "Mrs. Meagher's Own" because the general's wife presented the unit's colors just before it headed off for combat.) Before the brigade went into action at Malvern Hill, July 1, 1862, General Meagher made an inspiring talk to the men admonishing

Left: Brigadier General Michael Corcoran, leader of the Irish Corcoran Legion. Right: Brigadier General Thomas F. Meagher, who commanded the famed Irish Brigade, including the New York regiment known as "Mrs. Meagher's Own." No foreign group on either side won greater renown in battle than the Irish. (L: Library of Congress. R: Harper's New Monthly Magazine)

them to remember Fontenoy, where another Irish brigade had heroically fought for the King of France, and to remember that the eyes of Irishmen everywhere were upon them. The brigade gave a good account of itself in the fighting that followed.

At Fredericksburg, the Irish Brigade covered itself with blood and glory. By Meagher's order it went into action with every member wearing a sprig of green boxwood in his cap. It made repeated charges up the slope approaching Marye's Heights and each time encountered a murderous fire from Confederates posted behind the famous stone wall. But when Confederates walked over the field after the battle, the dead soldiers closest to the stone wall were those wearing sprigs of green in their caps. The brigade went into action on December 13th with 1,200 officers and men; when it was formed on the morning of the 14th only 280 were present. This heavy slaughter virtually ended the career of the unit as a brigade.

Confederates paid high tribute to the valor shown by the Irish at Fredericksburg. Major General George E. Pickett wrote to his fiancee December 14, 1862: "Your soldier's heart almost stood still as he watched those sons of Erin fearlessly rush to their death. The brilliant assault . . . was beyond description. Why, my darling we forgot they were fighting us and cheer after cheer at their fearlessness went up all along our line." Lieutenant General James Longstreet said of one of their charges: "It was the handsomest thing in the whole war." General Lee reported: "Never were men so brave."

An English correspondent of the London *Times* with Lee's army wrote: "Never at Fontenoy, Albuera or Waterloo was more undaunted courage displayed by the sons of Erin than during those six frantic dashes which they directed against the almost impregnable position of their foe."

On May 14, 1863, after Chancellorsville, Meagher, dispirited because of the diminution of his command, resigned. The remnant of the Irish Brigade, led by Colonel Patrick Kelly, took part in the fighting at Gettysburg on the second day. Here occurred one of the most dramatic incidents of the war. When the brigade was ordered to fall in to reinforce the hardpressed III Corps late in the afternoon, it was formed in close column by regiments. While the men waited in line, Father William Corby, brigade chaplain, stepped on a large rock and proposed to grant absolution to the men before they went into the fight. The soldiers dropped to their knees and uncovered their heads while Father Corby, with outstretched hands, pronounced the solemn words of general absolution. He then urged the men to do their duty and acquit themselves bravely. He concluded by telling them that the Catholic Church refused Christian burial to those who played the coward. The soldiers then went forward and gave a good account of themselves in the hard fighting that ensued near the base of Little Round Top, and which resulted in the loss of one third of their number.

In a number of engagements Union Irishmen fought Confederate Irishmen. At Fredericksburg a Georgia regiment, mostly Irish, held the portion of the line at which the attack of Meagher's Irish Brigade was directed. When the Confederate Irishmen saw the green sprigs in the caps of the attacking Federal Irishmen, they cried out, "Oh God! What a pity we have to fire at Meagher's men."

Sometimes the Irish of the opposing sides singled out each other in personal combat. Major Robert Stiles in *Four Years Under Marse Robert* tells the story of a Confederate Irishman named Burgoyne of the 9th Louisiana who loved fighting so well that when infantry firing slackened he would attach himself to an artillery crew still in action and help service the gun. At Gettysburg Burgoyne was acting as a cannoneer and screaming and jumping as he rammed home the charges. A recently captured Yankee Irishman standing on the other side of the gun was able to identify Burgoyne as a fellow son of Erin from his brogue. Disgustedly the Federal said: "Hey, ye spalpane! Say, what are yez doing in the Ribil army?"

Burgoyne immediately retorted: "Be-dad, aint an Irishman a free man? Haven't I as good right to fight for the Ribils as ye have to fight for the [damned] Yanks?"

The Federal Irishman replied: "Oh yes! I know ye, now you've turned your ugly mug to me. I had the plizure of kicking yez out from behind Marye's Wall, that time Sedgwick lammed yer brigade out o' there!"

"Yer a [damned] liar," said Burgoyne, "and I'll just knock your teeth down your ougly throat for that same lie."

Burgoyne thereupon leaped over the gun and took a swing at his opponent. The Yank was about to strike back when Stiles noted that his right hand was bloody. On examination he found that the prisoner had lost two fingers before he was captured. When Stiles stopped the fight and called the injury to the attention of Burgoyne, the latter replied: "You're a trump, Pat; give me your well hand. We'll fight this out some other time. I didn't see you were hurt."

The superb gallantry of the Irish is attested by the fact that on the Union side seventy-four of them won the Medal of Honor. Little wonder that a general who had first-hand knowledge of their battle performance in the Civil War stated:

"If tomorrow I wanted to win a reputation I would prefer Irish soldiers to any other; and I'll tell you why. First, they have more dash, more *élan* than any other troops that I know of; then, they are more cheerful and more enduring—nothing can depress them. Next they are more cleanly. The Irishman never failed to wash himself and his clothes. Not only were they cheerful but they were submissive to discipline. . . . And confidence was established the moment they saw their general in the fight with them. . . . I repeat, if I had to take from 1 to 10,000 men to make a reputation with, I'd take the same men as I had in the war—Irishmen from the cities, the levees, the rivers, the railroads, the canals, or from ditching and fencing on the plantations. They make the finest soldiers that ever shouldered a musket."

Among native Americans who donned the blue or the gray, the Indians were the most picturesque. Confederates recruited three Indian brigades, mostly Cherokees, Choctaws, Chickasaws, and Seminoles. One of the Cherokees, Stand Watie of Georgia, rose to the rank of brigadier general. The Union Army had one brigade of Indians, most of whom were Creeks. Indian muster rolls located in the National Archives contain such interesting names as Privates James Sweetcaller, George Hogtoter, Crying Bear, Flying Bird, Spring Water, Samuel Beinstick, Big Mush Dirt Eater and Bone Eater; listed among the Indian officers are Captain Spring Frog and Lieutenant Jumper Duck.

In combat, the Indians performed well, though their tactics tended to be unconventional and officers had occasion to complain of their scalping their casualties. At Wilson's Creek and Pea Ridge the "Rebel Yell" of white soldiers was blended with the savage war whoop of their Indian comrades. In the Battle of Elk Creek or Honey Springs, fought in the Indian Territory on July 17, 1863, Yankee Indians fought Rebel Indians and commanding officers on both sides paid high tribute to the gallantry of their Indian units.

Between battles, the demeanor of the Indian soldiers left much to be desired. They were slovenly in dress, neglectful of camp duties, careless of equipment and indifferent to prescribed routine, especially that governing furloughs and passes. Colonel William A. Phillips, who was as well acquainted with Indian soldiers as any Union officer, observed that absence without leave was a "chronic Indian weakness." He also complained: "The besetting sin of Indians is laziness. They are brave as death, active to fight but lazy." The Indians seemed inclined to support the side that appeared in strongest force among them, but this was no doubt due in large measure to two facts: first, few of them were deeply committed to the cause with

An International Indian Council convened at Tahlequah, Oklahoma. Among native Americans who fought in the Civil War, the Indians were the most picturesque. The Confederates recruited three Indian brigades; the Union had one brigade of Indians. (Smithsonian Institution)

which they were identified and, second, they received shabby treatment from both the Union and the Confederacy.

The discrimination experienced by Indians and foreigners was mild in comparison with that encountered by black soldiers, some 200,000 of whom served in Federal ranks. The Negroes who offered their services to the Union early in 1861 were told that the government had no need of them. Not until early 1863, after combat, disease and desertion had severely depleted Federal ranks, did Lincoln openly commit his government to the recruitment of Negroes.

From the very beginning black soldiers suffered much discrimination and abuse. Until June 1864 they received only about half the pay of their white comrades (black infantry privates, $7 a month; whites, $13), and their equipment and clothing were often inferior. Frequently they were subjected to insults and brutal treatment by white officers and enlisted men. During investigation by a military commission of a mutiny of the 4th Regiment, Corps d'Afrique, in December 1863, a white captain provoked by the brutality of Lieutenant Colonel Augustus W. Benedict testified:

> I have seen him strike them in the face with his fist, kick them, and in one instance, strike a man with his sword in the face. On the 19th of October, I was officer of the day; the guard was turned out for Lieutenant-Colonel Benedict and one man, Private Francis, of my company, did not dress properly, and Lieutenant-Colonel Benedict took the sergeant's sword and struck him in the face. I have frequently seen him at Fort Saint Philip, at guard-mounting, strike men in the face with his fist and kick them because their brasses were not bright or their boots not polished.

Another of Benedict's white subordinates told the commission:

> On the 7th of August, at Baton Rouge, when officer of the guard, I was ordered by Lieutenant-Colonel Benedict to take 2 men, have their shoes and stockings taken off, and to lay them down on the ground, straighten their legs and arms out, and stake them—tie them down. Then he told me to go to the commissary and get some molasses, and cover their faces, feet, and

COME AND JOIN US BROTHERS.

PUBLISHED BY THE SUPERVISORY COMMITTEE FOR RECRUITING COLORED REGIMENTS
1210 CHESTNUT ST. PHILADELPHIA.

Above: A recruiting poster circa 1863. The idyllic nature shown here was not representative of the realities of soldier life, especially for black recruits. (Library of Congress)

Below: Black teamsters pose near the signal tower at Bermuda Hundred, Virginia, in 1864. Black soldiers were largely restricted to labor and guard duty. (Library of Congress)

hands with molasses . . . the men had been stealing some corn to roast. . . . They were kept tied down from 10 a.m. until 7 p.m. or 7:30 p.m. They were tied down again the next morning. . . .

Benedict was sentenced to dismissal from service for "inflicting cruel and unusual punishment."

Typical of the attitude of many white Yanks toward their black associates was that registered by Lieutenant Charles H. Cox of the 70th Indiana Regiment in a letter to his sister, August 28, 1863:

> I saw a *nigger* Brigade this morning [near Nashville]. . . . I do not believe it right to make soldiers of them and class & rank with our *white* soldiers. It makes them feel and act as our equals. I do despise *them*, and the more I see of them, the more I am against the whole *black* crew.

The black troops were used mainly for cleaning camps, building defense works and manning garrisons. In June 1864, the War Department issued a general order forbidding excessive use of black troops for labor and picketing. The order was widely ignored. In the fall of 1864, Colonel James A. Hardie reported after an inspection of the Department of the Gulf:

> There are several Regiments of white Infantry . . . who have not yet been required to work a day since the receipt of this order, while colored troops have been required to work 8 hours a day. . . . The time which the colored troops would employ in drill and instruction is entirely taken up in performing not a share, but the whole of fatigue duty of the white troops.

In spite of the widespread practice of restricting black troops to labor and guard duty, some of them got into combat. While evaluation of their combat performance is difficult, owing to the bias of much of the evidence bearing on the subject, it seems reasonable to conclude that they fought as well as the white troops with whom they served. Some skulked or ran when subjected to the ordeal of battle, but the same was true of other troops, and especially those who lacked proper training or competent leadership.

In the Federal attack on Port Hudson, near Baton Rouge, May 27, 1863, two regiments of black troops, the 1st and 3d Louisiana Native Guards, numbering 1,080 officers and men out of a total force of 13,000, made six distinct charges over difficult terrain. The attack was repulsed, but the blacks won the commendation of Major General N. P. Banks for their meritorious performance. When Sergeant Anselmas Planciancois, a free Negro who carried the colors of the 1st Louisiana, fell mortally wounded during a charge, clasping the flag to his breast, two colored corporals vied for the honor of carrying the standard

onward. The contest was decided when one of them received a fatal wound.

At Milliken's Bend, June 7, 1863, near Vicksburg, when Confederates numbering about 1,500 attacked a Federal garrison of about 1,100, most of whom were Negroes, some of the fiercest fighting of the war ensued. Captain M. M. Miller, a Yale senior who led one of the black companies, wrote his aunt after the battle that he lost fifty killed and eighty wounded in "the horrible fight" and that he had "six broken bayonets to show how bravely my men fought."

The valor of black soldiers was demonstrated again on July 18, 1863, when a Federal force of about 5,000 made a bloody but futile night assault on Fort Wagner, near Charleston, South Carolina. The assault was led by a black regiment, the 54th Massachusetts, whose colonel, Robert Gould Shaw, a personable young aristocrat, had followed the example of a fellow Bostonian (Thomas Wentworth Higginson, Colonel of the 1st South Carolina Volunteers) in giving up the captaincy of an elite white company to assume command of a black regiment. Despite inadequate preparation for their assignment and difficulties resulting from darkness and rough terrain, the blacks went gallantly forward under heavy fire of rifles and artillery, supplemented at the peak of the assault by improvised hand grenades hurled from the fort by its defenders. One of the participants in the assault, Lewis Douglass, son of the renowned Negro orator, Frederick Douglass, wrote that at this point in the action, "I had my sword blown away . . . [and though] swept down like chaff, still our men went on and on." After Shaw fell, shot through the heart standing on the parapet waving his sword and urging his men forward, the regiment fell back. Its 272 casualties exceeded those of any of the ten white regiments participating in the attack.

The day before the 54th Massachusetts suffered its costly repulse at Wagner, another black regiment, the 1st Kansas, played a conspicuous role in a Union victory at Elk Creek, in the Indian Territory. There a force of seven Union regiments attacked eight regiments of Confederates. After two hours of stubborn fighting the Confederates were driven from the field. The Federal commander, Major General James G. Blunt, in his report of the battle stated:

> Much credit is due to all of them for their gallantry. The First Kansas (colored) particularly distinguished itself; they fought like veterans, and preserved their line unbroken throughout the engagement. Their coolness and bravery I have never seen surpassed; they were in the hottest of the fight, and opposed to Texas troops twice their number, whom they completely routed. One Texas regiment (the Twentieth Cavalry) that fought against them went into the fight with 300 men and came out with only 60.

Despite suffering much discrimination and abuse, some 200,000 blacks served in Federal ranks. Few black troops were organized by states. Rather, most were organized as regiments of "U.S. Colored Troops." Here, the 1st U.S. Colored Troops on November 16, 1864. (CWTI Collection)

Regardless of their color, the overwhelming majority of Rebs and Yanks were rural. Nearly half of those who wore the blue and well over half of their opposites in gray, were farmers. Going to war was an exciting experience for men who rarely had travelled any considerable distance from the fields that they tilled. Private J. B. Lance, a rustic Tar Heel who went from his native Buncombe County to the environs of Charleston, South Carolina, in 1861, wrote back to his father: "I have saw a rite Smart of the world Sence I left home But I have not saw any place like Buncomb and henderson yet." Many of the rural soldiers got their first train ride en route to the fighting zone. Private Joseph H. Diltz, a farmer from near Urbana, Ohio, wrote a friend back home shortly after his long ride to Maryland over the Baltimore & Ohio Railroad:

> Frank since I seen you last I hav seen the elephant. We started from urbana at three oclok p m. . . . we past within 4 mils of Whelling virginia. we past through some of the damdes plases ever saw by mortel eyes. We run under some of the god dames hills it was dark as the low regeons of hell We past through one tunel too miles long . . . as we was passing from tunelton to New Crick the cars run onto a stone that would weigh 500 lbs it was put on the track by rebels it was just whair the track runs close to the river if the engen had not bin so hevy we would have all went to hell in a pile or some other seaport.

In age, Rebs and Yanks ranged from beardless boys to venerable graybeards. Charles Carter Hay joined an Alabama regiment in 1861 at age 11; when he surrendered in 1865 he was one month short of his 15th birthday. Little (if any) older than Hay was a Yank named William Black; his age and unit are

unknown, but his picture plainly indicates that he was a mere boy.

The very young were usually drummer boys, though many teenagers fought in the ranks as full-fledged soldiers. Perhaps the most famous of all the drummer boys was Johnny Clem of Newark, Ohio, who went to war in 1862, when he was 10. The smashing of his drum by a Rebel shell at Shiloh won him the name "Johnny Shiloh." At Chickamauga Johnny swapped his drum for a sawed-off musket and rode into battle on an artillery caisson. For gallantry in that fight he was promoted to sergeant and henceforth was known as "The Drummer Boy of Chickamauga." Soon after his promotion he posed for the camp photographer in a new uniform sent by some admiring Chicago women. In subsequent battles he was twice wounded and following the cessation of hostilities he applied for admission to West Point. When his application was refused, President U.S. Grant appointed him a second lieutenant in the Regular Army. He retired from military service in 1916 as a major general.

The oldest Confederate found among hundreds of company rolls is E. Pollard, a 73-year-old man who, in July 1862, enlisted as a substitute in the 5th North Carolina. His military career lasted only three months and he was sick most of the time. His discharge papers stated that he was "incapable of performing the duties of a soldier on account of Rheumatism and old age." Among Yanks, Curtis King, who enlisted at 80 in the 37th Iowa in November 1862, was almost certainly the oldest common soldier in the Civil War. One man older than he, William Wilkins, 83, donned the Union blue in 1862, but he was a major general, commissioned in the Pennsylvania Home Guards. King's regiment, known as "The

Members of Company B, 9th Regiment, Mississippi Infantry, at Pensacola, Florida, in 1861. The excitement of war enticed men of all ages, from 10-year-old Johnny Clem to 73-year-old E. Pollard. Those who joined as youngsters matured rapidly. (Library of Congress)

Greybeards" and organized for non-combatant guard duty, was composed mainly of men over 45; 145 of them had passed their 60th birthday.

Most Rebs and Yanks were neither very old nor very young. On both sides 18-year-olds were the largest age group, and men ranging from 18 to 30 comprised about three-fourths of all the common soldiers.

The boys made better soldiers than the older men, and they matured rapidly in response to the challenges of marching and fighting. One of them, Private William W. Edgerton, who at 17 enlisted in the 107th New York in July 1862, wrote his mother eighteen months later from Chattanooga:

> It is strange how much a young man will learn from expeirance and study in a year and a half, one year and a half ago I dident have aney more calkulation than a last years birds nest, but haveing a great head or notion of studying human nature I have lernt a great deal, lernt to get all I can and ceep all I get, make as much out of every body as I can. I have no notion nor never did have, but I never untill now knew how to get around working all my lifetime, but now I know that buy working diligintly and not haveing aney holes in my pocket I neadent work very hard after I am 40 years old.

Reports of unit commanders in the *Official Records* contain many citations of boy soldiers for gallantry in

Many teenagers fought as full-fledged soldiers. Here: Confederate Private Jesse Murray, age 17, who was killed during the fighting at Seven Pines in 1862. (Library of Congress)

combat. At a critical point in a fight near Atlanta in July 1864, Eddie Evans, a stripling of the 24th Mississippi, seized the colors and, according to his colonel: "bore them with such conspicuous coolness and gallantry as to elicit the admiration of all. At one time he took his stand in advance of the line without any

A Virginia Military Institute cadet, Bengamin A. Colonna, typical of the teenagers who gallantly served the Confederacy. The Union, too, had many such soldiers. (Library of Congress)

protection . . . distant from the enemy's line not more than fifty yards, waving his colors defiantly and called upon his comrades to rally to the flag."

Many of the boys paid the supreme price for their gallantry, among them "Little Giffen of Tennessee," whose death near the end of the war, perhaps at Bentonville, was immortalized by the poet Francis O. Ticknor. But more youths died of disease than of hostile bullets. On July 9, 1863, Private James K. Newlin of the 14th Wisconsin wrote from near Vicksburg: "Henry Cady is dead . . . 'Little Cady,' as we called him, was universally acknowledged to be the best boy in the Comp'y. . . . We all loved him dearly, now he is taken from us; he was always so good, kind, and accommodating, that every one who saw him took an interest in him at once." "Little Cady" had scores of counterparts in both armies.

Some of the boy soldiers attained high rank during their Civil War service. William P. Roberts of North Carolina, who enlisted in 1861 at 19, was promoted brigadier in February 1865 at age 23, and thus became the youngest general in the Confederate Army.

On the Union side, Arthur MacArthur, father of General Douglas MacArthur of World War II, after winning the Medal of Honor at 18, for gallantry at Missionary Ridge, became colonel of the 24th Wisconsin; he led that valorous regiment with distinction through the bloody battles of Resaca and Nashville; after the war he rose to the grade of lieutenant general. Two other Billy Yanks who became colonels before reaching the age of 21 and who ably led their regiments in combat, were Henry W. Lawton of the 30th Indiana and John W. Forman of the 15th Kentucky. Galusha Pennypacker of the 97th Pennsylvania rose to colonel of his regiment and, one month before his twenty-first birthday, he was promoted to a brigadier, the youngest general in United States history.

Most of the common soldiers on both sides were poorly educated. Illiteracy ran as high as 50 percent in many Confederate units, and the average was probably between 15 and 25 percent. Yanks were more literate than Rebs, owing to the North's superiority in educational opportunity for the masses. But even on the Union side, that company which did not have from one to a half-dozen men who could not write their names on the muster roll was unusual.

In both armies spelling and grammar left much to be desired. A Yank of the Army of the Potomac wrote shortly after Lincoln ordered that organization to be broken up into corps: "They are deviding the army up into corpses."

Soldier accounts of camp illnesses led to a great diversity of misspelling. Pneumonia appeared in their letters as "new mornion," hospital as "horse pittle," erysipelas as "eri sipalous," typhoid fever as "tifoid fever," and yellow jaundice as "yaler ganders." One Yank who served under Brigadier General Frederick Lander wrote: "Landers has had the ganders but is getting well." After Lander died early in 1865, another of his men—and one who despised him—wrote: "Old Landers is ded. . . . I did not see a tear shed but heard a great many speaches made about him such as he was in hell pumping thunder at 3 cents a clap. . . . The report is that he killed himself drinking whiskey." An Ohio soldier informed his homefolk that he had been suffering from the "Camp Diary" and another Yank afflicted with the same malady wrote his wife: "I am well at the present with the exception I have got the Dyerear and I hope these few lines will find you the same." Surely this strange expression of hope was a slip of the pen. A Georgia soldier wrote his wife concerning his recent bout with diarrhea: "I have bin a little sick with diorah. . . . I eat too much eggs and poark and it sowered [on] my stomack and turn loose on me."

Francis M. Field of the 45th Ohio wrote his father in the fall of 1862: "the boys hant used wright; we have not drawed a cent of pay yet; we have to take it ruff and tumbel. . . . All the rest of the boys gits leters from home and i dont git any from home atall. . . . wright soon . . . excuse my poor writing and spelling . . . george huffman . . . has bin sick a good while [but] he is agiting better."

A Georgian stationed near Wilmington, North Carolina, wrote his wife: "This Countrie is so por it wolden hardle sprout pees." Another Reb informed his sister: "I will send you my fortograph and [I] want yourn without faill." A third Confederate complained to his spouse: "We have to drink wate[r] thick with mud & wigel tails."

Perhaps the champion misspeller of all those who wore the gray was Bartlett Yancey Malone of the 6th North Carolina. In his diary Gettysburg is "Gatersburg"; Blue Ridge is "Blew Ridg"; bean soup is "Been Soup"; adjutant is "adjertent"; bloody is "bludy"; some is "sum"; know is "no"; passing through is "passen threw"; peace is "peas"; tunnel is "turnel"; and missing is "misen." A cold day is a "coal day"; closer is "closter"; a court house is a "coat house"; where is "whar"; pretty is "pritty"; until is "untell"; accidentally is "axidently"; ford is "foad"; and verbs frequently are prefixed by the indefinite article as "the Yankies was arunning." Other speech characteristics which have a familiar ring to people who grew up in the rural South are exemplified by Malone's use of "a right smart force," of Federals, "we taken the turnpike," and "we will have a fight hear to reckly"—i.e., directly.

Individual motivation of the common soldiers varied greatly. Some had only vague ideas about their

Recruiting poster to fill the ranks of Colonel Lyle's 19th Regiment. Both North and South were forced to introduce conscription to bolster their volunteer systems. The Confederacy began conscription in 1862; the Union followed in 1863. (The Ohio Historical Society)

The 7th Regiment, New York Militia marches up New York City's Broadway in the spring of 1861. Many Northerners who joined up early in the war did so to fight slavery, but most were looking for adventure. Saving the Union was their first political concern. (CWTI Collection)

involvement in the conflict. Many signed up for service primarily because their friends and neighbors were enlisting. The prospects of release from family restraints and responsibilities, of travel, and of escape from the humdrum of farm and factory were tremendously appealing to the overwhelming majority of those eligible for military service.

Of Yanks, who in letters and diaries commented on their individual motivation, the overwhelming majority indicated that their basic reason for becoming soldiers was to save the Union. They identified the nation of their birth, or their adoption, with liberty, democracy, social justice, and equal opportunity for all; they associated the South with aristocracy, preference for the privileged, and suppression of the lowly; secession they viewed as unconstitutional, and armed resistance to national authority they deemed as traitorous.

Typical of the sentiments of many Yanks were these expressed by 21-year-old John H. Stibbs of Cedar Rapids, Iowa, to his parents in Wooster, Ohio, telling of his reasons for volunteering as a private in the 1st Iowa. On April 18, 1861, six days after Confederates launched their attack on Fort Sumter, he wrote: "The majority of our Citizens are full of patri-

otism and express their willingness to stand by the old Stars and Stripes and protect it from dishonour. . . . Most of . . . [those few who expressed sympathy for the South] have had their ideas scared out of them and have come out for the government and the balance have been given to understand that Young America can't tolerate a traitor and that they must come out and make a decided stand on one side or the other." The next day he wrote his father: "I did not ask the consent of you and Ma in my yesterday's letter as to whether you would be willing to have me voulenteer and I don't propose to do it now. *I take it for granted* I am doing right and that when my Country needs my services to protect her flag from dishonour and disgrace that my parents will be the *last* ones to object to my enlisting." Two days later he reported: "I have thought the matter over cooly and have counted the cost and if my life is needed for the defense of my Country I am ready to give it up, and do it freely." On April 23 he informed his father: "I am very anxious to get into action and am as ready as ever to go and do all I can even to giving up my life for the protection of the old Union that has given me and my Father our liberties and has made America the greatest nation in the world." Stibbs's subsequent

HURRAH FOR TEXAS!

The Land of Milk and Honey

The 1st Battalion, 2d Regiment R. I. Cavalry, under command of Major A. W. Corliss, has been ordered to join the Expedition of General N. P. Banks, destined for Texas. Now is the time to join this Crack Regiment. By so doing you will escape the mud and snow of Virginia, and the cold winter of the North.

Bounty, $25
WHEN SWORN INTO SERVICE.
300 DOLLARS WHEN YOU LEAVE THE STATE!
And 15 Dollars when Discharged!

A good opportunity to settle on the Rich Prairies of this noble State is offered at the close of the Rebellion.

RECRUITING OFFICERS:

Capt. R. C. ANTHONY, Corner of Orange and Westminster Sts., Up Stairs; Capt. G. A. SMITH, Dorrance Street; Capt. WILLIAM H. STEVENS, Corner of North Main Street and Market Square.

The Fourth Company is recruiting at Camp Mauran.

A. W. CORLISS, Major Com'dg.

service, during which he rose to the rank of colonel, proved that his patriotic utterances of April 1861 were not empty words, but expressions of deep-seated devotion to flag and country. At Fort Donelson, Shiloh, Tupelo, Nashville and other engagements, he fought gallantly for the Union and not once did he express any doubt about the cause for which he repeatedly risked his life.

Yanks of foreign birth found the cause of the Union no less appealing than native Americans. On July 22, 1861, Philip Smith, an immigrant member of the 8th Missouri, wrote in his diary:

> As I lay in my bed this morning I got to thinking. . . . I have left home and a good situation . . . and have grasped the weapon of death for the purpose of doing my part in defending and upholding the integrity, laws and the preservation of my adopted country from a band of contemptible traitors who would if they can accomplish their hellish designs, destroy the best and noblest government on earth, merely for the purpose of benefiting themselves on the slave question.

Thousands of other foreign recruits expressed sentiments corresponding to those registered by Philip Smith.

Some Yanks, though always a decided minority, were fighting primarily for the emancipation of the slaves. One of these was Chauncey H. Cooke, a young Wisconsin private, who wrote his father early in 1863: "I have no heart in this war if the slaves cannot be free," and who stated soon after the fall of Vicksburg: "I tell the boys right to their face I am in the war for the freedom of the slave. When they talk about saving the Union, I tell them that is Dutch to me. I am for helping the slaves if the Union goes to smash." Similar views were held by Urich N. Parmelee of Connecticut, who left Yale in 1861 "to free the slave" and who wrote after issuance of the Emancipation Proclamation: "I do not intend to shirk now there is really something to fight for. I mean *Freedom*."

Most Rebs who commented on their individual motivation indicated that they were fighting to protect their families and homes against foreign invaders. Some mentioned their concern for the growing power of the central government and the increasing impingement of Federal authority on state prerogatives as Northerners acquired the lion's share of the country's population and wealth. Charles E. Smith of the 32d Ohio, an emigré from the South, told in his diary of receiving a friendly letter from a Confederate cousin in April 1863, in which the Reb stated: "I

always thought some of . . . [my cousins] were in the [Union] army that was to crush this rebellion if it could but I do not think that it can, for although you have so many more men than we have, you have not those in power to manage things right. We are fighting for the Constitution that our forefathers made, and not as old Abe would have it."

Undoubtedly many Rebs were fighting for slavery, not so much as an economic institution, but as an established and effective means of perpetuating white supremacy, and members of the non-slaveholding class (to which about three-fourths of the Johnny Rebs belonged) were just as much interested in keeping the South a white man's country as were any other group in Southern society. As a general rule Rebs did not openly avow that their main reason for going to war was to uphold "the peculiar institution" but wrote instead of defending state sovereignty (under which they thought slavery would be more secure than under a national government dominated by

Alabama Private James L. Greer. Most common soldiers ranged in age from 18 to 30. (Alabama Department of Archives & History)

Facing page: A Union Cavalry poster offers a bounty and tries to entice recruits with appeals to "escape the mud and snow of Virginia, and the cold winter of the North." (CWTI Collection)

This Alabama soldier displays a fancy hat . . . and steely-eyed determination. (Mississippi Department of Archives & History)

wemmen and children tell I get home and we'll all have a chance. . . . I want you to go . . . and see my wife and children, but I want you to take your wife with you when you go."

Private William W. White of the 18th Georgia, on April Fool's Day, 1862, wrote his cousin, from near Yorktown:

> Camp Wigfall, Thirteen Hundred Miles From
> Any Place,
> April, the one, 1800 &
> awful cold
>
> Good Morning "Plug Ugly"
> Your loving Epistle in which you vented all your spleen and heaped upon me all the base cognomens of which your ninny-head was master reached me. . . . I had hoped and prayed that when I entered the army . . . our associations would there be sundered . . . but it seems in that I am disappointed, for no sooner did you learn my whereabouts than you favored me with one of your soul-stirring, love-reviving, gizzard-splitting productions. . . . But you, Thomas, like all *long-eared animules* would not stick to one side. . . . You need not blame me for not writing to you . . . [for] there is a little Blue-eyed Beauty in Georgia who writes to me every week and it consumes nearly all of my spare moments to answer her sweet and interesting letters; however, I expect to see you again in about fifty years provided I should live that long, and then I will tell you enough lies to last you one season. . . . Give my respects . . . to all inquiring friends and my wool dyed, double and twisted love to the girls.

Billy Yanks sometimes advertised for correspondents through the personal columns of the newspapers. Some of these notices are obviously the work of mischief makers. The Chattanooga *Gazette* of March 6, 1864, for example, carried this advertisement: "Any young lady not sufficiently homely to frighten a dog out of a butcher shop nor sufficiently beautiful to bewitch the idle shoulder straps about town can get up considerable fun by commencing a correspondence with *Aaron*, Chattanooga Post Office." The New York *Herald* of March 8, 1863, under the heading "Matrimonial," printed this notice: "Two young gentlemen possessed of large fortunes, but rather green, wish to open correspondence with young ladies of the same circumstances with a view to matrimony—brunettes preferred—but no objection to blondes provided they are perfect past all parallel. Address Harry Longsworth and Charley B.B., Camp Denison, Ohio."

A Vermont Yank who had not heard from a friend in a long time wrote: "Ans[wer] this as soon as you get it and let me know w[h]eather you are alive are [or] not if you are dead I shall like to know it." And an Ohioan who lacked postage because of arrearage of pay wrote on an envelope addressed to his homefolk:

Northerners) or "the Southern way of life." One Reb who forthrightly stated that he was fighting for slavery was Private G. G. Holland, a non-slaveholder, who wrote to a friend in September 1863:

> You Know I am a poor man having none of the property said to be the cause of the present war. But I have a wife & some children to rase in honor & never to be put on an equality with the African race.

One of the most notable traits of Civil War soldiers was their humor. Their sensitivity to the ludicrous and the spontaneity of their mirth gave them escape from their troubles and made the hardships of soldiering more tolerable. Rebs and Yanks liked to tease relatives and friends in their letters. Private William R. Stilwell of Georgia, after a year's absence from home wrote his wife: "If I did not write and receive letters from you I believe that I would forgit that I was marrid. I dont feel much like a maryed man but I never forgit it sofar as to court enny other lady, but if I should you must forgive me as I am so forgitful." William Sprinkle, a North Carolina Reb, wrote a young married man of his home community: "Thomy I want you to be good and tri to take cear of the

The 3d Kentucky at mess before fighting at Corinth, Mississippi, on May 11, 1862. Camplife was often marked by pranks, horseplay, and other expressions of humor as the men sought to escape from the hardships of soldiering. Painted by Conrad Chapman. (Library of Congress)

Postmaster please to pass this through,
I've nary a cent, but three months due.

In camp, fun-loving propensities were manifested in pranks and horseplay. Green recruits were sent to supply sergeants with instructions to demand their umbrellas, or were honored by election to the high but fictitious position of fifth lieutenant and then put to catching fleas and carrying water. Visitors who came to camp wearing stovepipe headpieces were hailed vociferously with such greetings as "Come out of that hat! I see your legs," or "Look out, that parrot shell you're wearing's going to explode." Wearers of shiny new boots were apt to be told to "Come up outer them boots; . . . I know you're in thar; I see your arms sticking out." Anyone who rode through company streets sporting an elegant mustache was almost sure to be hailed with suggestions to "Take them mice out'er your mouth; take em out no use to say they aint thar, see their tails hangin' out"; or, "Come out'er that bunch of har. I see your ears a workin'."

Civilians and dull-witted comrades were the usual

victims of such horseplay. But officers, especially those who held staff positions, or who were incompetent, overbearing, or given to putting on airs, were considered fair game by pranksters. Indeed, soldiers were able when they set their minds to the task to ridicule intolerable superiors into resignation.

The humor of the common soldier was so irrepressible as frequently to manifest itself in battle. At Chickamauga a chaplain who, as the shooting started, exhorted his charges to "remember, boys, that he who is killed will sup tonight in Paradise," was urged by a Reb to "come along and take supper with us." When the parson refused the invitation and galloped to the rear, a resounding shout went up from the advancing ranks, "The parson isn't hungry, and never eats supper."

In another battle Rebel George Lemmon in his excitement fired his musket too close to comrade Nick Watkins' head, shooting a hole in his hat. Whereupon Nick turned and said: "George Lemmon, I wish you'd look where you're shooting—I'm not a Yankee." Many similar incidents occurred among the men in blue. In 1863, a Pennsylvania private wrote his homefolk, "We laugh at everything. . . . The roughest jokes I ever heard were perpetrated under a heavy fire."

Some of the best jokes were made about clothing and food. A Reb of General Joseph E. Johnston's army wrote from near Atlanta in June 1864: "In this army one hole in the seat of the breeches indicates a captain, two holes a lieutenant, and the seat of the pants all out indicates the individual is a private." Hardtack, the big thick cracker or biscuit that was the standard bread ration during periods of active campaigning, inspired many humorous sallies. A Kansas Yank reported the following camp dialogue:

> Sergeant: Boys I was eating a piece of hard tack this morning, and I bit on something soft; what do you think it was?
> Private: A worm?
> Sergeant: No by G-d, it was a ten penny nail.

The crackers were delivered to camp in barrels or boxes marked "B.C."—which probably was an abbreviation for "Brigade Commissary." But the consumers claimed with mock seriousness that the letters represented the hardtack's date of manufacture. The crackers were often so wormy that soldiers nicknamed them "worm castles," and one soldier stated: "All the fresh meat we had came in the hard bread . . . and I preferring my game cooked, used to toast my biscuits."

A Yank, annoyed by the brevity of a letter he had recently received from home, wrote back to the sender: "Yore leter was short and sweet, jist like a rosted maget." A third Yank, reporting his first encounter with Rebs, wrote his father: "Dear Pa. . . . Went out a Skouting yesterday. We got to one house where there were five secessionists, they broke & run and Arch holered out to shoot the ornery suns of biches and wee all let go at them. They may say what they please, but godamit Pa it is fun."

Another impressive quality of the plain folk was their ability to give colorful and forceful expression to their thoughts, and this despite the serious deficiencies of most of them in grammar and spelling. Some of their figures of speech were pungent and vivid. One Reb commented that "the Yankees were thicker [th]an lise on a hen and a dam site ornraier," while another reported that his comrades were "pitching around like a blind dog in a meat hous," and a third wrote that it was raining "like poring peas on a rawhide." An Ohioan reported that Rebel dwellings near Fredericksburg looked like "the latter end of original sin and hard times," and another Yank wrote from Chattanooga that he was so hungry he "could eat a rider off his horse and snap at the stirrups."

Choice comments were inspired by the boredom and monotony of camp life. "You wanted to know how I like it," wrote an Ohioan to a friend; "i ain't home Sick i don't no What home Sick is but i no the diferens between home and Soldieren."

Efforts to recount battle impressions and experiences also gave rise to vivid passages. An Illinois Yank reported after the Battle of Jackson, Mississippi, that "the Balls . . . Sung Dixey around our years [and] the grape and Canister moed hour Ranks down like grass before the Sithe"; and a New York soldier wrote after the Williamsburg, Virginia, fight that "the air perfectly whistled, shrieked and hummed with the leaden storm." A Texan who was at Chickamauga noted in his journal that "if ten thousand earthquakes had been turned loose in all their power they could not have made so much racket."

Camp rations inspired some of the most picturesque comments. A Reb complained that the beef issued to him must have been carved from a bull "too old for the conscript law," while a comrade declared that the cows that supplied the meat for his unit were so feeble that "it takes two hands to hold up one beef

Soldiers found various diversions to relieve the boredom and deprivation of camp. Here, Mississippi soldiers practice throwing Bowie knives. Songfests, gambling, sports, and reading were other popular pastimes. (Harper's Weekly)

to shoot it." Yanks also found much fault with their meat ration, which they commonly referred to as "salt horse"; but their choicest remarks were directed at the hardtack that comprised their bread ration. "Teeth-dullers" and "sheet iron crackers" were favorite designations for hardtack, and one Yank suggested that it "would make good brest works."

Common soldiers of both sides achieved exceptional pungency in denouncing their officers. An Alabamian wrote his wife that "Gen. Jones is a very common looking man who rides just like he had a boil on his stern." Another Reb declared that his colonel was "an ignoramus fit for nothing higher than the cultivation of corn." A Floridian stated that his superiors were "not fit to tote guts to a Bear."

Yanks registered comments even more caustic. Private Hezekiah Stibbs of Iowa wrote his brother in January 1863: "We have got a good many officers in this regiment that never had a square meal until they came into the service." Another Yank characterized those who commanded him as "woss than worthless." A Massachusetts soldier who seems to have been a prototype of Bill Mauldin wrote: "The officers consider themselves as made of a different material

from the low fellows in the ranks. . . . They get all the glory and most of the pay and don't earn ten cents apiece on the average the drunken rascals." Private George Gray Hunter of Pennsylvania declared: "If there is one thing that I hate more than another it is the Sight of a Shoulder Strap, For I am well convinced in My own Mind that had it not been for officers this war would have Ended long ago." But the peak of denunciatory expressiveness on either side was attained by the Yank who wrote: "I wish to God one half of our officers were knocked in the head by slinging them Against A part of those still Left."

A third conspicuous trait was pride. The soldier's predominant fear when he faced battle was not that he would be maimed or killed—though concern for safety was very great—but that he might play the coward and bring disgrace on himself and his family. "I did not know whether I had pluck enough to go through [it]," wrote an Iowa Yank to his brother shortly after his baptism of fire at Fort Donelson, "but now I have no fear but I can do my duty, although I know the danger is great." A similar sentiment was registered by a Georgian who wrote his wife after his first fight, "it was a pretty severe anniciation . . . but thank god I had nerve to stand it."

On the day after the First Battle of Bull Run a Federal soldier wrote proudly to his father: "We got the worst of it but . . . I didn't run." And following the terrible fight at Franklin, Tennessee, in 1864 a Rebel informed his brother: "One of Old Abe's boys pluged me in the right foot making a severe wound, [but] I am proud to say that there was no one between me and the Yankees when I was wounded."

When deprivation, sickness, and war-weariness caused spirits to sag, pride in self and family kept soldiers at their posts. Private John Cotton of Alabama wrote his wife in May 1863: "I want to come home as bad as any body can . . . but I shant run away . . . I don't want it throwed up to my children after I am dead and gone that I was a deserter . . . I don't want to do anything if I no it will leave a stain on my posterity hereafter." And despite enormous hardship and anxiety both to himself and his family, he remained faithful to his cause until the end.

A fourth quality impressively demonstrated by the common soldiers of the Civil War was courage. This is not meant to suggest that all Rebs and Yanks were heroes, for there was a considerable amount of malingering, skulking, and running in every major battle. When Colonel John C. Nisbet of the 66th Georgia saw a soldier streaking to the rear in a fight near Atlanta in 1864, he yelled at the fugitive, "What are you running for?" Without slowing his pace the soldier shouted back, "Bekase I kaint fly." At Shiloh thousands of Yanks abandoned their comrades and

The decisive charge of the 78th Pennsylvania and 21st Ohio volunteers at the Battle of Stone River on January 2, 1863. The desperation and the deadliness of Civil War combat is attested by the heavy casualty rates suffered by both Federals and Confederates in many engagements. (CWTI Collection)

took refuge beneath the bluff of the Tennessee River and at Chickamauga, when Longstreet broke through the Union lines, hordes of officers and men fled the field in panic. At Missionary Ridge a similar panic swept through Bragg's forces and Rebs ran *en masse* from the scene of action. But on both sides such conduct was exceptional.

The Civil War required more raw courage than most conflicts of recent times. For in that war men marched to battle in massed formation with a minimum of protection and supporting arms. Until the middle of the conflict they disdained to dig trenches and throw up hasty fortifications. Fighting was open, and closing with the enemy was more than a colorful phrase. Contests were decided by desperate charges in which muskets were fired at such close range as to burn the faces of contestants, and the climax was frequently a savage tussle in which men pitched into each other with bayonets, clubbed muskets, rocks, and fists. An Iowa soldier who took part in the fight at Allatoona Pass in October 1864 wrote: "When the battle was over one of our boys was found dead facing the enemy who had killed him. Both of them lay with their faces nearly touching . . . with their bayonets run through each other." This incident was by no means unique.

The desperation and the deadliness of Civil War combat is attested by the casualty rates. At Balaklava the Light Brigade, whose charge was immortalized by Tennyson, suffered a loss in killed and wounded of 36.7 percent. But at Gettysburg the 1st Minnesota and the 26th North Carolina each sustained a loss of about 85 percent. These were the heaviest losses of any regiments in any Civil War engagement, but the

1st Texas had 82.3 percent of its officers and men killed or wounded at Antietam, and the total number of regiments on both sides suffering losses of more than 50 percent in a single battle ran to well over one hundred.

In some battles the gallantry of common soldiers was so impressive as to inspire cheers from their opponents. History has recorded no greater displays of heroism than the Confederate assaults at Malvern Hill, Corinth, Gettysburg, and Franklin, and the Federal attacks at Fredericksburg, Kennesaw Mountain, Vicksburg, and Second Cold Harbor. In this last fight men of Winfield Scott Hancock's II Corps, when informed of the order to charge a seemingly impregnable Confederate position, wrote their names on slips of paper that they pinned to their uniforms so that their homefolk might be promptly informed of their fate. About fifteen minutes after the assault was launched three thousand soldiers of this battle-scarred organization lay dead or wounded on the field.

In the hard-fought contests of the Civil War innumerable plain Americans who ordinarily would have lived uneventfully and obscurely, without ever knowing the stuff of which they were made, attained the heights of heroism. Official reports of unit commanders which record the details of their gallantry tell of humble soldiers on both sides volunteering to perform perilous tasks, shrieking defiance at their foes, denouncing and even striking officers who played the coward, vying with comrades for the privilege of carrying the colors, taking over command when officers were all disabled, and refusing to leave the field when seriously wounded.

Two examples must suffice to illustrate the gallantry displayed by some of these noble men. Rebel Private Mattix, wounded so severely in the left arm at Murfreesboro that he could not wield his musket, went to his regimental commander and said: "Colonel, I am too badly wounded to use my gun but can carry the flag, may I do it?" Private Mattix knew that carrying the colors was the most dangerous of all combat assignments. He also knew that three color bearers of his regiment had already been shot down in that furious battle. But when the colonel nodded assent, Mattix seized the flag staff with his good arm, stepped in front of the regiment, and kept the colors flying through the remainder of the battle.

Near the close of the fight at Hanover Court House, May 27, 1862, a wounded Yank called out feebly to a regimental commander who was passing by. The officer turned around and stooped low over the prostrate soldier thinking that he wanted to send a farewell message to some loved one. But what the wounded man whispered instead was the inquiry:

"Colonel, is the day ours?" "Yes," replied the officer. "Then," responded the soldier, "I am willing to die." And he did die and was buried on the field where he gave his life. This common soldier may never have heard of the Plains of Abraham and heroic statements made there by the dying Montcalm and Wolfe. But his words were as glorious as theirs and his valorous death deserves no less than theirs to be immortalized on the pages of history.

The greatness of this heroic Yank, of Rebel Private Mattix, and of their comrades who comprised the rank and file of the Union and Confederate armies was recognized and acclaimed by contemporaries. Joseph C. Stiles, a distinguished minister who accompanied Lee's army on the Antietam Campaign, wrote afterward to his daughter: "I could tell you a thousand thrilling incidents indicative of the glorious courage of our [common] soldiers." And he quoted a Federal prisoner as remarking: "*A Confederate soldier! I believe the fellow would storm hell with a pen-knife.*" After the battle of Chickamauga a Confederate brigade commander, William B. Bate, reported: "The private soldier . . . [vied] with the officer in deeds of high daring and distinguished courage. While the 'River of Death' shall float its sluggish current to the beautiful Tennessee, and the night wind chant its solemn dirges over their soldier graves, their names, enshrined in the hearts of their countrymen, will be held in grateful remembrance."

In his official report of the Murfreesboro Campaign Major General W. S. Rosecrans, after noting the splendid conduct of his officers, stated: "But above all, the sturdy rank and file showed invincible fighting courage and stamina, worthy of a great and free nation." A few days after Rosecrans made his report Braxton Bragg, the commander who had opposed him at Murfreesboro, wrote the Confederate adjutant general:

> We have had in great measure to trust to the individuality and self-reliance of the private soldier. Actuated only by a sense of duty and of patriotism, he has, in this great contest, justly judged that the cause was his own, and gone into it with a determination to conquer or die. . . . No encomium is too high, no honor too great for such a soldiery. However much of credit and glory may be given . . . the leaders in our struggle, history will yet award the main honor where it is due—to the private soldier, who . . . has encountered all the hardships and suffered all the privations.

Bragg's prediction that history would award principal honor to the private soldiers has not yet been borne out. The generals and political leaders continue to dominate writings about the Civil War. Bragg was right, however, in his appraisal of the character of the Confederate private. And what he said about

Johnny Reb's individuality, self-reliance, and dependability was equally applicable to Billy Yank.

The Civil War was in large degree a soldier's war. In that struggle the determination, self-sufficiency, and endurance of the individual in the ranks were of utmost importance. Officer casualties were heavy, and in the hurly-burly of combat those who survived often were able to exercise little control over their units. In the crucial, climactic stages of battle the common soldiers were to a large extent on their own, and it was often their courage and tenacity, individual and collective, that ultimately decided the contest.

Still another trait conspicuously manifested by the common soldiers was a deep-seated devotion to duty. The words "honor" and "duty" appear with impressive frequency in their correspondence. The duty to which Rebs and Yanks generally seemed to be most sensitive was that involving their associates in arms. With few exceptions they considered themselves honor-bound to perform their allotment of camp chores, to share equally the inconveniences and deprivations of army life, and to stand firmly by their fellows in the hour of peril.

The sense of obligation to comrades in arms found frequent and forceful expression in home letters. In 1863, a Mississippi private wrote his wife: "I have never had a mark for any neglect of duty Since I have been in the Service—and I dont intend that I ever Shall if it can be avoided." And he lived up to his pledge until honorably released by a Federal bullet at Franklin. In May 1864, one of Lee's soldiers wrote his mother: "I have been quite sick with fever for the last 4 or 5 days. They wanted me to go to Richmond but I am determined to see this fight out if it costs me my life." A similar sentiment was registered by an ailing Yank who, in response to his sister's inquiry if he had applied for a discharge, wrote: "I have not, and never shall. I would feel ashamed if I should succeed even in getting it . . . and I would love to join my Reg't soon. You don't know how sorry I feel I am not there now, as they no doubt will again be thrown into the fight with their decimated ranks, and share the *glory* with them. I really feel ashamed at my situation."

Duty to cause and country, while never as frequently expressed as obligation to companions in arms, was deeply felt by many soldiers of both sides. Many Rebs saw a parallel between the struggle that they were waging and that conducted by their Revolutionary forefathers, and when hardship weighed heavily on them, they derived much comfort from recalling the triumph over similar sufferings of Washington's army at Valley Forge.

Shortly after the costly defeats at Gettysburg and Vicksburg, Sergeant John W. Hagan of Georgia wrote his wife: "I & every Southern Soldier should be like the rebbil blume which plumed more & shinned briter the more it was trampled on & I beleave . . . we will have to fight like Washington did, but I hope our people will never be reduced to destress & poverty as the people of that day was, but if nothing elce will give us our liberties I am willing for the time to come." This humble man fought on in the face of increasing adversity, and when his lieutenant played the coward in the early stages of the Georgia Campaign, Sergeant Hagan took command of his company and led it heroically through fight after fight until he was captured in the battle for Atlanta.

Billy Yank's patriotism, like that of Johnny Reb, was a compound of loyalties to home and country. The dual attachment was forcefully expressed by Private John F. Brobst of the 25th Wisconsin in a letter to his sweetheart shortly after his unit arrived in Dixie early in 1863: "Home is sweet and friends are dear, but what would they all be to let the country go in ruin, and be a slave. I am contented with my lot . . . for I know that I am doing my duty, and I know that it is my duty to do as I am now a-doing. If I live to get back, I shall be proud of the freedom I shall have, and know that I helped to gain that freedom. If I should not get back, it will do them good that do get back."

On September 16, 1861, Samuel Croft of Pennsylvania, after a long march over difficult country, wrote his sister: "I did not come for money and good living, my heart beats high, and I am proud of being a soldier, when I look along the line of glistning bayonets with the glorious Stars and Stripes floating over them . . . knowing that the bayonets are in loyal hands that will plunge them deep in the hearts of those who have disgraced . . . that flag which has protected them and us, their freedom and ours, I say again I am proud and sanguine of success." Croft's patriotism was sorely tried by the mismanagement and reverses that bedeviled the Army of the Potomac for the next two years, but he served his country faithfully until he was shot down at Gettysburg.

Sergeant Edmund English of New Jersey, the son of an Irish immigrant, on January 8, 1862, wrote his mother: "Though humble my position is—gold could not buy me out of the Army until this Rebellion is subdued. A man who would not fight for his Country is a scoundral!" Sergeant English also experienced periods of discouragement, but his shining patriotism always restored his spirit. In April 1863, he wrote: "The blind acts of unqualified generals and Statesmen have had no lasting impression on the motives which first prompted me to take up arms or chilled my patriotism in the least. I cannot get tired of soldiering while the war lasts. . . . As long as God

spares my health and strength to wield a weapon in Freedom's defense, I will do it." His life and health were spared, and when his three-year term of service expired in 1864 he re-enlisted and fought on to the end of the war.

The sense of duty manifested by these men and countless others who wore the blue sustained the Union through the first years of bungling, gloom, and disaster. And when the expiration of the original terms of enlistment approached early in 1864, and the nation stood in grave danger because of the threatened loss of their proven courage, hardiness, and experience, they came forward by company, regiment, and brigade to pledge their continued service. By thus freely offering themselves for what they knew would be another season of bloody sacrifice, they gave the nation one of its most glorious moments. To them and their kind the Union will ever owe an overwhelming debt of gratitude.

Another quality demonstrated by the common soldiers, blue and gray, was an enormous capacity for hardship. Because of their limited resources, Southerners were required to endure far more of suffering than were Northerners. But many Northerners experienced great misery, and when put to the test they bore their lot with no less fortitude than Confederates.

Soldiers of both sides had their starvation times, though Rebs were far more intimately acquainted with hunger than Yanks. Many men in gray went for days without any food save a few grains of corn picked up from the places where the horses fed and parched over the glowing embers of their campfires. Yanks on the Knoxville Campaign of late 1863 and Rebs at Nashville marched for miles over rocky, ice-coated roads in bare feet leaving traces of blood behind them.

The sick and wounded of both armies experienced enormous hardship, and in Confederate hospitals inadequate facilities, shortage of food, and dearth of medicine led to unspeakable agonies. Literally thousands of Rebs were subjected to the ordeal of having limbs sawed off without benefit of anesthesia. But the sick and wounded bore their miseries and tortures with remarkable courage and patience.

An Alabama nurse wrote her superior from a Virginia hospital in 1861: "The fear that my *womanly* nerves would give way within the hearing of the 'groans of the wounded' almost made me shrink from the position I occupy, but while I grow sick at the sight of the amputated limbs and ghastly wounds, I must testify that a groan has rarely reached my ears and the heroism of our men has developed itself more thoroughly and beautifully in enduring bodily suffer-

The Chimborazo Hospital at Richmond, Virginia, in 1865. The sick and wounded of both armies experienced enormous hardship; mortality rates among them were high. (National Archives)

ing . . . and want of home comforts that of necessity attaches to a war hospital."

Phoebe Pember, an administrator in Richmond's Chimborazo Hospital 1862–1865, in her memoir, *A Southern Woman's Story*, pays high tribute to the fortitude of the lowly patients. She relates in some detail the experience of a young soldier named Fisher, who won the admiration and affection of all those who came in contact with him by the patience and cheerfulness of his ten-month convalescence from a hip wound. On the night following his first success in walking from one end of the ward to the other, Fisher cried out with pain as he turned over in his bed. Examination revealed a small stream of blood spurting from his wound; a splintered bone apparently had cut an artery. Mrs. Pember stopped the blood flow with her finger and sent for the surgeon. The doctor promptly concluded that the severed artery was too deeply imbedded in the fleshy part of the thigh to be repaired.

When informed of the hopelessness of his plight the young man gave the matron his mother's address and then asked: "How long can I live?"

"Only as long as I keep my finger upon this artery," Mrs. Pember replied.

Then followed a silence broken by the simple remark, "You can let go——."

"But I could not," wrote Mrs. Pember in her memoir. "Not if my own life had trembled in the balance. Hot tears rushed to my eyes, a surging sound to my ears, and a deathly coldness to my lips."

"The pang of obeying him was spared me," she added, "and for the first and last time during the trials that surrounded me for four years, I fainted away."

As previously indicated love of family and home was one of the most notable attributes of the common soldiers, and this sentiment found frequent expression in their correspondence. The heartache produced by the severance of family ties was vividly reflected in the letters of Private William Elisha Stoker, a semi-literate Texan who spent most of his two-year service in Arkansas. In September 1862, about six months after leaving home, he wrote his wife Betty: "When I think of the pleasure that we have enjoyed and then think of the situation that I am now placed in, it almost breaks my heart. . . . I am constern[tly] dreaming about home. I am afraid I am going to hear something unfavorable."

The following month Stoker wrote: "I was in hopes some time ago that we would hav peace now. . . . I want to come home. I want to see you and [my little daughter] Priscilla. I can't tell you how bad I want to see [you]. . . . When you write, fill a sheet every time if you can and if you cant think of nothing, get Priscilla to say some thing and write it. You wrote that she was as smart & as pretty as ever. I wish I could see you & her. I am afraid that you & hers features I will for get I have wis[hed] lots of times that I had of had your likeness taken & brought with me. Betty Shew Priscilla my ambletipe [ambrotype] and write what

A Confederate soldier and his loved one. Love of family and home was one of the most notable attributes of the common soldiers, a sentiment that found frequent expression in their correspondence. (Mississippi Department of Archives & History)

Rebs and Yanks. In May 1863, a Maine soldier stationed in Virginia wrote his homefolk: "I have seen men in the army [whose] . . . sickness and even death . . . was caused chiefly [by] discontent and homesickness."

Yanks and Rebs who were fathers repeatedly registered grave concern and deep affection for their children. Robert M. Gill of Mississippi wrote his wife Bettie in 1862: "I often ask myself whether our little Callie speaks of her Pa. Does she remember me? You must not whip her. I have a perfect horror of whipping children." Gill was exceptional in opposing whipping, because most fathers of his time sincerely believed that to spare the rod was to spoil the child. But his fatherly love had countless parallels in both armies. Some of the tenderest letters of Yanks and Rebs were addressed to their children. An Alabama soldier closed a letter to his wife thus: "I will say a few words to the Children Willia I waunt you to Bee a good Boy and minde youre Mother Markus I waunt you and Willia to Bee smarte and make smarte men and all ways tell the Truth and mind what you are told and minde your'e Mother."

Innumerable Rebs and Yanks repeatedly urged their children: "Be good, mind your mother and dont neglect your books"; and this advice reflected the most earnest desires of humble folk for their offspring.

The lovely Ellie Swain, daughter of the president of the University of North Carolina, had numerous Southern admirers. But after the Civil War ended, she was wooed and won by a Union Brigadier General. (North Carolina Collection, University of North Carolina Library)

she says about it." In February 1863, he informed Betty: "I dont know what kind of blessings I would have to come home & come walking up into the yard. . . . I think I must get about half tight to keep from Fainting when I get there, with over joy."

Stoker considered deserting, but when some of his comrades decided to go home and urged him to accompany them, he could not take this drastic step. "I told them no," he wrote Betty afterward, "[that] I loved my rib as well and would do as much as any boddy to see them [his family] on honerable terms but to desert and go it would throw a stigmey on me & her to[o] & it would be thrown up to Priscilla for years that her Par deserted the armey & wouldent fight for his cuntry. . . . I aint going to come home untell I can come like a white man. . . . I want to come so bad [that] I am nearley ded but that dont help the case any." Stoker apparently received a mortal wound at Jenkins' Ferry, April 30, 1864.

Stoker's distress at being separated from his family, extreme as it was, was exceeded by that of some other

The almost universal concern of Rebs and Yanks for the conventionality and piety of their families did not mean that they were uniformly decorous and refined in their tastes and customs. Indeed many of them were earthy in their interests and salty in their expressions. In their home letters they made frequent mention of the elemental functions of nature. Some referred to diarrhea as "The Virginia Quickstep" or "The Tennessee trots," but more called it "the sh-ts." One Yank wrote his wife: "I expect to be as tough as a knott as soon as I get over the Georgia Shitts," and another, heading his letter "Camp Sh-t," informed his spouse: "To tell the truth we are between a sh-t and a sweat out here." A North Carolina Reb wrote his wife concerning a comrade: "Marke Kelley . . . hant a friend in the company, it is thought that he will be put out of office for some misbehaveure with a woman on the cars and beter than all he shit in his briches and it run down his legs and filled his shoes."

An Illinois private wrote his wife early in 1862: "You say that our little Patty does not grow enough, well you must feed her well and give her lotts of 'titty'." A Reb, annoyed by reports that neighbors were criticizing him for alleged misconduct in camp, wrote his spouse: "The people . . . that . . . speakes slack about me may kiss my—. . . . Mollie please excuse my vulgar language."

Many Yanks and Rebs, and especially the younger ones, wrote friends back home about their amorous experiences with prostitutes and camp followers, and some spared no detail. One Reb even told what the fancy women of Petersburg charged him for their favors.

Evil, or, more specifically, activities regarded as evil by Americans of a century ago, abounded in Union and Confederate camps, and some of the most convincing testimonials as to the prevalence of sin came from the chaplains. The most rampant evils were swearing, gambling, drinking, thieving, and Sabbath breaking. But some soldiers stood fast against the devil's allurements. One of those was Private Orville Bumpass of Mississippi who wrote his wife near the end of his service: "Uncontaminated I left home & so I expect to return."

The overwhelming majority of soldiers on both sides were volunteers; indeed, the principal value of conscription, initiated by both Union and Confederacy in 1862, was to keep men already in uniform from going home, and to stimulate further volunteering.

After the volunteers signed up for service they proceeded to a nearby camp for completion of the transition from civilians to soldiers. Physical examination was a prescribed feature of induction, but in many instances medical scrutiny was so casual as to

Mrs. Sarah Emma Edmonds Seelye, alias Private Franklin Thompson. A native of Canada, she was unmarried when she served in disguise in the Union army. She was one of a considerable number of women who donned male attire, enlisted as men, and served for weeks or even years before officers discovered their sex. (Michigan Department of State Archives)

make it a mockery. Proof of perfunctoriness was found in the considerable number of women who donned male attire, enlisted as men, and served for periods ranging from weeks to years before officers discovered their sex. The most amazing instance of masquerade was that of "Albert Cashier," a farm woman of Irish background who, in August 1862, at 19, enlisted as a private in the 95th Illinois. She served throughout the remainder of the war and in 1865 returned to civilian life, still posing as a man.

In 1911, an automobile accident required her hospitalization and it was then that her sex was revealed. In 1899 she had qualified for a pension, and filed with her papers in Pension Bureau Records of the National Archives is a report of three physicians who examined her at that time stating that she was afflicted with piles that were so sensitive as to "bleed on slight touch," but containing no indication that she was a woman. After her sex was discovered thirteen years later, pension authorities reviewed her claim; they were told by one of her former comrades that "Cashier was very quite in her manner and she was not easy to get acquainted with. . . . When I was examined for enlistment, I was not stripped, and a woman would not have had any trouble in passing the examination." The reviewers, convinced that she had performed full service as a soldier, including participation in the Vicksburg, Red River, and Nashville Campaigns, recommended continuation of her pension; she drew it until her death in 1915.

After undergoing physical examination, however cursory, recruits were formally mustered into service. Many were inducted twice, first as state troops and a short time later as Union or Confederate soldiers. Induction into national service consisted of undergoing inspection (by companies) by the mustering officer, pledging allegiance to the United States or the Confederacy, promising to obey orders, and swearing to abide by the Articles of War, numbering 101, which were read as the concluding feature of the induction ceremony.

At some point in the transition from civilians to soldiers, the recruits chose their officers. As a rule the rank and file elected only their company officers (lieutenants and captains), who in turn chose the field grade officers (majors, lieutenant colonels, and colonels), but in some regiments soldiers elected all officers, from corporal to colonel. Usually they perfunctorily elected persons who had taken the lead in raising the units. Sometimes, though, elections were hotly contested affairs, with competitors using promises, food, and liquor to promote their candidacy.

Private A. Davenport of the 5th New York wrote his parents May 1, 1861: "The other night we held an election for 1st Lieut. Collins was our favorite but the officers of the Reg. wanted someone of their own class, in education, &c. Collins resigned in favor of Lieut. Hamblin, our Adjt. a fine man & a Scholar who was unanimously elected. . . . Hamblin made a very good Speech and invited us to join with him in a social glass of Brandy & water. The Col. [Abram Duryée] said that it was against the rules to allow any drinking, but as this was an especial occasion he would allow it."

Permitting men to choose their officers was a concession to new world individualism and democracy, and the consequences were often costly. This was true less often among Confederates than among Federals, because in the South's stratified society, recognized leaders generally raised units and got elected to office. Even so, some Confederate units had cause to complain of the ill effects of elections. Early in 1862 an intelligent and patriotic Mississippi lieutenant wrote his wife: "The want of capacity among our Company and Regimental officers is terrible. Some Captains cant read; others there are whose chirography would shame the heiroglyphics that bedeck the slopes of the

Egyptian pyramids. Regimental officers are scarcely any better."

During their first days in camp recruits drew clothing and equipment. For Confederate privates, uniforms consisted of gray coat—double-breasted and hip-length initially, but gradually replaced by a short-waisted single-breasted jacket (which gave Rebs the nickname "Gray Jackets"); gray trousers (throughout the war Confederate *Army Regulations* specified pants of sky blue color, but these apparently were never issued); cotton shirt of unspecified color; drawers; socks; shoes; cap (modeled after the French kepi); cravat of black leather; and double-breasted overcoat or "great coat" of gray flannel, fitted with cape.

Uniforms drawn by Yanks in 1861 were similar to those of Rebs, the principal difference being the color, which for Federals was dark blue for coats and light blue for trousers. Union overcoats were single-breasted and blouses were of two types—a long dress coat with high, stiff collar, and a short blue jacket, which was much preferred for field wear.

On both sides uniforms were trimmed with colors indicating branch of service—red for artillery, blue for infantry, and yellow for cavalry. Mounted troops had shorter coats than the infantry, preferred boots to shoes, and wore trousers reinforced in seat and legs.

Left: Confederate sergeant, cavalry. Right: Union private, infantry. For their regulation uniform, the South chose a gray tunic over light blue trousers. The Union chose a dark blue coat over light blue trousers. (Both: CWTI Collection)

Branch of service was also indicated on the buttons of officers by appropriate emblems for ordnance and engineers, and letters A, I, and C for artillery, infantry, and cavalry. Buttons of Union enlisted men were adorned with a spread-eagle design; those of the Confederate rank and file contained the number of their regiment, except for artillery, whose buttons bore the letter A.

In both armies headgear was decorated with branch insignia and colors: Union officers and non-commissioned officers below the grade of general wore crossed cannon for artillery, a bugle for infantry, crossed sabers for cavalry, turreted castle for engineers, and flaming shell for ordnance, along with a brass numeral designating regiment and, when applicable, a brass letter specifying company. Union privates wore brass letters and numerals, the latter beneath the former, indicating company and regiment; on the Confederate side branch was designated by the color of the cap crown.

Rank was also designated by trimmings and insignia. On the Union side the insignia, worn on shoulder straps, was virtually the same as that used in the U.S. Army today. On the Confederate side general officers of all grades wore the same markings—three stars in a wreath on the collar and four rows of braid on the sleeves. Confederate colonels wore three stars without the wreath; lieutenant colonels, two stars; majors, one star; captains, three bars; first lieutenants, two bars; and second lieutenants, one bar. Noncommissioned ratings in both armies were indicated by two or three chevrons on the sleeve.

Soldiers were generally nonchalant in their observance of uniform regulations, and as recruits seasoned into veterans they became less concerned with appearance than with comfort. Rebs generally substituted soft hats for caps and shortage of commercial dye and factory-made cloth caused them to shift to garments spun and woven by relatives and friends and colored with home-made dye. Coats and trousers, dyed with the juice of walnut hulls, had a yellowish tint suggestive of butternuts; this distinctive hue gave to Rebs the popular nickname "Butternuts."

Ties were worn by very few soldiers on either side; the general aversion to neckwear was reflected in a Reb's acknowledgement of a package from home: "I can put everything to advantag except the cravat—If I was to put it on the Boys would laugh at it." Drawers, generally ankle-length, were more widely used than ties, since they provided a safeguard against chafing of the flesh from rubbing of trousers on long marches. But many soldiers, especially rural Rebs unaccustomed to undergarments at home, felt no need of donning them when they went to camp.

Both Yanks and Rebs who went to war in 1861 wore heavy leather belts fastened with brass buckles.

Mississippi Private Joseph C. White. Both Confederates and Federals who went to war in 1861 wore heavy leather belts fastened with brass buckles. (CWTI Collection)

Some of the buckles were of fancy design, but enlisted men generally wore simple types stamped "U.S." or "C.S." As the Northern blockade tightened, both leather and metal became so scarce that most Rebs had to dispense with belts and use homemade galluses—or nothing at all—to hold up their pants.

Early in the war Rebs and Yanks normally carried extra articles of clothing—along with stationery, toilet articles, books, and photographs—in a knapsack. But in the course of campaigning most of them discarded their knapsacks and wrapped the contents, greatly diminished, in blankets draped from left shoulder to right hip and tied at the ends. Knapsacks made of canvas, rubberized cloth, or leather, and strapped to the back, were only one of several "trappings" with which new soldiers burdened themselves. Some took along to camp drinking tubes equipped with filters for use in sucking water from creeks and springs. Many Federals carried ponchos at one time or another, and Confederates appropriated for their use a considerable number of these raincoats.

Members of the 4th Michigan Infantry. Like all Union troops, they were better uniformed and equipped than their Confederate counterparts, particularly as the war progressed. (U.S. Army Military History Institute)

The veteran soldier—Union or Confederate—considered himself well equipped if he possessed a blanket rolled in tent canvas or an India-rubber cover; a cloth or rubber haversack, known also as a "bread bag," which resembled an old-fashioned school satchel; a canteen, usually of canvas-covered metal, though those of Confederates were sometimes homemade wooden containers which had the appearance of flattened kegs (at least one Reb improvised a canteen from a gourd); a musket; a leather cartridge box, loaded with forty rounds; a leather cap box; a bayonet in its sheath; a sewing kit; and mess equipment—hooked to the belt—consisting of metal plate, knife, fork, spoon, and cup, and sometimes a light skillet. The weight of all this impedimenta ranged from forty to fifty pounds.

Private A. Davenport, 5th New York, estimated the weight of his own equipment thus: "40 rounds ammunition, belt, &c . . . 4 lbs; canteen of water 4 lbs; Haversack of rations, 6 lbs; Musket, 14 lbs; Knapsack at least 20 lbs; besides the clothes we have on our backs." Most veteran Federals, and nearly all experienced Confederates, carried considerably less weight than this. Elimination of the knapsack and reduction

of its contents to ten pounds or less would produce a result that accorded more closely with established practice. Rare was the Southerner after the war's first year whose knapsack and food weighed six pounds. But even the lightest-traveling Confederate had to carry gun and ammunition, and he usually toted rations, water, blanket, tin cup and plate, and a few personal articles; all of these added up to about thirty pounds.

Shelter for Civil War soldiers varied considerably with time, seasons, location, and other circumstances. When the weather was balmy or the army on the march, the men often lived and slept under the open skies. Partly because of their prior mode of life and partly because of the Confederacy's limited resources, this unsheltered existence was considerably more common among Southerners than among their opponents.

The normal shelter, except in winter, was a tent. In the first months of the war, Sibley and wedge tents were in common use. The Sibley tent, shaped like a bell (one Confederate wrote that "it looked like a large hoop skirt standing up by itself on the ground"), was supported by an upright center pole. Its ten to twenty occupants slept with their feet to the center and heads near the edge, like spokes in a wheel.

Below: Confederate winter quarters at Centreville, Virginia, in 1862. Except in winter, the normal shelter of the common soldier was a tent, though in warm weather and during marches men often slept under open skies. (Library of Congress)

Wedge tents, commonly known as "A" tents, because from the end they looked like a capital A without the bar, were pieces of canvas stretched over a horizontal ridgepole, staked at the ground on both sides, and closed at the ends.

After 1861 the standard summer shelter of the rank and file was the shelter tent, widely known as the dog tent. In its most common version this was a two-man habitation made by buttoning together the half-shelters and stretching them over a horizontal pole supported at each end by a pronged stick or a musket stuck in the ground with bayonet fixed. Occasionally three or four soldiers would combine their half-shelters to make a larger tent; and if a man wanted to go it alone he simply tied the corners of his canvas to the tops of four upright sticks and crawled under.

During the winter months trench warriors took to "bombproof" dwellings that resembled the dugouts occupied by soldiers of recent wars. But the number of soldiers involved in trench warfare in winter was relatively small until the siege of Petersburg and Richmond. The winter quarters of most Civil War participants were log huts or "barricaded" tents. Logs of the huts' walls were horizontally laid after the fashion of frontier cabins or vertically arranged like those of a stockade. Cracks were daubed with mud and roofs were covered with boards or thatch. Barricaded or "winterized" tents were made by superimposing wedge or shelter tents on log bases. Like the log huts, they were usually occupied by four men. Spaciousness

and comfort were sometimes increased by digging out the earth floor to a depth of several feet. Tent roofs were waterproofed by stretching rubber blankets or ponchos over the canvas.

Heat was normally provided by fireplaces built of sticks and daubed with clay. Chimneys, similarly constructed, frequently were topped with commissary barrels to increase the draft.

The most important item in Johnny Reb's or Billy Yank's equipment was his gun. Early in the war this was sometimes a shotgun, a squirrel rifle, a Tower of London musket (dating back to the War of 1812), a Belgian rifle (calibre .70), an Austrian rifle (calibre .54), or a Harpers Ferry Model 1849 (also called a Mississippi Rifle). But after 1861 most Yanks and Rebs were armed with Springfield (calibre .58) or Enfield (calibre .577) rifled muskets. These were cumbersome weapons, firing conical, hollow-based minie bullets, but they were sturdy, dependable weapons, accurate at ranges of 200-300 yards and capable of killing a man at a distance of a half mile or more. Some soldiers were equipped with breech-loading rifles such as the Sharps, Maynard, Burnside, Morse or Star, and a few were fortunate enough to obtain seven-shot Spencer or sixteen-shot Henry repeaters. Cavalrymen usually were armed with short-barreled carbines.

In their letters Rebs and Yanks sometimes commented on their guns. They were sharply critical of the antiquated imports with which many of them were armed early in the war. A Wisconsin soldier described the Dresden rifles issued to his company as "miserable old things . . . [which] do about as much execution to the shooter as the shootee." A Hoosier private, who characterized his Belgian musket as "the poorest excuse of a gun I ever saw," complained: "I dont believe one could hit the broadside of a barn with them . . . the guns kick, oh my! no wonder they have cheek pieces in the stocks." Little wonder that soldiers referred to their outmoded muskets as "mules" and "pumpkin slingers."

Most Rebs and Yanks wrote approvingly of Enfield and Springfield guns. Concerning the former, one Yank stated: "We went out the other day to try them. We fired 600 yards and we put 360 balls into a mark the size of old Jeff [Davis]."

Repeating rifles received the highest praise. A Mississippian whose company in 1862 drew five-shot Colt rifles informed his homefolk: "It is right funny to see the boys [of other companies] come over . . . to see our guns, take hold of them and say 'by golly boys if we all had guns like these we would clean the Yankees up in six months'." A Connecticut soldier, whose regiment was armed with Spencer repeaters,

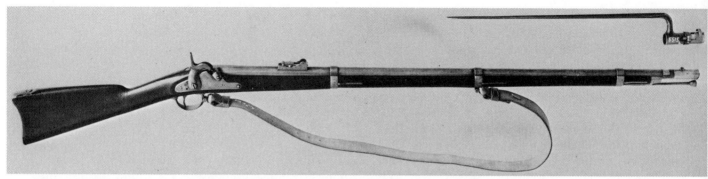

Confederate Richmond muzzleloading musket, caliber .69. (West Point Museum Collection)

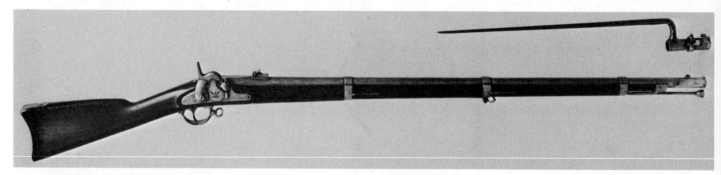

U.S. Springfield muzzleloader, Model 1855, caliber .58. (West Point Museum Collection)

His gun was a soldier's most important piece of equipment. Here: Pennsylvania Lancers, in camp, with the wagon of famed Civil War photographer Mathew Brady in the background. First armed with lancers, these cavalrymen later switched to pistols and carbines. (Library of Congress)

wrote from near City Point, Virginia, May 19, 1864: "Our Reg't. has been under fire from the Rebs 8 days. . . . The Rebs made 3 charges on us but we stood up to the rack with our 7 Shooters & repulsed them each time & we piled the Rebs in heaps in front of us. The Rebs hate our guns they call them the Yankes 7 Devils They say see the G. D. Yankeys stand up there with their G. D. Coffy mills wind em up in the morning run all day. . . . We are as good as a Brigade."

While learning to use their guns and other military equipment, Rebs and Yanks had to adjust to a regimented routine that differed markedly from civilian practice. Life in camp was regulated by drum or bugle calls, and these normally ran to about a dozen a day. The first was reveille, sounded at dawn or thereabouts, to rouse the men from their slumber and summon them to roll call. After lining up and responding to their names, they might be put through a brief and rapid drill, but usually they were left on their own until the second call about thirty minutes later hailed them to breakfast. The third signal shortly afterward sent the ailing to the regimental surgeon and the well to such fatigue duties as cleaning quarters, policing company grounds, and cutting wood.

At guard mounting, sounded about 8 o'clock, the first sergeant of each company called out and inspected his detail for the next twenty-four-hour stint, and marched them to the regimental parade ground. There, to the accompaniment of music provided by the regimental band, the guards were formed into line, inspected by the adjutant, and sent off to their respective posts. The next signal was for drill, which frequently lasted until the call, sometimes known as "roast beef," announced the time for lunch.

After a brief interval of free time came another call for drill, which normally lasted one to two hours. Drill over, the men returned to their quarters, brushed uniforms, polished buttons and buckles, and cleaned their weapons in anticipation of the call to retreat, which consisted of roll call, inspection, and dress parade. Both officers and men took great pride in the dress parade, held sometimes by regiment and sometimes by brigade, and always to the accompaniment of music.

The call to supper was sounded shortly after retreat. Then came another period of free time, after which tattoo brought companies back into line to answer roll. Upon dismissal the men returned to their quarters. The day was officially concluded by the sounding of taps, which signaled the extinguishing of lights and the cessation of noise.

This was typical routine for an infantry regiment during a period of quiet. Practices varied, of course, in different commands and with changing circumstances. Sunday routine was different from that of any other day. The big event of the Sabbath was a general inspection of personnel, equipment, quarters, grounds, kitchens, hospitals, and other facilities. Preliminary checks were made by the units' own officers. But the climax was inspection of the regiment by an outsider, usually the brigade commander or one of his staff. The inspector marched up and down the open ranks scrutinizing uniforms and arms, but he also poked into the knapsacks that the men had unslung, opened, and laid on the ground for his examination. Detection of the smallest particle of dirt or the slightest deviation from uniform regulations was almost certain to bring sharp reproof from the inspector and a tongue lashing from the captain after return to quarters.

This inspection and the preparations that it required consumed most of the morning. "Knapsack drill," as the Confederates and Federals called the Sunday exercise, was an exhausting experience, and the soldiers of the sixties regarded it with dread. But like the other aspects of the regimentation of which it was a part, it helped mold undisciplined individuals into smoothly functioning organizations.

As the novelty of camp life wore off, recruits lost most of their initial enthusiasm for soldiering, and many complained of their regimentation. Charles H. Thiot of the 1st Georgia quoted approvingly a comrade's observation that "if he lived to see the close of this war he meant to get two pups and name one of them 'fall in' and the other 'close up' and as soon as they were old enough to know their names right well he intended to shoot them both, and thus put an end to 'fall in' and 'close up'." A Louisiana Reb wrote from an Alabama camp December 25, 1862:

"A soldier is not his own man, he has given up all claim on himself. He has placed his life in the hands of his superiors, he is as a checker player uses his men, if they see a chance to swap one for two they do it. I will give you a little information conserning evry day business. consider yourself a private soldier and in camp. you are not allowed to go outside the lines without a pass from your Comp commander approved by the cornel of the Reg. Well, you get youre pass more than once you go in some shop. in comes a guard with his muskett and says have you got a pass. you pull her out, she is all right. you go sauntering around and the first thing you know you are in somewhere where you have no business. you are very abrubly asked by a man with a muskett if you belong there. you very politely tell him you do not. he tells you to leave. you immediately obey or be sent to the guard house. you go back to camp. the drum beats for drill. you fall in and start. you here feel youre inferirority. even the Sargeants is hollering at you close up, Ketch step, dress to the right, ans sutch like.

Band of the 114th Pennsylvania Infantry at Brandy Station in March 1864. Like other Zouave regiments, these soldiers were colorfully dressed, each wearing a short jacket, broad sash, loose pants, and fez. (U.S. Army Military History Institute)

Similar sentiments were expressed by D. P. Chapman of the 93d Illinois, who wrote from Camp Douglas in 1862: "They keep us very strict here, it is the most like a prison of any place I ever saw. There is a high board fence around the grounds and a guard also with muskets loaded. . . . It comes rather hard at first to be deprived of liberty."

Rebs and Yanks found various diversions to relieve the boredom and deprivations of camp. One of the most satisfying recreations was singing. Soldiers of the sixties were the "singing-est" soldiers in American history, and the Civil War inspired more "sing-able" songs of the sort that endure than any other conflict. Letters and diaries indicate that the songs enjoyed most were "When This Cruel War Is Over," "The Girl I Left Behind Me," "Just Before the Battle Mother," and "Tenting on the Old Camp Ground," along with such old favorites as "Annie Laurie," "Auld Lang Syne," "Juanita," "Lilly Dale," "Sweet Evalina," and "Listen to the Mocking Bird."

Also rating high in camp popularity were the grand old hymns, "All Hail the Power of Jesus' Name," "How Firm a Foundation," "Rock of Ages," "Jesus Lover of My Soul," "Nearer My God to Thee," and "On Jordan's Stormy Banks I Stand."

Patriotic and martial songs were sung with great gusto on the march and about the campfire. Top favorites of this category among Yanks were "Battle Hymn of the Republic," "John Brown's Body," "Happy Land of Canaan," "Gay and Happy Still," "Tramp, Tramp, Tramp," "Battle Cry of Freedom," "Yankee

Doodle," and "Star Spangled Banner." Among Rebs "Dixie" and "Bonnie Blue Flag" ranked highest but great favor was also accorded "Maryland, My Maryland" and "All Quiet Along the Potomac Tonight." Perhaps the favorite of all Southern sentimentals was the sweet and plaintive "Lorena."

Both sides had their comic songs: Yanks favored "The Blue Tail Fly," "Shoo, Fly, Shoo," "Pop Goes the Weasel," and "The Captain and His Whiskers"; Rebs enjoyed these too, along with "Oh How I Hate to Get Up in the Morning" and "Goober Peas." Without doubt the most popular of all songs among both soldiers and civilians of the Civil War era was "Home Sweet Home."

Songfests were supplemented by instrumental music. Regimental and brigade bands provided music on ceremonial occasions and sometimes gave concerts in the evening. Informal groups entertained their comrades with minstrel performances featuring stringed instruments. Almost every company had one or more talented violinists or banjoists who liked to render such rollicking tunes as "Billy in the Low Grounds," "Arkansas Traveller," "My Old Kentucky Home," and "Oh Lord Gals One Friday."

Another favorite diversion was gambling. Yanks and Rebs "shot craps" and rolled dice in a banking game known as chuck-a-luck, sweet-cloth, or birdcage. Around campfires, at breaks on the march, and even while awaiting orders to advance in battle they brought out cards to risk their meager pay at poker, twenty-one, euchre, or keno. They also gambled on horse races, wrestling matches, boxing contests, cockfights, and louse races. When, in the Confederacy, paper shortage and dearth of funds made it impossible for Rebs to buy cards, they made their own, decorating them sometimes with likenesses of Jeff Davis.

In both armies religious men were shocked and grieved by the pervasiveness of gambling. A Mississippian wrote his mother shortly after a pay day late in 1862: "chuck-a-luck and Faro banks are running night and day, with eager and excited crowds standing around with their hands full of money. Open gambling has been prohibited, but that amounts to nothing." Early in the same year, John A. Harris of the 19th Louisiana wrote his wife: "This is the worst place [in] the world for men to get into bad habits. . . . I had no idea when I left home that Sullivan would even Gamble, but he has done so. . . . John Dance . . . is playing cards regular, but dont play for money yet. He plays for Coffee and such as that. He is just now what I would call a Student of Gambling. I . . . have tried to shame him. At first he was Shigh about it but now he is bold."

Checkers, dominoes, and chess also had their dev-

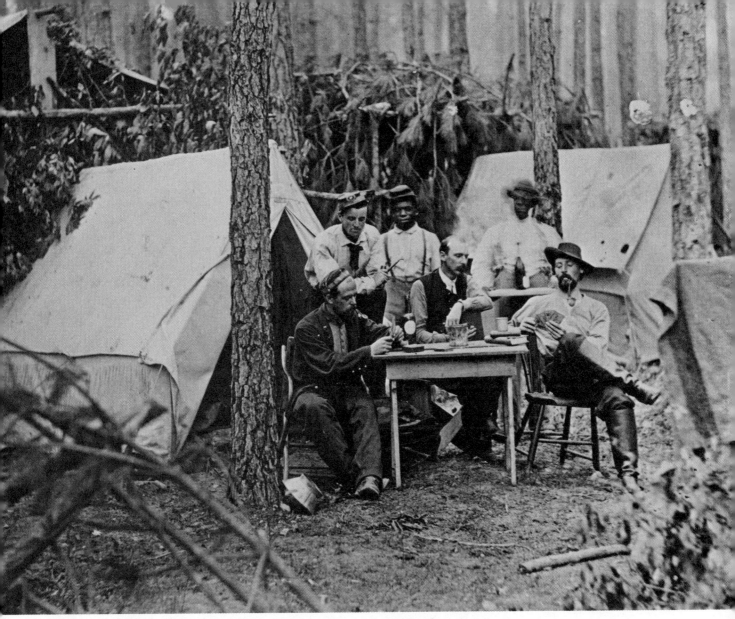

The "Four Guardsmen's Mess": Officers of the 114th Pennsylvania Infantry in front of Petersburg, August 1864. Playing cards, from left: Captains A.H.G. Richardson, G.W. Bratton, and H.E. Rulon. Watching are Captain J.S. Crawford and two Negro soldiers. (CWTI Collection)

otees, but were never as popular as card games. Both Rebs and Yanks played early versions of baseball, but the sports most commonly enjoyed were foot races, broadjumping, leapfrogging, boxing, and wrestling. In winter, snowball fights occurred, with participants battling in companies and regiments, under command of their officers. Prisoners were taken as in regular combat and when snow pellets were loaded with rocks or bullets, as was sometimes the case, painful casualties resulted.

Reading provided recreation for many. Newspapers and magazines were passed around in camp until they were literally worn out and the same was true of some books and pamphlets. Shakespeare, Milton, Hugo, and Dumas had some appreciative readers, but classic writers were far less popular than "Bill Arp," "Mr. Dooley," and the authors of Beadle's "Dime Novels,"

and paperback comics such as "Phunny Fellow" and "Budget of Fun." Rebs and Yanks, like soldiers of other wars, spent some of their leisure reading "racy" booklets and poring over pictures of nude or scantily attired females. Yanks, owing to their better pay and the more abundant offerings of Northern printers, had greater opportunity for indulging pornographic tastes than did Rebs.

In the absence of travelling troupes (the Hutchinson Family Singers, who toured the Army of the Potomac, was a notable exception) and organized recreational programs, Rebs and Yanks had to provide their own entertainment. Usually diversions were spontaneous and informal, but some units had enough initiative and talent to present theatricals of considerable merit. Even so, camp life was for most a dull and dreary existence.

Card games were popular among soldiers on both sides. When their store-bought playing cards wore out, the men made their own cards. (Special Collections, Emory University Library)

Largely because of this unhappy situation, breaches of discipline were frequent. Perhaps the most common offense was absence without leave, though liquor-inspired brawling ran a close second. Major General George B. McClellan early in 1862 declared that "drunkenness is the cause of by far the greater part of the disorders which are examined by the courts-martial." Another common offense frequently associated with drinking was insubordination. This usually consisted of enlisted men speaking disrespectfully to their superiors. One Yank, when placed under arrest, told his lieutenant: "You ain't worth a pinch of sh-t" and another, offended by a reprimand, said to the rebuking officer, "You kiss my arse, you God damned louse." A Louisiana artilleryman, annoyed by loud singing emanating from an officer's tent, shouted angrily "Shut up." Another Reb told a lieutenant who ordered him punished for disobedience, "No one but a damned coward would have a soldier bucked . . . if you will pull off your insignia of rank I will whip you on the spot." Rebs and Yanks applied a great variety of epithets to officers who offended them, including, "damned puppy," "sh-t-house adjutant," "bugger," "skunk," and "whore-house pimp," but their favorite expletive was the time-honored "son of a bitch."

Drinking generally was forbidden in the camps of both armies. Nonetheless, both officers and their men drank. Drunkenness frequently led to brawls and insubordination, the latter usually consisting of speaking disrespectfully to superiors. (Library of Congress)

Another military offense to which the restriction and monotony of camp often contributed was desertion. Soldiers who unlawfully left the service aggregated about 100,000 Confederates and 200,000 Federals. On both sides hunger was a factor in desertion; this was especially true of Confederates in the latter part of the war. "If I ever lose my patriotism," one Reb wrote his homefolk, "then you may know the 'Commissary' is at fault. Corn meal mixed with water and tough beef three times a day will knock the 'Brave Volunteer' under quicker than Yankee bullets."

Inadequacy of food also was the cause of much of the theft and pillage that abounded in Northern and Southern camps. Soldiers stole money, watches, jewelry, and clothing from each other in order to obtain means for supplementing their meager rations. For the same purpose some roamed battlefields under cover of night rifling the pockets of the dead. Individually and in groups they scoured the countryside preying on helpless civilians and giving little if any consideration to whether their victims were friends or foes. Hungry soldiers repeatedly raided pig pens, chicken roosts, orchards, and gardens located near their camps, and the propensity for "foraging"—the military euphemism for such depredation—was about as great in one army as it was in the other. Not all theft and pillage was motivated by hunger, of course;

Military authorities resorted to a variety of punishments in an effort to maintain discipline. Particularly painful was tying men up by the wrists or thumbs with a rope thrown over a limb, tightening the rope until only the toes touched the ground. (Library of Congress)

much of it had its origins in human depravity and the degenerating tendencies of army life.

Military authorities resorted to a great variety of punishments in an effort to maintain discipline. For minor offenses one of the most widely used penalties was confinement in the guard house, which usually was not a house at all, but a tent, a stockade, or a small plot of ground watched over by one or more armed guards. Confinement ranged in duration from a few hours to a month, depending on the seriousness of the offense; sometimes prisoners were limited to bread-and-water rations during all or a part of their incarceration.

Another common punishment was the wearing of a ball and chain. The ball was normally a cannon ball, weighing from six to thirty-two pounds, and it was attached to the leg by a chain two to six feet long. Culprits were required to walk about the camp, for varying periods, dragging the shackles behind them.

A similar penalty was the carrying of a heavy object of some sort—a log balanced on the shoulder, a bag of dirt or bricks tied to the back, or a rock or cannon ball held in the hands—for repeated stints of one to four hours interspersed by brief periods of rest. This could be a very painful punishment. A Texan told of a comrade who, for firing his gun in camp, had to carry a heavy log for three hours: "The first hour he done well, the second hour he was walking slow and looking serious and changing the stick from right to left and from left to right and calling for the time of day, and long before the third hour was out he was begging for mercy."

A corrective frequently applied by unit commanders was to force men to parade the company streets wearing large placards specifying their offense, such as "Coward," "Thief," or "I stole a skillet." A Union cavalryman had to walk up and down the parade ground carrying on his back a saddle that he had stolen. A Confederate who appropriated a citizen's pig had to wear the porker's skin around his neck in the presence of his comrades; and another Southerner who got the jitters while on picket and shot a dog had to lug the dead animal about the camp at double quick pace. A Confederate found guilty of selling whiskey in camp was placarded with the notice "Ten Cents a Glass," and ridden about the camp on a rail, with three bottles dangling from his feet.

Many petty misdoers were subjected to the humiliation of "wearing the barrel shirt." The barrel was fitted by cutting a hole in the bottom, so that it could be slipped over the wearer's head, and by making openings in each side through which to pass his arms. Usually a sign indicating the misdeed was attached to the outside of the "shirt."

Other lesser punishments were assignment to extra guard duty, though some officers condemned this practice on the ground that it tended to degrade a responsible function intimately associated with soldierly honor; digging ditches; grubbing stumps; riding the wooden horse, a horizontal pole held aloft by two upright beams; standing on some conspicuous pedestal, such as a barrel, stump, or box; and cleaning the company grounds.

A penalty frequently imposed for insubordination was bucking and gagging. This consisted of placing the offender in a sitting position, tying his hands together and slipping them over his knees, inserting a pole or musket beneath the knees and over the arms and tying a stick or bayonet in the mouth with a string. When prolonged for several hours, as frequently was the case, this was a terrible punishment. An officer who witnessed the bucking and gagging of a Federal artilleryman at Memphis in 1864 wrote afterward to his wife: "[after] 4 hours he was sobbing and crying as if suffering greatly. When untied he was not able to walk. . . . He was *carried* to his quarters."

Even more inhuman was the punishment, frequently meted out for "back talk," of tying men up by their wrists or thumbs with a rope thrown over a limb. Sometimes the victims were allowed to rest their full weight on their feet, but the general practice was to tighten the rope until only the toes touched the ground, thus placing a great strain on the wrists or thumbs and causing the cord to cut into the flesh. Little wonder that men subjected to this torture after a while groaned and screamed in agony and that comrades, incensed by the brutality, angrily demanded their release and even cut them loose, sometimes at the risk of being subjected to the same punishment themselves.

A cruel punishment used in the artillery was to strap a culprit, with arms and legs extended in spread-eagle fashion, to the spare wheel carried on the rear of the caisson. If the vehicle remained stationary, and if the victim lay with his head at the top of the wheel for no more than an hour or two, the discomfort might be relatively mild. But if the wheel was given a half-turn so as to place the prisoner in a horizontal position, the time extended to several hours, and the caisson driven over rough roads, as was sometimes the case, it became an excruciatingly painful punishment.

The Federal and Confederate Congresses by acts passed respectively in August 1861, and in April 1862, prohibited the flogging of soldiers. But the injunction was sometimes ignored. Both North and South accepted branding as a legal punishment throughout the war, and courts-martial records show that it was widely used. The brand was usually the

A capital offense: The military execution by firing squad of James Griffin, alias John Thomas Barnett, a private of the 11th Pennsylvania Cavalry, for "desertion and highway robbery," at Portsmouth, Virginia, on September 17, 1863. (Library of Congress)

144

first letter of the offense committed—"D" for desertion, "C" for cowardice, "T" for thievery, and "W" for worthlessness—and it was either stamped on with indelible ink or burned into the skin with a red-hot iron. The usual place of application was the hip, hand, forehead, or cheek.

Deserters, cowards and other serious offenders sometimes were required as a part of their punishment to have half or all of their head shaved. To this and other penalties occasionally was added the provision that the victims be dishonorably discharged, stripped of their buttons and insignia, and drummed out of the camp. Drumming out was done to the tune of "The Rogue's March"—Confederates sometimes substituted "Yankee Doodle"—with soldiers in front and behind carrying arms reversed—in the presence of the regiment, brigade, or division to which the culprit belonged.

Another punishment frequently prescribed for serious offenses was imprisonment. Terms varied from a few years to life, and the place of confinement usually was a penitentiary or a military prison like the Federal "Rip-Raps" near Norfolk or the Dry Tortugas off the coast of Florida.

A few capital offenders (deserters, murderers, rapists, mutineers, spies, and the like) were hanged, but most soldiers who paid the death penalty were shot by firing squads. The shooting of soldiers was an awful spectacle, described in gruesome detail by many in their letters and reminiscences. The horror of these affairs was frequently enhanced by the clumsiness that required as many as three rounds of firing before the victims were finally put out of their misery.

Sleeping on sentry was a capital offense. Officers did a great deal of talking about its seriousness, and a considerable number of men adjudged guilty of dozing at their posts were sentenced to be shot. But the records do not show a single instance of a Civil War soldier actually paying the death penalty for sleeping on sentry.

While punishment was the principal reliance of commanders for combating crime and gross immorality, chaplains and the men to whom they ministered leaned heavily on religion to promote order and decency among the soldiers. In general the quality of Civil War chaplains left much to be desired, since the best ministers usually were reluctant to give up the security and comforts of civilian life for the uncertainty and hardship of camp. There were many notable exceptions, of course, among them such chaplains as John A. Brouse of the 100th Indiana and Charles T. Quintard of the 1st Tennessee.

Religious services, like diversions, were in large part provided by the soldiers themselves. Groups of them assembled on Sunday, usually in the afternoon or evening to avoid conflict with morning inspection, for preaching, singing, and prayer. Often the sermon was given by a company or regimental officer, or by one of the enlisted men.

After listening to Colonel Granville Moody, a distinguished minister who commanded the 74th Ohio, a Yank stated: "It was one of the most eloquent sermons I ever heard." Brigadier General William N. Pendleton, Confederate artillery chief, who at Manassas allegedly exclaimed while drawing a bead on the Yankees, "Lord preserve the soul while I destroy the body," often preached to his men. A sergeant who heard him speak in a log tabernacle late in 1864, wrote afterward: "I never listened to more solemn and impressing remarks."

When the military situation permitted, religiously inclined soldiers held informal week-day meetings,

featuring prayers, testimonies, and songs. During months when the armies were in winter quarters, religious activities were intensified, with the result that great, emotion-charged revivals swept through the camps leading many sinners to repentance.

In some instances unit commanders led their men in prayer before taking them into battle. At religious services, and during intervals between worship, chaplains and colporteurs distributed tracts, made available in great quantities by church presses. These bore such titles as "Why Do You Swear?," "The Gambler's Balance Sheet," "Sufferings of the Lost," "Satan's Baits," "The Temperance Letter," and "A Mother's Parting Words to her Soldier Boy." Both the tracts and the religious periodicals distributed in camp were widely read, not primarily because they aroused soldier interest but rather because of a dearth of secular books and papers.

The abundant exposure of Rebs and Yanks to re-

ligious literature, sermons, and prayers undoubtedly led to some improvement in discipline and morals. However, reform in most instances seems to have been limited both in scope and endurance. Certainly in most Civil War camps, evil was far more pervasive and persistent than righteousness.

Chaplains and others interested in promoting piety in Civil War camps placed great emphasis on the precariousness of life among men in arms. In stressing this direful note they were well within the bounds of fact.

The principal killer of Civil War participants was sickness. Indeed, the number of Yanks and Rebs who died of disease was more than twice the number who died of battle causes. The great prevalence of disease and the shockingly high death rate among those stricken by sickness, resulted from a combination of factors. First, the fact that a majority were rural meant that many, if not most, of them had not previously been exposed to measles and other diseases common among urban children. When they were crowded into camp these contagious maladies struck with epidemic force. The victims, unaware of the danger, did not take proper care of themselves, and many developed complications that proved fatal.

A second reason for the frequency and deadliness of disease was ignorance of both cause and treatment on the part of physicians and patients. Bacteriology was an undeveloped science. Malaria and other illnesses were attributed to "miasms" arising from the lowlands and poisonous vapors permeating the atmosphere. Largely because of ignorance, sanitation and other safeguards against the contraction and spread of infectious disease were grossly inadequate.

A third cause of the widespread susceptibility to sickness was diet. Camp fare was usually deficient in fruits and vegetables, and milk was very difficult to obtain. This was especially true on the Confederate side, and the frequency of Johnny Reb's complaints of suffering from "the sh-ts" afforded abundant evidence of his dietary deficiencies.

And finally on both sides filth contributed greatly to dysentery and other maladies that plagued the camps. Most Yanks and Rebs thought only of convenience when disposing of waste and responding to the call of nature. A Reb wrote in his diary December 8, 1863: "On rolling up my bed this morning I found I

Father Thomas H. Mooney conducts Sunday morning mass in the camp of the 69th New York. Civil War chaplains and the men to whom they ministered leaned heavily on religion to promote order and decency among the soldiers. (Library of Congress)

had been lying in . . . something that didn't smell like milk and peaches."

Refuse and offal accumulating in and around camps attracted hordes of flies that crawled over food and spread germs far and near. An Alabamian wrote his wife in June 1862: "There are more flies here than I ever saw any where before, sometimes I . . . commence killing them but as I believe forty come to everyone's funeral I have given it up as a bad job."

Germ-spreading mosquitoes, fleas, and body lice tormented soldiers even more than flies. A New Englander stationed in Louisiana wrote his homefolk in 1863: "We are in sore trouble with poisonous animals in the water, fleas on the ground and mosquitoes in the air." About the same time a Pennsylvanian encamped near Fredericksburg, Virginia, wrote his brother: "I do not believe [that after Antietam] there was a man in our brigade . . . but was lousy."

Medical reports show an aggregate of 6,029,564 cases of sickness on the Union side. Confederate records are incomplete, but if illnesses were half as numerous among Southerners as among the Federals (who outnumbered them by more than two to one), as they undoubtedly were, cases on both sides totalled something over 9,000,000. The most common maladies were "looseness of the bowels," (diarrhea, dysentery, "flux," and scurvy), and measles and malaria (generally called "the shakes"). Pneumonia, smallpox, yellow fever, and tuberculosis were of less frequent occurrence, but all of them took a heavy toll of lives.

The principal killers on both sides, however, were typhoid and intestinal infections. Typhoid probably was responsible for one fourth of all deaths from disease among Civil War participants. On the Confederate side, and possibly among Federals as well, as many soldiers died of what they called "the sh-ts" as were killed in combat.

Civil War surgeons, reflecting the scientific backwardness of their time, often did their patients more harm than good. They amputated limbs and probed wounds with dirty instruments, dosed diarrhea patients with whiskey and strong purgatives and bled both sick and wounded with lancet or leech. The

The precariousness of life: A soldier's drawing of the inside of a Union hospital tent. The principal killer of Civil War soldiers was not battle but disease. (National Archives)

Wounded soldiers rest near Marye's house during the Battle of Chancellorsville. The man on the litter has just had his foot amputated. Civil War surgeons, reflecting the scientific backwardness of their time, often amputated limbs and probed wounds with dirty instruments, thereby doing their patients more harm than good. (National Archives)

victims of such ministrations were quick to denounce their tormentors. An Ohioan wrote from near Vicksburg in March 1863: "hell will be Filde with doters and offersey when this war is over," and one Reb complained that "the Doctors kill more than they cour" while another rated surgeons as the "most unworthy of all the human famaly."

It is not meant to suggest that medical practices in Civil War armies were uniformly bad or that surgeons were universally incompetent, for such was not the case. Lessons learned from war experience and experimentation led to some decided improvements: notably in evacuating battle casualties; in transporting the wounded from combat zones by rail and ship; in developing pavilion type hospitals; and, on the Confederate side especially, in improvising substitutes for scarce drugs. Particularly outstanding were the achievements of Doctors Samuel H. Stout and Joseph Jones on the Confederate side and of William A. Hammond and Jonathan Letterman among the

Federals. Even so, the plight of Rebs and Yanks who were sick or wounded was generally terrible and the suffering that they endured exceeded that of participants in other American wars.

Though ignorance, germs, exposure, and hunger caused far more suffering and death than combat, fighting was the aspect of soldiering that caused greatest concern to most Civil War participants. Ralph Ingersoll aptly noted that for soldiers in World War II "the battle is the payoff." He might well have said the same of Johnny Rebs and Billy Yanks, for closing with the enemy was for most the principal reason for entering the service and the climactic episode of their army experience. Generally they contemplated initiation into combat with a mixture of eagerness, nervousness, and dread. A Tennessee Reb wrote in his diary of his baptism of fire at Williamsburg, May 5, 1862:

I was not much surprised when we received the order to fall in. . . . I can never forget my thoughts as I stood there and looked around. . . . It was the first time I had ever been called upon to face death. I felt in a few moments some of us standing here, vainly trying to jest and appear careless, would be in eternity. . . . The feeling called *fear* did not enter my breast, but it was painful, nervous anxiety, a longing for action . . . and a dull feeling about the chest that made breathing difficult. All the energies of my soul seemed concentrated in the one desire for action. We were not kept long in suspense for very soon orders came for us to go forward. . . . We advanced slowly . . . when the crack of a rifle and the falling of a man announced to us that we were in the range of the enemy's sharpshooting.

A Mississippian wrote his sweetheart in June 1862, after his first fight near Corinth: "I am glad to say that i was not scarde though i felt sorter curies. . . . though i did not run i mite have run if i had thought of it in time." Concerning his baptism of fire at Shiloh another Mississippian wrote in his diary:

We are moving in line of battle cautiously and slowly. I have the shakes badly. Well I am not alone—in fact we all look like the shaky Quackers. Scared? Oh, no; only an old fashioned rigor. . . . Oh how I wish I was a dwarf, just now, instead of a six-footer.

A Yank anticipating his first fight wrote his father: "I have a marked dread of the battle field, for I . . . have never seen a person die . . . & I am afraid that the groans of the wounded & dying will make me shake nevertheless I hope & trust that strength will be given me to stand & do my duty."

So great was the anxiety of soldiers awaiting their baptism of fire that when finally they entered into battle they experienced a sense of relief. "With your first shot you become a new man," wrote a Reb after First Manassas. "Fear has no existence in your bosom. Hesitation gives way to an uncontrollable desire to rush into the thickest of the fight. . . . You become cool and deliberate, and watch the effect of bullets . . . and [cannon] balls as they rake their murderous channels through your ranks . . . with a feeling so callous . . . that your soul seems dead to every sympathizing . . . thought."

A similar reaction was experienced by a Massachusetts private who wrote his mother after his first battle: "As . . . the bullets began to whiz about us, I thought to myself, 'now the test is coming' & I wondered if I should meet it bravely. I nerved myself up . . . and moved forward at the command, expecting to be hit. . . . After the first round the fear left me and I was as cool as ever I was in my life."

In the trenches: Union troops await the call to combat at Petersburg, 1865. Photograph by Mathew Brady. (U.S. Army)

The seasoning that came after their first exposure to combat enabled Yanks and Rebs to go into battle with less anxiety about "playing the coward," and with increasing indifference to the fate of their comrades. Many gained composure by taking the fatalistic view that every man had an appointed time to die and until that time arrived life was secure regardless of the fury of enemy fire. Religiously inclined soldiers tended to interpret successive battle survivals as evidence of God's purpose to see them safely through the war. But the dread of battle lingered on in the minds of most soldiers and in some it increased, owing largely to a belief that luck could not last always and that they would be victims of the law of averages.

The metamorphosis experienced by many veterans on both sides was vividly expressed by a Georgian of Lee's army, in a letter of November 19, 1864, to his wife:

> I do not know what is getting into me but I am getting more and more scary every fight I go into. . . . In the first two or three engagements I shared in, I felt a sort of exultation in moving about unhurt when others about me were shot down, but all that seems to be done away with now & I am getting . . . as nervous about the whistling of bullets as any person I know of & I actually *suffer* when going into a fight, particularly when I have been looking forward to it for several days. Fortunately this feeling wears off very rapidly when once really in for it.

Both in their baptisms of fire and in their subsequent battles soldier experiences and reactions varied greatly. Representative of the actions and impressions of many Civil War soldiers in many engagements were those recorded by 16-year-old Private William H. Brearley of the 17th Minnesota, after Antietam, his second battle, and by Private Edmund D. Patterson, age 20, in the wake of his fourth fight, Gaines's Mill. On September 26, 1862, Brearley wrote:

> It was rather strange music to hear the balls Scream within an inch of my head. I had a bullet strike me on the top of the head just as I was going to fire and a piece of Shell struck my foot—a ball hit my finger and another hit my thumb. I concluded they ment me. the rebels played the mischief with us by raising a U.S. flag.

Building a pontoon bridge under fire at Fredericksburg. Many soldiers gained composure by taking the fatalistic view that every man had an appointed time to die. (Library of Congress)

we were ordered not to fire and as soon as we went forward they opened an awful fire from their batteries on us we were ordered to fall back about 1/2 miles, I staid behind when our regiment retreated and a line of skirmishers came up—I joined them and had a chance of firing about 10 times more—in about an hour we had to fall back to the regiment—it was then about 6 P.M. I have heard and seen pictures of battles—they would all be in line all standing on a nice level field fighting, a number of ladies taking care of the wounded &c. &c. but it isent so, much, in both of these battles the rebels had Stone walls to get behind and the woods to fall back in. Our generals say they (the rebels) had as strong a position as could *possibly* be and we had to pick into them through an old chopping all grown up with bushes so thick that we couldent hardly get through—but we were so excited that the 'old scratch' himself couldent have stopt us. We *rushed* on them evry man for himself—all loading & firing as fast as he could see a rebel to Shoot at—at last the rebels began to get over the wall to the rear and run for the woods. the firing encreased tenfold then it sounded like the rolls of thunder and all the time evry man shouting as loud as he could—I got rather more excited than I wish to again. I dident *think* of getting hit but it was almost a miricle that I wasent the rebels that we took prisoners said that they never before encountered a regiment that fought so like "Devils" (so they termed it) as we did—every one praised our regiment—one man in our company was Shot through the head no more than 4 feet from me he was killed instantly. after the battle I took care of the wounded until 11 P.M. I saw some of the horidest sights I ever saw—one man had both eyes shot out—and they were wounded in all the different ways you could think of—the most I could do was to give them water—they were all very thirsty. . . . I was so dry at one time I could have drank out of a mud puddle—without stopping to ask questions—Our Colonel . . . is just as cool as can be, he walked around amongst us at the battle the bullets flying all around him—he kept Shouting to us to fire low and give it to them.

After the action at Gaines's Mill, near Richmond, June 27, 1862, Patterson wrote in his diary:

About five O'clock in the evening the order was given; 'Forward Guide, Center March, Charge Bayonets.' Up to the crest of the hill we went at a double quick, but when we came into view on the top of the ridge we met such a perfect storm of lead right in our faces that the whole brigade literally *staggered* backward several paces as though pushed by a tornado. The dead lay in heaps, and two minutes in that position would have been utter annihilation. Just for one moment we faltered, then the cry of Major Sorrell, 'Forward Alabamians,—Forward!', and the cry was taken up by the officers of the different regiments and we swept forward with wild cheers over the crest and down the slope, and though at every step some brave one fell, we did not falter. Just as we reached it [a deep ravine] we poured a volley into the front lines of the Yankees, and then some of the more active cleared it at a bound; others jumped in and scrambled up the opposite side. Immediately in front of me was a log or piece of timber thrown across. I crossed on it as did many others.

By the time we had gotten across, the front line, broken by our fire, frightened by our screams which sounded like forty thousand wild cats, had reached their second line and thrown them into confusion, and they, panicstricken, left their works and crowded to the top of the hill, thus preventing their artillery from firing into us, and then commenced a scene that only the pen of an Abbot or a Victor Hugo could describe. The assaulting column consisted of six brigades, ours occupying the extreme right of the line, and each brigade had been successful. And the enemy, completely routed at every point, now lost all order and every man only thought of saving himself. They threw down their arms and ran in one grand mass, out of the woods and down the valley beyond. In vain their officers tried to rally them; they could not stand the terrible fire poured into them. We ran over their artillery, killing the gunners at their guns, and as this confused mass of fugitives fled down the long open valley we kept close to them and shot them down by the hundreds and thousands. We were so close to them that pistol did as much good as guns, and we could not miss them for they were at least twenty deep, and very few of them offering to fire a shot.

By the time we had gone half a mile we were as much confused as the Yankees, for no one had paid any attention to company or regiment, but each had devoted his entire attention to loading and firing as fast as possible. At this critical juncture a large body of the enemy's cavalry appeared on the field, bearing down upon us. Quickly we closed our ranks and presented a pretty good front to the enemy, not such a line as would have stood an infantry charge, but plenty strong to resist cavalry. When the head of their columns had gotten within about fifty yards of us we gave them a well directed and murderous fire that emptied many a saddle, and sent them flying in the opposite direction. . . .

The sun had set looking through the dust and smoke and fire of the battlefield, of a blood red color. We had won a complete victory, and now the scattered remnants of the various regiments and brigades that had been engaged had nothing to do except care for the wounded and to concentrate, that is, each man to find his proper command.

I did not know how tired I was until the excitement of the battle was over. I was almost too weak to stand, and my cheeks as hollow as though emaciated by a long spell of sickness. I dropped down under a bush and slept such a sleep as comes only to a tired soldier after a battle.

As soon after battle as convenient, most Rebs and Yanks wrote the folk at home to relieve apprehensions about their fate and to share experiences with loved ones. Typical of many communications was that written by a Hoosier on October 9, 1862, the day after Perryville:

Dear Wife I seat myself on the ground with a drum for a writing desk to write you a few lines to let you know that i am yet on top of the soil and not hirt. . . . There was plenty of men killed on both sides of me and not a ball struck me, the nearest I came to being hit was with a cannon ball it knocked me down it came so close to my head . . . but it did not hurt me much. . . . I should like to give you a description of the fight if i had the time and space but i havent either. . . . The rebels lost more than we did about two to one. . . . I was sent on the battle feild the next morning to take water to the wounded . . . and it was an awful sight to see there men torn all to pieces with cannon balls and bom shells the dead and wounded lay thick in all directions.

When telling homefolk of their battle experiences Yanks and Rebs sometimes alluded to the combat performance of their foes. When they conceded gallantry to the enemy they usually did so grudgingly. An Indianan, for instance, wrote his sweetheart after the fight at Ezra Church, near Atlanta, July 28, 1864: "The rebels were nearly every man drunk and some of the prisoners taken were so much intoxicated that they had to be led." But occasionally they revealed unstinted admiration of the courage displayed by their opponents. Following a sharp encounter near Richmond in May 1864, a New Yorker wrote:

Two full regiments of rebs . . . made a rush at us from the woods. . . . You should have seen the rascals, as clad in their threadbare suits of gray with short jackets . . . tight stockings, slender shanks and enormous yells and gesturing they advanced like so many crazy demons. Jer-usa-lem. What a storm of bullets they let fly at us. Overpowered we fell back double quick across a plowed field to the cover of a wood but quickly rallied and charged forward again with a hearty old Union cheer. Johnny Reb peppered and we peppered. Our fellows dropped fast. At length the secesh got a crossfire on us . . . and we were scattered a second time.

Many soldiers commented on the confusion and the noise of battle. After Fredericksburg, a Minnesota sergeant reported that before the end of the day's fighting his regiment was "scattered from Hell to Breakfast," and a Georgian who was at Malvern Hill wrote his aunt: "I never heard such a noise in all my life. It sounded like a large can[e] break on fire and a thunder storm with repeated loud thunder claps one clap following another." Ten days after the Williamsburg fight of May 5, 1862, a Minnesota sergeant wrote his sister: "The air perfectly whistled, shrieked and hummed with the leaden storm. . . . So loud [was] the rattle of musketry we could not hear the artillery."

Some recalled humorous incidents of battle, such as Rebel private Joseph Adams losing his pants from a shell burst at Murfreesboro and of M. D. Martin having his two haversacks of hardtack fragmented by a cannon ball at Chancellorsville and scattering crackers in such profusion that "several of the boys were struck by the biscuits and more than one thought he was wounded."

Lingering uppermost in the minds of most participants was the gruesomeness of battle, and incidents of horror and tragedy received major emphasis in letters to loved ones. "You doant no what kind of a-feeling it put on me to see men shot down like hoges & See a man tore all to peases with a Shell after he is dead," wrote a Georgian to his wife after the Battle of Chickasaw Bluffs.

Another Georgian who walked over the field following Lee's victory at Chancellorsville reported: "It looked more like a slaughter pen than anything else. . . . The shrieks and groans of the wounded . . . was heart rending beyond all description." A Mississippi cavalryman, recounting to his mother a sharp clash during the retreat from Shiloh stated: "I shot men . . . until my heart was sick at the slaughter. . . . One fellow made a pass at me with his bayonet and . . . in an instant I wheeled and shot him through the breast and he tumbled over like a beef."

After Gettysburg, a Maine soldier wrote his parents: "I have Seen . . . men rolling in their own blood, Some Shot one place, Some another. . . . our dead lay in the road and the Rebels in their hast to leave dragged both their baggage wagons and artillery over them and they lay mangled and torn to pieces so that Even friends could not tell them. You can form no idea of a battle field . . . no pen can describe it. No tongue can tell its horror I hope none of my brothers will Ever have to go into a fight." An Ohio soldier who walked over the field of Antietam two days after the fight described the scene thus to his father:

The smell was offul . . . their was about 5 or 6,000 dead bodes decaying over the field and perhaps 100 dead horses . . . their lines of battle Could be run for miles by the dead they lay long the lines like sheavs of Wheat I could have walked on the boddes all most from one end too the other.

Horror and tragedy found most vivid expression in individual instances observed by the soldiers. S. L. Loving of the 3d Michigan wrote his sister of what he saw while strolling over the battlefield of Williamsburg: "In one instance a Michigander and an Alabamian [who had] thrust a bayonet through each other lay dead, [each] still grasping his bayonet. . . . A Catholic died with a cross in his hands, and some with a string of beads. . . . Another had undone his knapsack and taken out his Testament and died with it grasped in his hands . . . opened to some promise. Others . . . held letters from home . . . as though loath to part with the last messengers from loved ones."

After Seven Pines, a New Yorker wrote to his homefolk: "I saw [Confederate] Father & Son side by side wounded. They both died where they lay." A Confederate colonel in recounting the experience of the 5th Texas at Gettysburg stated: "There were two twin brothers belonging to Company C . . . [who] came up to where I was standing and commenced firing. In a moment one of them is shot down by my side. The other brother caught hold of him as he fell and gently laid him down on the ground, and as he did so, he also received a death shot."

Of all soldier's commentaries on the horror of battle, the most moving is the following letter written to A. V. Montgomery of Camden, Mississippi, by his mortally wounded son.

> Spottsylvania County, Va.
> [May 10, 1864]
>
> Dear Father
>
> This is my last letter to you. I went into battle this evening as Courier for Genl Heth. I have been struck by a piece of Shell and my right shoulder is horeribly mangled & I know death is inevitable. I am very weak but I write to you because I know you would be delighted to read a word from your dying Son. I know death is near, that I will die far from home and friends of my early youth but I have friends here too who are kind to me. My Friend Fairfax will write you at my request and give you the particulars of my death. My grave will be marked so that you may visit it if you desire to do so, but [it] is optionary with you whether you let my remains rest here or in Miss. I would like to rest in the grave yard with my dear mother and brothers but its a matter of minor importance. Let us all try to reunite in heaven. I pray my God to forgive my sins & I feel that his promises are true that he will forgive me and save me. Give my love to all my friends. My strength fails me. My horse & my equipments will be left for you. Again a long farewell to you. May we meet in heaven.
>
> Your dying son,
> J. R. Montgomery.

Fairfax kept his promise, and his letter, dated May 15, 1864, is filed with that of Montgomery in the Museum of the Confederacy at Richmond. Fairfax's letter reveals that Montgomery was taken to the hospital in the field but the surgeons after examining his wounds decided that an operation would be useless. He lingered until the morning of the 14th of May 1864, when he died peacefully. "On the evening he was wounded," Fairfax wrote the bereaved father, "his strength was sufficient to write you a letter which I enclose. . . . I have never witnessed such an exhibition of fortitude and Christian resignation as he showed. . . . No word of complaint escaped his lips. . . . He retained his consciousness to the last."

Thus a brave boy died, and in this poignant record of his death he bore eloquent witness to the tragedy of the Civil War.

Burial of the dead at Spotsylvania in May 1864. Of the 618,000 Union and Confederate soldiers who lost their lives in the Civil War, 204,000 were killed during battle. (CWTI Collection)

What conclusions can be drawn from the record of J. R. Montgomery and of all the other common soldiers involved in the great American conflict of 1861-1865? That record, as written by the soldiers themselves and by the officers who led them, indicates that lowly folk are as richly endowed with the qualities essential to good citizenship as any other class in American society.

The Civil War made enormous and unprecedented demands on the American masses. Never before or since was so much of hardihood, sacrifice, and suffer-ing required of them. And the magnificent manner in which most of them acquitted themselves in their time of testing justified the faith that had been reposed in them by Thomas Jefferson and the other Founding Fathers. Their admirable conduct in the nation's greatest crisis proved the soundness of democratic government and convincingly affirmed the hope expressed by Lincoln at Gettysburg that "a new nation, conceived in Liberty and dedicated to the proposition that all men are created equal . . . can long endure."

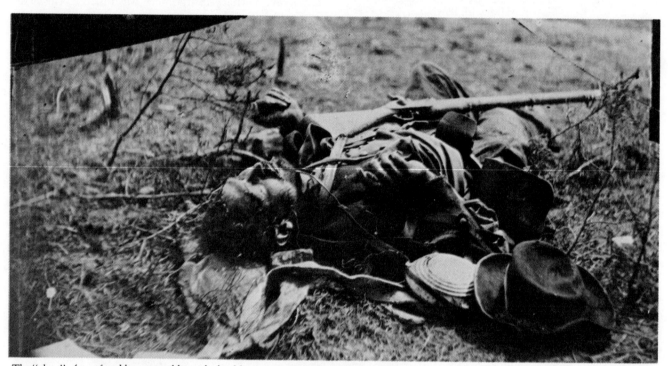

The "glory" of war faced by every soldier, whether Union or Confederate. (Library of Congress)

From Union to Nation

The entire North—and even parts of the South—went into profound mourning at Lincoln's death. Thousands paid their last respects at the White House on April 19 as Lincoln lay in state and General Grant wept openly by his catafalque. Seven million men, women, and children lined railroad tracks from Washington to Springfield to view Lincoln's funeral train carrying the sixteenth president to his final resting place.

A different railroad and horseback journey took place through Virginia, the Carolinas, and Georgia as Jefferson Davis fled southward toward Texas, hoping to rally scattered Confederate armies to continue fighting for the victory that Davis still thought possible. Through April he issued appeals for southerners to fight on, "operating in the interior" where the enemy's extended lines of communication "would render our triumph certain." But few southerners paid much attention, while one Confederate commander after another followed Lee's example and surrendered his army. On May 10, Union cavalry captured Davis himself in Georgia. They imprisoned him at Fortress Monroe in Virginia, to stand trial for complicity in Lincoln's assassination.

The United States government had discovered evidence of the role of Confederate agents in the plot to kidnap Lincoln. The government thought it also had evidence of the involvement of Confederate officials including Davis in that plot and the related one to assassinate the president. But as it became clear that this evidence would not stand up in court, the government gradually dropped plans to try Davis. (Recent research has turned up circumstantial evidence that high Confederate officials, perhaps including Davis, were aware of the assassination plot and may have approved it.) The only people tried and convicted were those directly involved in the assassination attempts against Lincoln, Seward, and Johnson, and those who helped Booth try to escape. Four of them, including Mrs. Surratt, were hanged on July 7, 1865. The other four were imprisoned. One died in prison; the other three received pardons from President Andrew Johnson in 1869.

Jefferson Davis remained in prison for two years while the government pondered whether to try him for treason. They finally let him go, recognizing that a jury in Virginia (where, according to the Constitution, Davis would have to be tried) was unlikely to convict him. Davis returned to Mississippi, where he lived quietly until 1889, writing his memoirs and a history of the Confederacy in which he insisted that the South was right, secession was legal, and the Confederacy should have had its independence. But the U.S. Supreme Court had ruled secession unconstitutional in 1869, a rather superfluous decision since Union victory in the Civil War had already decided the question as a practical matter in 1865. Individual states and regions have occasionally attempted since then to defy the national government, but none has ever again tried to secede. At the cost of at least 620,000 soldier lives—nearly as many Americans as have died in all of the country's other wars combined—the United States preserved its integrity as a nation.

The Union was not only preserved; it was transformed. The old decentralized republic in which the federal government had few direct contacts with the average citizen except through the post office became a nation that taxed people directly and created an internal revenue service to collect the taxes, drafted men into the army,

At the cost of at least 620,000 soldier lives, the United States preserved its integrity as a nation. The problem of secession was solved, slavery was gone from the land forever, and the federal government became the supreme authority. (CWTI Collection)

increased the powers of federal courts, created a national currency and a national banking system, and confiscated at least three billion dollars of personal property by emancipating the four million slaves. Eleven of the first twelve amendments to the Constitution had limited the powers of the national government; six of the next seven, beginning with the Thirteenth Amendment in 1865, vastly increased national powers at the expense of the states.

The first three of these postwar amendments spoke to another radical transformation accomplished by the Civil War: the abolition of slavery (Thirteenth Amendment) and the granting of equal citizenship (Fourteenth Amendment, 1868) and equal voting rights (Fifteenth Amendment, 1870) to former slaves and all other black Americans. This matter became the central issue of the troubled twelve-year Reconstruction period after the Civil War, during which the promise of equal rights was fulfilled for a brief time and then abandoned, to be revived again in the second half of the twentieth century, when it still remains one of the most important and divisive issues facing the American people.

The war tipped the sectional balance of power in favor of the North for a half century or more. Prior to the war, from the adoption of the Constitution in 1789 down to 1861, slaveholders from states that joined the Confederacy had served as President of the United States during forty-nine of the seventy-two years—more than two-thirds of the time. Twenty-three of the thirty-six speakers of the House and twenty-four of the presidents pro tem of the Senate had been southerners. The Supreme Court always had a southern majority before the Civil War; twenty of the thirty-five justices to 1861 had been appointed from slave states. After the war a century passed before a resident of an ex-Confederate state was elected president. For a half-century *none* of the speakers of the House or presidents pro tem of the Senate came from the South, and only five of the twenty-six Supreme Court justices named during that half century were southerners.

The United States went to war in 1861 to preserve the *Union*; it emerged from war in 1865 having created a *nation*. Before 1861 the two words "United States" were generally used as a plural noun: "the United States *are* a republic." After 1865 the United States became a singular noun. The loose union of states became a single nation. Lincoln's wartime speeches marked this transition. In his first inaugural address he mentioned the "Union" twenty times but the "nation" not once. In his first message to Congress, on July 4, 1861, Lincoln used the word "Union" thirty-two times and "nation" only three times. But in his Gettysburg Address two and one-half years later, the president did not mention the Union at all but spoke of the "nation" five times to invoke a new birth of freedom and nationhood. And in his second inaugural address on March 4, 1865, Lincoln spoke of the South seeking to dissolve the *Union* in 1861 and the North accepting the challenge to preserve the *nation*.

Was it worth the cost in lives lost and maimed? Few of the four million emancipated slaves who joyously celebrated the Day of Jubilee in 1865 doubted the answer. Nor did the millions of northerners who celebrated the news of Lee's surrender. Nor did Lincoln, who spoke in his second inaugural address of God's will for the United States. "Fondly do we hope—fervently do we pray—that this mighty scourge of war may speedily pass away. Yet if God wills that it continue, until all the wealth piled by the bondman's two hundred and fifty years of unrequited toil shall be sunk, and until every drop of blood drawn with the lash shall be paid by another drawn with the sword, as was said three thousand years ago, so still it must be said 'the judgments of the Lord are true and righteous altogether.'"

Even most southerners eventually came to share the sentiments expressed by young Woodrow Wilson, who had experienced the war as a child in Georgia. When he was a student at the University of Virginia law school in 1880, Wilson said that "*because* I love the South, I rejoice in the failure of the Confederacy. . . . Conceive of this Union divided into two separate and independent sovereignties! . . . Slavery was enervating our Southern society. . . . [Nevertheless] I recognize and pay loving tribute to the virtues of the leaders of secession . . . the righteousness of the cause which they thought they were promoting—and to the immortal courage of the soldiers of the Confederacy." These words expressed themes that would help reconcile generations of southerners to defeat: their forebears had fought bravely for what they believed right; perhaps they deserved to win; but in the long run it was well that they had lost.

Why? Because the Civil War resolved the two corrosive problems left unresolved by the American Revolution. The first was the question whether this new nation, this republic born in a world of kings, emperors, tyrants, and oligarchs, could survive. The republican experiment launched in 1776 was a fragile entity. The founding fathers—indeed all Americans for the next three generations—were fearful about the prospects of its survival. They knew that most republics through history had been overthrown by revolution or *coup d'etats*, or had collapsed into dictatorships or civil war. Americans alive in 1860 had twice witnessed French republics succumb to emperors and once to a restoration of the Bourbon monarchy. South of the border they had seen numerous Latin American republics repeatedly overthrown. The same thing, they feared, could happen here.

The Civil War was the great challenge to the survival of the American republic.

When President Abraham Lincoln was assassinated, the man who filled his place and took up his unfinished work was Vice President Andrew Johnson of Tennessee. (CWTI Collection)

"Our popular government has often been called an experiment," said Lincoln on July 4, 1861. "Two points in it, our people have already settled—the successful *establishing*, and the successful *administering* of it. One still remains—its successful *maintenance* against a formidable internal attempt to overthrow it." Or as Lincoln expressed it in the Gettysburg Address, the Civil War was the great "testing" whether a "government of the people, by the people, for the people" would survive or "perish from the earth." It did not perish. Northern victory preserved the nation created in 1776. And since 1865 no disaffected region has tried to secede from the United States. That question has been settled.

At Gettysburg Lincoln also spoke of a "new birth of freedom" for the United States. This referred to the other problem left unresolved by the Revolution of 1776—slavery. The Civil War settled it. The Thirteenth Amendment to the Constitution, ratified in 1865, declared that "neither slavery nor involuntary servitude . . . shall exist within the United States." It was this achievement, above all others, that has caused the Civil War to be labeled as the Second American Revolution. Mark Twain put it best, a half-dozen years after the war. That cataclysm, he wrote, "uprooted institutions that were centuries old, changed the politics of a people, and wrought so profoundly upon the entire national character that the influence cannot be measured short of two or three generations." Five generations have passed, and we are still measuring the influence of the Civil War.

—James M. McPherson

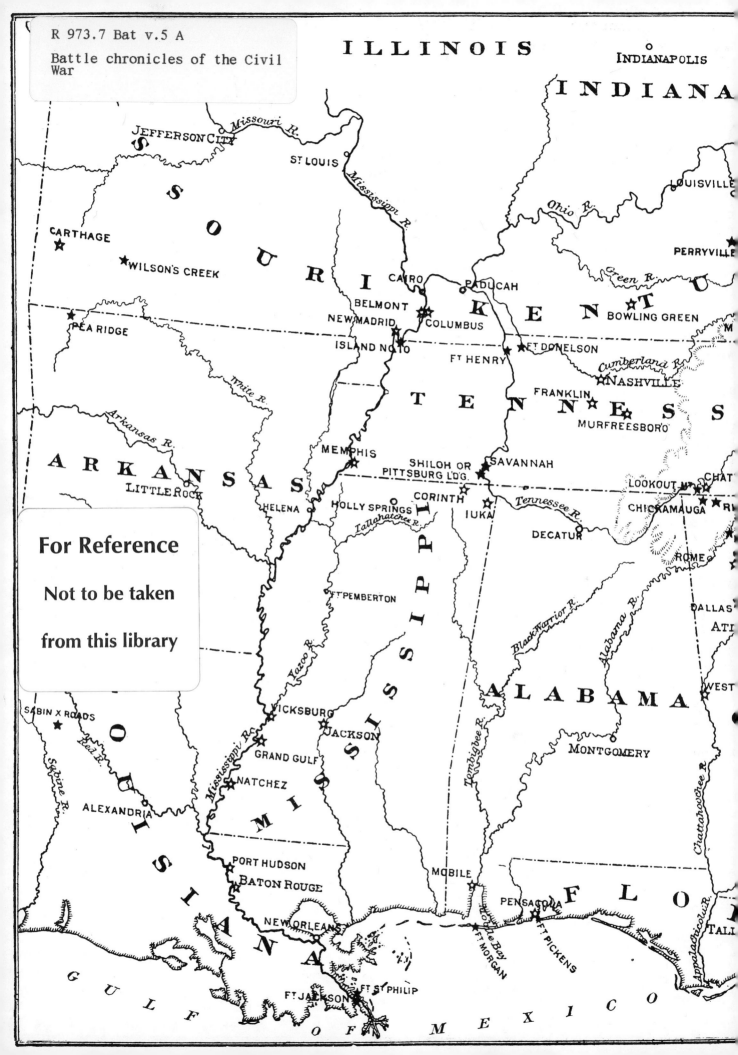